The President's
Kitchen Cabinet

★ ★ ★

The President's Kitchen Cabinet

The Story of the
AFRICAN AMERICANS
Who Have Fed Our First Families,
from the WASHINGTONS *to the*
OBAMAS

★

Adrian Miller

THE UNIVERSITY OF NORTH CAROLINA PRESS

Chapel Hill

This book was published with the assistance of the
JOHN HOPE FRANKLIN FUND
of the University of North Carolina Press.

The University of North Carolina Press has been a
member of the Green Press Initiative since 2003.

Cover illustrations: newly remodeled White House kitchen, 1902 (courtesy
Library of Congress); Obama State Service Plate (courtesy White House
Historical Association); Gilbert Stuart, *Portrait of George Washington's Cook*,
ca. 1795-97. © 2016 Museo Thyssen-Bornemisza / Scala, Florence.

Library of Congress Cataloging-in-Publication Data
Names: Miller, Adrian, author.
Title: The president's kitchen cabinet : the story of the African Americans who
have fed our first families, from the Washingtons to the Obamas / Adrian Miller.
Description: Chapel Hill : The University of North Carolina Press, [2017] |
Includes bibliographical references and index.
Identifiers: LCCN 2016042812| ISBN 9781469632537 (cloth : alk. paper) |
ISBN 9781469632544 (ebook)
Subjects: LCSH: African American cooks—Biography. | Cooks—
United States—Biography. | White House (Washington, D.C.)—
Employees. | Presidents—United States—Staff—History. | Presidents—
United States—History. | White House (Washington, D.C.)—History.
Classification: LCC TX649.A1 M55 2017 | DDC 641.5092/2 [B] —dc23
LC record available at https://lccn.loc.gov/2016042812

To all of the past, present, and future
presidential cooks of African heritage:
Your light shines bright despite persistent efforts
to keep you in the shadows.

To the late WALTER SCHEIB III,
White House executive chef (1994–2005),
whose enthusiasm for my work
kept my pilot light lit.

CONTENTS

ILLUSTRATIONS

A section of color photographs follows page 106

PREFACE

Dear President Obama,
I have a few questions for you. Nothing that will affect the world
situation, but I was wondering . . . I love shrimp and pineapple pizza.
What are your favorite foods? I am not allergic to anything, not any
kind of food or any animals. Are you allergic to anything? There are a
lot more questions I'd like to ask you, but I don't want to bug you. You
probably have more important earth-shattering questions to deal with.[1]

When eleven-year-old Malaysia wrote the letter above to President Barack Obama circa 2009, she expressed a desire widely shared by many Americans. We want a personal connection to our presidents and First Families, and we believe that food—what presidents like to eat (or refuse to eat), what they serve to their guests, and what they cook—can be a leading indicator of presidential character. This predicament leads to what I call the "presidential pickle." We want our presidents to be extraordinary people, but we also want them to be a lot like us. In our system of government, where power ultimately derives from its citizens, a president's popularity is the bread and butter of maintaining political power.

Savvy presidents carefully use food to ordain and establish in the public consciousness that they are regular people, just like you and me. It's an enterprise that is fraught with peril, and the stakes are high. Any missteps could make a president seem aristocratic (dining on too much fancy food), out of touch (not knowing the price of common groceries), weird (cottage cheese and ketchup, a combination that President Nixon loved), or just plain boring (having a strong affinity for iceberg lettuce or saltine crackers). Presidents' food personas often publicly take shape on the campaign trail as they spend their days visiting working-class restaurants, county fairs, and other community events to talk to voters. Though these moments are managed as much as possible by a candidate's staffers, there remains enough spontaneity to get a feel for those seeking the Oval Office. We scrutinize how they answer questions, how they emote with concerned citizens, and, probably more important, what they eat, their table manners, and how they chew their food. Remarkably, the latter is often not pretty. The stakes can be high because failure at good manners gives a president's political enemies an opportunity to sear an aristocratic image of said president in the public's consciousness. Several chief executives have suffered a political "kiss of death" because of a poor food image. Depending on how successful presidents are at crafting their image, they may leave the American public hungering for more information about them—or not.

That's how the presidential food story often plays out in the public, but what happens in private is a much different matter. In this sphere of their lives, the First Families simply want food that will make them happy and keep them healthy. Depending upon the president, the public persona and the private reality may go together like beans and rice, or they may seem like alternate universes. Whether acknowledged or not, presidents and the public are in constant dialogue, and food helps the American public avoid the chemical aftertaste left by staged events and scripted speeches. Through food, we get an authentic taste of our president's personality.

African Americans, as private and professional cooks, have been called upon time and time again to multitask in the following ways: cooking superb, comforting food for the First Family; dazzling presidential guests with the same; aiding and abetting a positive presidential food image; all while maintaining their professionalism and asserting their humanity, often under difficult conditions. In turn, presidents and First Ladies have often leaned on their African American cooks to burnish their reputation for private entertaining, for friendship, and for a unique perspective on African American life. This book will feast upon the legacy of African Americans who have been involved in various aspects of presidential food service. Though it will focus primarily on chefs and cooks, we will learn of many other people who are important to the president's culinary team. This book is truly a group biography.

One would think that I got interested in this subject while I worked in the White House in the late 1990s. I had a high-security clearance, and I could have gone into the executive kitchen during down times in activity and chatted up the chefs. But I didn't. Not for several years would I become fascinated in the presidential food history of our nation.

For fourteen months at the very end of his second term, I worked in the White House for President William Jefferson Clinton on something called "The President's Initiative for One America." This was an outgrowth of "The President's Initiative on Race" that President Clinton also launched. Clinton's bold idea was that if we just talked to one another and got to know one another, we might find out that we have a lot more in common than what supposedly divides us. I got the job thanks to Kathleen Ahn, a Georgetown University Law Center classmate, who was already working on the initiative. I was practicing law in Denver, Colorado, when she called and asked me if I had any friends back in Washington, D.C., who might want to work with the initiative. I asked about the job and quickly figured out that this was a "once-in-a-lifetime" opportunity. I took the approach that Dick Cheney did when presidential candidate George W. Bush asked him to recommend a vice presidential candidate: as the head of the search committee, I submitted only my own name.

I thoroughly enjoyed my time in the White House but at first had only limited access to presidential cooking. By the end of my tenure, however, I was elevated to a position that gave me White House Mess privileges (I highly recommend the cheeseburger), and I regularly ate in a small cafeteria on the first floor of what is now called the Dwight D. Eisenhower Executive Office Building—back then we called it the "Old Exec." I never dined at a state dinner nor noshed in any of the presidential dining rooms. Though I passed it several times walking through the West Wing to the White House's East Wing, I never took a peek into the White House kitchen.

At the change of an administration, the outgoing president's political appointees write a resignation letter and submit it to the incoming president's staff, a task I undertook at the end of Clinton's term. Shockingly, President-elect Bush accepted mine. I was now back in the private sector seeking a job in either Washington, D.C., or my beloved hometown of Denver. The employment market was slow at the time, and I was watching way too much daytime television. I thought to myself, "I guess I should read something." I went to a D.C. area bookstore and purchased the late John Egerton's *Southern Food: At Home, on the Road, in History*. That book launched the journey to writing my first book, *Soul Food: The Surprising Story of an American Cuisine, One Plate at a Time*. During the decade that I researched *Soul Food*, African American presidential chefs kept jumping out at me from the pages of dusty books and from the soft glow of digitized newspapers and periodicals on my computer screen. I was immediately intrigued, but I didn't have enough information to tell more than a handful of stories.

Fast-forward to late 2008 when Ari Weinzweig of Zingerman's Roadhouse and Deli in Ann Arbor, Michigan, asked me to speak at the upcoming African American annual dinner at the restaurant. I was originally charged with talking about soul food, but I had a change of heart once I found out the date of the event: 20 January 2009, the inauguration day for Barack Obama, our nation's first African American president. I looked over my files, convinced myself there was enough material to do a presentation, and then persuaded Ari that we should change course. Fortunately, he agreed. That night, Chef Alex Young, the Roadhouse's winner of the James Beard Award, prepared a themed dinner utilizing historical recipes, and I introduced each course by telling stories about the particular African American presidential chef who inspired the dish. It was a wondrous night, and it inspired me to continue my quest to bring to light the personalities and capabilities of African American presidential chefs.

It's been an amazing journey but not without some stumbling blocks along the way. Though presidential cooks have worked for some of the most powerful people on earth, history writers have provided significant details on the lives of only a tiny handful of them. This book offers plentiful detail for more of the 150 African American presidential culinary professionals I've identified in my research, but for many, the historical record gives only glimpses of their lives by way of incomplete name references, quick anecdotes, praises from satisfied diners, and pictures without captions. First-person accounts by African American presidential chefs are scarce because they spoke infrequently about what they did in the presidential kitchen (either by choice or by claims for confidentiality). Some valuable information comes from presidential biographies, cookbooks, and the recollections of the presidents themselves, their families, and their trusted aides. For most of what you'll find in this book, we must thank numerous presidential observers who wrote about these culinary professionals in books, magazines, and newspapers. Regrettably, there are fewer contemporary African American voices in the historical sources. It's a real challenge to interview presidential chefs currently on the job and recent alums involved in presidential food service due to an understandable culture of discretion and nondisclosure agreements. Still, I encourage these chefs to share their stories. I can personally attest to the fact that there is intense public interest in them as people, in their path to the White House, and in what they do at work and during their leisure time. These culinary professionals, these people, deserve more than to be historical silhouettes. Let's give more life to their legacy.

White House executive chef Walter Scheib was tremendously helpful while I was researching this book. I came across his website and e-mailed him some initial questions. To my surprise, he called me within a few hours, and we had a great conversation. After this, we stayed in occasional contact. I eventually persuaded him to team up with me for a "Black Chefs in the White House" event for the Stanford Black Alumni Association of Washington, D.C. The event was held on a lovely spring night in May 2011 at Johnny's Half Shell Restaurant. Chef Ann Cashion did a great job replicating and reinterpreting presidential recipes, and John Fulchino was a fantastic host. I gave the history of African American presidential chefs, and Chef Scheib provided a highly entertaining perspective on his experiences in the contemporary White House kitchen. After Scheib saw me in action, he came up afterward and said, "I don't lend my name to many things, but I love what you're doing. You have a fascinating project, and I can tell that you have integrity. If you give me enough notice, and my calendar is open, I'll do as many of these events as I can with you. I think we'd be a good team." In short, he immediately got what I was trying to accomplish.

We collaborated on a few events and projects, including pitching a television documentary on this subject. Scheib was quick to take my phone calls and texts and was generous with his time, giving me a great insider's view of how the White House kitchen worked. We were scheduled to do another event in July 2015. But in June, on my birthday, as it sadly happened, Scheib went for a solo hike in the mountains outside of his part-time home in Taos, New Mexico, and disaster struck. A fast-moving storm moved in, and Scheib drowned in a flash flood. I miss his counsel, fun personality, and graciousness and wish we had had the opportunity to become better friends. That's why this work is dedicated, in part, to him.

I thank the following people for helping in various ways as I worked on this project: Maureen Farkash for letting me interview her daughter Kiana; Shai Halbe and Manjusha Kulkarni; Nelson Hsu and Kimberly Kho; Jeannette LaFors and Matt Kelemen; Kary and Nanette LaFors; Dan Manatt; Angie and Johnny Mosier; Caroline Park; Ellen Sweets; and Marques and Roopa Tracy.

I also greatly appreciate the research and editorial help from Kelly Bates, Carrie Hale, Shawn Hallinan, Deborah Nicholson, and Mary Russell. I give a special thank you to my editor, Elaine Maisner, copyeditor Julie Bush, and managing editor Mary Carley Caviness for using their keen eyes and sharp minds to improve the manuscript. I also thank the anonymous readers who critiqued an early draft of this book. They kept me from making some woeful historical errors and gave me helpful guidance on striking the right tone. I also thank Sue Zimmerman for testing some recipes on short notice, Kristi and Andres Espiñeira for hosting a drink-recipe-tasting party, and Cynthia Chen for giving me a laser printer at just the right time in my writing life.

Thanks again to my White House colleagues in the President's Initiative for One America office: Kathleen Ahn; Karen Scott, for many laughs and an enduring friendship; and especially to Robert "Ben" Johnson, who took a chance on me and did things to advance my career that he really didn't have to do. I also thank President Bill Clinton for the glorious opportunity to work in the White House.

I thank my law school buddy Don Graves for giving me the serious White House hookup. Former Colorado governor Bill Ritter Jr. created an opportunity for me to speak with Chef Sam Kass while he worked in the White House and gave President and Mrs. Obama a copy of my first book while describing this one. Ramin Ganeshram and Tavis Smiley presented me with the opportunity to write my first essay about African American presidential chefs in the *America I AM Pass It Down Cookbook*. I thank Joe Yonan, food and dining editor at the *Washington Post*, for giving me the space to write and further flesh out some themes found in this book; former White House assistant chefs John Moeller and Frank Ruta for taking the time to share experiences and answer my questions; Kris Browning-Blas, the former food editor at the *Denver Post*; Patricia Calhoun of *Westword* for showing me and this project so much love in my hometown media; and freelance writer Ruth Tobias for getting the word out on my work nationally. Deep thanks go to Walter Scheib IV, one of Chef Scheib's sons, for being so willing to give me access to his father's culinary files. It was great to see a White House chef's mind at work.

Writing this book was greatly aided by those who, on my behalf, helped organize numerous Black Chefs in the White House presentations around the country, where I got to test out theories, storytelling approaches, and puns and corny jokes: Claud Cloete, Lee and Charles Everding, Jesi Jones and the good folks in the Denver Eclectics, Dr. Joy Simmons, and Ari Weinzweig. Also, my thanks go to all who helped organize the events that I did for various Stanford University Alumni Clubs around the country (in Atlanta, Chicago, Los Angeles, New York, Northern California, Philadelphia, the Rocky Mountains, San Diego, and Washington, D.C.): Magnus Christon, Jane and Cam Collins, John Drive, Eric Fortner, Lauren Graham, Saidah Grayson, Amanda Johnson, James Jordan,

Lisa Park, Mary Beth Walpole, Lyzette Wallace, Yale University Dining Services, and the Virginia Club of New York.

I also thank the staffs at the following presidential centers and libraries for helping me with research requests in person and from afar: the George Bush Presidential Library and Museum; the George W. Bush Presidential Center; the Jimmy Carter Presidential Library and Museum; the William J. Clinton Presidential Center; the Dwight D. Eisenhower Presidential Library, Museum and Boyhood Home; the Gerald R. Ford Presidential Library and Museum; the Benjamin Harrison Presidential Site; the Rutherford B. Hayes Presidential Center; the Lyndon Baines Johnson Presidential Library and Museum; the John F. Kennedy Presidential Library and Museum; the Richard Nixon Presidential Library and Museum; the Ronald Reagan Presidential Library and Museum; the Franklin D. Roosevelt Presidential Library and Museum; and the Harry S. Truman Presidential Library and Museum. I also thank the University of Denver for maintaining an excellent and thorough culinary collection and for making all of its resources readily available on-site for independent researchers like me.

As I continue to discover and unearth more information on African American presidential culinary professionals, I'll post it on my website: www.blackchefswhitehouse.com. If there is a presidential cook somewhere in your family history or social circles, I encourage you to reach out.

Finally, I thank God for the blessing to pursue one of my passions, to commune with these intriguing personalities, and to share their stories with you.

The President's
Kitchen Cabinet

★ ★ ★

African American Presidential Culinary Professionals

The following is a list of the African Americans, by presidential administration and position, who have had a hand in presidential food preparation. Some presidential administrations and people are not listed because the African Americans who participated in food service were not identified by name in the sources I consulted.

GEORGE WASHINGTON
(1789–97)
Samuel Fraunces (steward)
Hercules (enslaved family cook)
Paris (enslaved apprentice cook)
Richmond (enslaved family cook)

JOHN ADAMS
(1797–1801)
Dinah (cook, last name unknown)

THOMAS JEFFERSON
(1801–9)
Edith ("Edy") Hern Fossett
(enslaved cook)
Peter Hemings
(enslaved cook, brewer)
Frances "Fanny" Gillette Hern
(enslaved cook)
Ursula (enslaved pastry cook)

JAMES MADISON
(1809–17)
"Old Black" Joe (enslaved cook)
Sukey (enslaved cook)

JAMES MONROE
(1817–25)
Augustus Jackson (cook)
Jennie Trigger
(enslaved head cook)

JOHN QUINCY ADAMS
(1825–29)
Augustus Jackson (cook)

ANDREW JACKSON
(1829–37)
Augustus Jackson (cook)

WILLIAM HENRY HARRISON
(1841)
George DeBaptiste (steward)

JAMES POLK
(1845–49)
Coakley (male cook [first name
unknown])
Mary White (cook)

JAMES BUCHANAN
(1857–61)
Cornelia Mitchell (cook)

ABRAHAM LINCOLN
(1861–65)
Peter Brown (cook, butler, waiter)
Mary Dines
(Old Soldiers' Home cook)
Cornelia Mitchell (cook)
Rosetta Wheeler
(cook, seamstress)

ANDREW JOHNSON
(1865–69)
Lizzie Mitchell (family cook)
William Slade (steward)

ULYSSES S. GRANT
(1869–77)
Edgar (or Edward) Beckley
(cook/steward)
Sarah Brooks (cook)
Lucy Fowler Latimer (cook)
Amos Thompson
(assistant head of pantry)
Janie Warmack (cook)

RUTHERFORD B. HAYES
(1877–81)
William T. Crump (steward)
Jane Humphreys (head cook)
Lucy Fowler Latimer (cook)
Winnie Monroe (family cook)
John A. Simms (steward)

JAMES GARFIELD
(1881)
Joe Brown (railroad cook)
William T. Crump (steward)
Lucy Fowler Latimer (cook)

CHESTER A. ARTHUR
(1881–85)
Joe Brown (railroad cook)
Gabriel A. Coakley
(assistant cook)
Lucy Fowler Latimer (cook)
Howard Williams (steward, cook,
and messenger)

GROVER CLEVELAND
(1885–89, 1893–97)
Joe Brown (railroad cook)
Marcus Edwards (railroad cook)
Dollie Johnson (cook)
Susan Sebastian (cook)
William T. Sinclair (steward)
William Wells (steward)

BENJAMIN HARRISON
(1889–93)
Joe Brown (railroad cook)
Dollie Johnson (family cook)
Mary Robinson (pastry cook)
William T. Sinclair (steward)

WILLIAM MCKINLEY
(1897–1901)
Mrs. Benjamin
    (noted cook from S.C.)
Joe Brown (railroad cook)
Marcus Edwards (railroad cook)
Alice Howard (assistant cook)
Katie G. Seabrook (caterer/cook)
William T. Sinclair (steward)
William Wells (steward)

THEODORE ROOSEVELT
(1901–9)
Joe Brown (railroad cook)
Mrs. Julia Davis (cook)
Charles Harris (cook)
Alice Howard (assistant cook)
Mary (second cook)
Henry Pinckney (steward)

WILLIAM H. TAFT
(1909–13)
Joe Brown (railroad cook)
Mary (second cook)
Major Arthur Brooks
    (wine cellar keeper)
Jim Carter (assistant cook)
Marcus Edwards (railroad cook)

Charles Harris (cook)
Alice Howard (assistant cook)
John Smeades (railroad cook)

WOODROW WILSON
(1913–21)
Major Arthur Brooks
    (wine cellar keeper)
Joe Brown (railroad cook)
Charles H. Browne
    (dining room servant)
Jim Carter (assistant cook)
Marcus Edwards (railroad cook)
Alice Howard (assistant cook)
Delefasse Green (railroad cook)
Tom Jackson (railroad car cook)
Letch Wilson (railroad cook)

WARREN G. HARDING
(1921–23)
Major Arthur Brooks
    (wine cellar keeper)
Joe Brown (railroad cook)
Charles H. Browne
    (dining room servant)
Marcus Edwards (railroad cook)
Alice Howard (assistant cook)

CALVIN COOLIDGE
(1923–29)
Major Arthur Brooks
    (wine cellar keeper)
Joe Brown (railroad cook)

HERBERT HOOVER
(1929–33)
Joe Brown (railroad cook)

FRANKLIN DELANO
ROOSEVELT
(1933–45)
Ida Allen (chief cook)
Armstead Barnett (pantryman)
Elizabeth Blake (assistant cook)

Daisy Bonner
    (Warm Springs, Ga., cook)
James Carter (assistant cook)
Loretta Deans (cook)
Lizzie McDuffie
    (maid / assistant cook)
Elizabeth Moore (assistant cook)
Catherine Smith (assistant cook)

HARRY S. TRUMAN
(1945–53)
Eugene Allen (pantryman)
Armstead Barnett (pantryman)
William Dallas (Blair House chef)
Alonzo Fields (maître d'hôtel)
Vietta Garr (family cook)
Samuel "Mitch" Mitchell
    (railroad cook)
Allena Price (assistant chef)
William "Dad" Smith
    (assistant chef)

DWIGHT D. EISENHOWER
(1953–61)
Armstead Barnett (pantryman)
Ellen K. Charles (cook)
Jessie H. Goddis (butler/cook)
George L. Johnson (cook)
John H. Johnson (butler/cook)
Donald Major (cook)
Dolores Moaney
    (family cook at Gettysburg)
Sgt. John Moaney Jr. (valet/cook)
Willie A. Payne (cook)
Eunice J. Perkins (cook)
Allena M. Price (cook)
William "Dad" Smith (cook)
Fate Suber (butler/pantry)
Pearl Wiggins (pantry)
Isaiah Wilson (cook)

JOHN F. KENNEDY
(1961–63)
Eserline Dewberry
  (assistant cook)
Raymond Jackson (assistant cook)
Pearl Nelson (family cook)
Allena Price (assistant chef)

LYNDON BAINES JOHNSON
(1963–69)
Lucy M. Addison (pantry)
Fannie Allen (pantry)
Jessie D. Beals (pantry)
Alise Berry (pantry)
Franklin H. Blair (kitchen)
Mrs. Vernell Butler
  (kitchen helper)
Sallie Ann Davis (kitchen)
Eserline Dewberry (assistant chef)
Julia Farrow (kitchen)
John Ficklin (maître d'hôtel /
  wine steward)
Jessie Hall (pantry)
Margaret Harris (kitchen)
Raymond Jackson (assistant cook)
James T. Jeffries (pantry)
Dorothy L. Johnson (pantry)
Lottie Luckett (pantry)
Mary Lumpkin (pantry)
Eric R. Martin (kitchen)
Johnny E. Miller (pantry)
Delois Parks (kitchen)
Allena Price (assistant chef)
James E. Selmon (pantry)
Mary T. Smith (pantry)
John Stewart (pantry)
Willie P. Taylor (kitchen)
Helen C. Terry (pantry)
John F. Wiggins (pantry)
Pearl Wiggins (pantry)
William F. Wilkerson (pantry)
Ethel Wilson (pantry)
Zephyr Wright (family cook)

RICHARD M. NIXON
(1969–74)
Franklin H. Blair (pantry)
Eserline Dewberry
  (assistant cook)
John Ficklin (maître d'hôtel /
  wine steward)
Ronald Jackson
  (White House Mess)
Lee Simmons
  (*Air Force One* steward)

GERALD R. FORD
(1974–77)
Loraine Bivings (assistant cook)
Eserline Dewberry
  (assistant cook)
John Ficklin (maître d'hôtel /
  wine steward)
Ronald Jackson
  (White House Mess)

JAMES E. CARTER
(1977–81)
Eserline Dewberry
  (assistant cook)
John Ficklin (maître d'hôtel /
  wine steward)

RONALD REAGAN
(1981–89)
Adam Collick (kitchen steward)
Eserline Dewberry
  (assistant cook)
John Ficklin (maître d'hôtel /
  wine steward)

GEORGE H. W. BUSH
(1989–93)
Adam Collick (kitchen steward)
Sr. Master Sgt. Wanda Joell
  (*Air Force One* flight attendant)

WILLIAM J. CLINTON
(1993–2001)
Adam Collick (kitchen steward)
Anthony S. Holiday
  (assistant chef)
Sr. Master Sgt. Wanda Joell
  (*Air Force One* flight attendant)
Nathan McMackle (assistant chef)
Paula Patton-Moutsos
  (assistant chef)
Exec. Chef Charlie Redden
  (White House Mess)
Jason Stitt (assistant chef)

GEORGE W. BUSH
(2001–9)
Denzil Benjamin (assistant chef)
Adam Collick (kitchen steward)
Sr. Master Sgt. Wanda Joell
  (*Air Force One* flight attendant)
Paula Patton-Moutsos
  (assistant chef)
Exec. Chef Charlie Redden
  (White House Mess)
Stephen W. Rochon (chief usher)
Kathleen Willis (assistant chef)

BARACK H. OBAMA
(2009–17)
Denzil Benjamin (assistant chef)
Tafari Campbell (assistant chef)
Adam Collick (kitchen steward)
Sr. Master Sgt. Wanda Joell
  (*Air Force One* flight attendant)
Angella Reid (chief usher)
Stephen W. Rochon (chief usher)

1
The Key Ingredients of Presidential Foodways

❦❧

*As I always told the Negro servants and dining room help
that worked for me, "Boys, remember that we are helping to make history.
We have a small part, perhaps a menial part, but they can't do much
here without us. They've got to eat, you know."*

ALONZO FIELDS,
My 21 Years in the White House, 1961

You have probably heard a number of presidential conspiracy theories full of foreign intrigue, but perhaps not one that is as American as apple pie. President William Howard Taft was an apple-loving man, and it ran in the family. One newspaper reported, "The Taft family are fond of apples in almost any form. It is not publicly known that one of the invariable rules of the President and all of his brothers is to eat apples just before bedtime. This custom was started by Alonzo Taft, the father of the President, and his children have followed it consistently. Whether traveling or at home the President is never without apples."[1] One of President Taft's favorite ways to consume the fruit was in the form of apple pie, and when he traveled by train he could get, arguably, the best apple pie on earth. President Taft owed this possibility to John Smeades, an African American man who ran the kitchen on the presidential train. One newspaper described Smeades's apple pie as "a glory, a Lucullan feast, an eighth wonder of the world."[2] Though President Taft's heart, mind, and stomach said "yes" to that famous apple pie, those who surrounded him—his wife, physician, and staffers—said "no" because they felt the president really needed to stay on his diet.

This temptation for President Taft presented a serious quandary for members of his staff. How could they be so close to apple pie greatness and not indulge? After all, *he* was the one who had to watch his weight, not them. In due time, the "Secret Order of the Apple Pie" was born with a membership consisting of the president's key staffers: Surgeon Major Thomas L. Rhoads, Jimmie Sloan of the Secret Service, Charles D. Hilles, and Major Archie Butt. Their sole purpose was to devise a variety of schemes to eat Chef Smeades's apple pie without President Taft ever knowing about it. But Taft invariably knew what was happening (as all presidents seem to)—when it came to food, he was hard to fool. At one point, he playfully confronted his deceptive doctor who had crumbs on his face from a recently devoured piece of pie: "'Major [Rhoads], it is better to practice than to preach. Can't I have a bit of that pie?'"[3] Evidently, President Taft didn't win this time, but he wasn't always left disappointed.

Sometime around 1912, President Taft boarded a midnight train to his native Ohio and thought he was going back to a simpler place in time when he wasn't on a strict diet. Fortunately for him, the First Lady and the president's physician weren't on the same train. Once the train left the station, presidential staffers Ira T. Smith and Joe Alex Morris relate, President Taft summoned the train's conductor for an urgent request: "'The dining car . . .' Mr. Taft began shyly, 'Could we get a snack?' The conductor looked surprised. 'Why, Mr. President, there isn't any dining car on this train.' The President's sun-tanned face turned pink, with perhaps a few splashes of purple. His normally prominent eyes seemed to bulge." Taft loudly beckoned his secretary, Charles D. Norton, to solve this problem, but Norton reminded the president of his dietary strictures and that he had already eaten dinner and wouldn't miss breakfast. This only deepened Taft's resolve as he continued to lobby the conductor: "'Where's the next stop, dammit?' he asked. 'The next stop where there's a diner [car]?'"[4] The conductor informed him that it would be Harrisburg, Pennsylvania, and Taft responded epically, "'I am the President of the United States, and I want a diner attached to this train at Harrisburg. I want it well stocked with food, including filet mignon. You see that we get a diner. . . . What's the use of being President,' he demanded, 'if you can't have a train with a diner on it?'"[5]

As one might guess, the presidential train made an unscheduled stop at Harrisburg, and a dining car was attached. Right around midnight, President Taft was happily dining on filet mignon. History is silent on what cook the railroad company roused from his slumber for the awesome, probably annoying (this time at least), and nerve-wracking task of preparing the president's late-night meal. In all likelihood, it was an African American man. Now, *My presidency for a dining car!* isn't a political slogan that's going to win a lot of votes with the general public, but this food-related anecdote involving President Taft poignantly shows that the presidential food story can be a mix of joy and pain, of luxury and deprivation, and usually there was an African American cook right in the middle of things.

White House family kitchen, circa 1901.
Mrs. John Logan, Thirty Years in Washington.

· · ·

This book explores the role that African Americans have had on "presidential foodways"—places where culture, history, cooking, eating, and the presidency intersect. Presidential foodways involve a lot of moving parts. Rather than go into great detail about how those parts apply and interact with each other as the story unfolds, I'll first describe them in this chapter. Each aspect of presidential foodways will be peppered with relevant anecdotes involving African Americans that are pulled from two centuries of presidential history. With some exceptions, the presidential food story that follows is told from the perspective of the African Americans who made those meals.

First, a few housekeeping notes. Because this work spans two centuries, some common terminology has changed over time, and I use several words interchangeably throughout the book. Thus, "Executive Mansion," "Executive Residence," and "president's house" all designate the actual home the president had while living in New York, Philadelphia, and Washington, D.C. Only the 1600 Pennsylvania Avenue location in Washington, D.C., has ever been called the "White House."

Depending upon the historical source that I cite, "African American," "black," "colored," and "Negro" indicate people of African heritage. And I use "chef" and "cook" interchangeably (which might be a bit controversial for some), because I draw upon the original definition of the term *chef de cuisine*, which simply meant the person "who presides over the kitchen of a large household" or "head cook"—regardless of whether or not the person had professional training.[6] Indeed, many African Americans throughout early American history were called cooks when they might have properly been called chefs. This all changed in the United States when in 1976, "the position of executive chef moved from a 'service' status to a 'professional' classification in the U.S. Department of Labor's *Dictionary of Occupational Titles*."[7] Today, the term "chef" is used to identify someone who has had some professional culinary education or training. Historically speaking, this has been a distinction without a difference. Rather than getting caught up in titles, President Lyndon Johnson's personal cook Zephyr Wright summed it up nicely when she said, "'Oh, I'm no chef . . . I just like to cook.'"[8]

Also, one should note that there are several types of cooking in the White House complex: the large, formal entertaining that happens in the building's grand spaces, such as the State Dining Room; the small-group entertaining of VIPs in the President's Dining Room; the family meals prepared and served in the private kitchen and dining areas on the Executive Residence's second and third floors; the White House Mess, which provides a private dining space in the West Wing for high-level staffers (primarily run and operated by U.S. Navy cooks); and the small cafeteria in the Dwight D. Eisenhower Executive Office building. Though African Americans have their fingerprints on all aspects of the presidential cooking described above, this book primarily focuses on the behind-the-scenes cooking done for the First Family rather than on the high-profile state dinners.

In culinary school, right after a course on kitchen safety, students are taught how to get organized before they start cooking. Most cooks I know fall into one of two camps. The first camp consists of those who pull ingredients from the pantry and the refrigerator as they go along, hoping that they have everything they need to prepare a certain dish. If they don't, it's not too big a deal because they are confident that they can improvise a good result—usually without precise measurements. These people are called "dump cooks" or "scratch cooks." I am not among them. I fall into the second camp, where I need to have all of my ingredients previously measured and laid out before me. This subdues the panic that would overcome me if I didn't have everything that I needed in order to cook. This latter approach is called *mise en place*, which is French for "everything in its place."

Let me borrow from the culinary world and declare that what follows is a literary *mise en place* comprising four major "ingredients" that make up presidential foodways.

First Ingredient: The President's Influences on Foodways

THE PRESIDENT'S PALATE

What a president craves to eat is first, last, and everything in between for the White House kitchen staff. Most presidents have been wealthy people with their own personal cooks. Since familiarity bred culinary comfort, they often brought their own personal cooks with them to the Executive Mansion once they became president. If they didn't have their own cook, they often tasked their First Lady with finding one. Given that assignment, a First Lady would dutifully tap her personal networks to find and vet someone who was capable of performing well in such a demanding job. Thus, for most cooks, the path to the presidential kitchen depended primarily upon on two things: whom they knew and how well they cooked.

Before installing their own cooks, First Families rely on the White House kitchen staff cooks to feed them in the interim—and to get it right. The staff cooks, working closely with the White House's steward and chief usher as well as with the butlers, pride themselves on anticipating the needs of an incoming presidential family, especially concerning what they might first request to eat and drink as they settle in for those first few days of the presidency. Usually such requests are met without a hitch, but there have been some nerve-wracking moments when the staff missed the mark.

As longtime White House butler Alonzo Fields, an African American, recalled, White House chief usher Howell Crim faced a similar challenge: "One day the President [Eisenhower] gave the crew an unexpected problem. The chief usher, Mr. Crim, was told to get some yoghurt, and the housekeeper and Charles [Ficklin, the maître d'], like Mr. Crim, did not know what yoghurt was. This little incident nearly prevented my transfer [to become head butler] from being O.K.'d."[9] Fortunately, Fields was welcomed at work the next day.

Besides what presidents put in their stomach, how they think about food affects their cook's job. Most presidents have been extremely hands-off about White House food operations and have usually delegated such things to their spouse with the understanding that they would consistently get good food to eat. There have been exceptions. We have had gourmet presidents who were extremely interested in what they ate (Presidents George Washington, Thomas Jefferson, James Monroe, Chester Arthur, and Dwight D. Eisenhower). We've had others, like President Abraham Lincoln, who seemed fundamentally uninterested in food. One observer noted, "When Mrs. Lincoln, whom he always addressed by the old-fashioned title of 'Mother,' was absent from home, the President [Lincoln] would appear to forget that food and drink were needful for his existence, unless he were persistently followed up by some of the servants, or were finally reminded of his needs by the actual pangs of hunger."[10]

Herbert Hoover exemplified the "food as fuel" perspective to the point of hilarity. Lillian Rogers Parks, an African American woman who served for decades as a White House maid, had the rare opportunity to witness presidential personality quirks up close. In her taboo-shattering memoir of her White House experiences, Parks wrote, "The President [Hoover] hardly took enough time to eat, so anxious was he to get back to work. All the servants and kitchen staff made bets on how long it would take him to eat. He averaged around nine to ten minutes, and he could eat a full-course dinner in eight minutes flat. They would come back saying, 'Nine minutes, fifteen seconds,' or what the time had been. Eight minutes seemed to be his record. For State dinners, though, he would slow down for the benefit of the guests."[11]

Obviously, how finicky the boss is about how the food tastes can make the cook's job very difficult. No president was nosier about kitchen operations than President Calvin Coolidge. Parks remembered,

> Mama came home with a million funny stories having to do with the President's sense of economy. He was always coming into the kitchen and personally instructing the help on how to cut the meat. He sought out Mrs. Jaffray [who supervised the kitchen staff] and gave her lessons in cutting corners, and once, when he heard the

kitchen help griping about his interference, he fixed them with a beady eye and asked them, "Do you have enough to eat?" "Yes, Mr. President," they agreed, snapping to attention. "Fine," he said, and walked out.[12]

This high level of intervention was quite remarkable since President Coolidge built his public persona on being laissez-faire ("let do") on everything else. Fortunately, most cooks did their job without such intense presidential oversight.

THE PRESIDENT'S SCHEDULE

If there has been a consistent thorn in the side of the presidential kitchen staff, it has been cooking for a commander in chief who is chronically late. Except for special occasions like a state dinner, where everyone knows the night will be long, members of the kitchen staff expect to work a manageable, almost routine, schedule and be home in the evening to spend time with their own families. From the Founding Fathers until the dawn of the twentieth century, our chief executives considered punctuality for meals to be a presidential virtue, which was good news for the kitchen staff. President Washington set the tone when he told a couple of congressmen who arrived late for a dinner he hosted at his presidential residence in New York City, "Gentlemen, we are punctual here. My cook never asks whether the company has arrived, but whether the hour has."[13] But by the twentieth century, the demands on the modern presidency often upset the place and timing of presidential meals. Theodore Roosevelt may have been the first president who implemented a "working lunch" by taking meals at his desk in the newly created Oval Office. Years later, his distant cousin Franklin Delano Roosevelt often ate his lunch from a heat-retaining enclosed cart that was wheeled by a butler from the basement kitchen to the Oval Office.

Working late or feeding a large number of unexpected guests has been the biggest source of irritation for the staff. As Parks wrote of Taft's presidential kitchen, "No cook would stay. No wonder: the President was forever keeping the kitchen off balance by bringing any number of guests home with him without advance warning. This coupled with Mrs. Taft's habit of looking into their pots and pans, made them decide that the honor of working in the White House wasn't worth the strain on their nervous systems. Even the cooks who cooked for the help wouldn't stay."[14] The kitchen staffs of Presidents Lyndon Baines Johnson and Bill Clinton would have certainly commiserated with their predecessors in Taft's kitchen. The strain of working in the presidential kitchen often took a toll on the cooks and their families, but the African American cooks suffered on because there were few alternative jobs that carried the same prestige and relatively stable income.

Sometimes a cook's rapport with the president allowed him or her to "turn the tables" and boss around "the boss." This can happen only after years of familiarity, as was the case between Zephyr Wright (discussed in chapter 4) and President Lyndon Johnson, which Jim Bishop chronicled while observing Johnson for a day: "Mrs. Zephyr Wright, a middle-aged Negro who has worked as a cook for the Johnsons for twenty-five years, is a lady of poise. She is unimpressed with the Presidency, and is probably the only person who if a President is late for a meal can tell him, 'Go sit in the kitchen until I fix you something.'"[15] All is not lost, though, regarding punctuality in the modern age, for Presidents George W. Bush and Barack Obama reportedly stuck to their schedules in ways that would have made President Washington proud.

THE PRESIDENT'S WEALTH

In 1858, the *Circular* reported something that most people probably didn't know: "For all domestic servants, . . . except steward and fireman, the President must pay for his own cooks, his butler, his table-servants, his female servants, his coachman and grooms, [etc.], as any other person does who employs such a retinue of servants. He supplies his table, with the exception of garden vegetables, as any other private person does by his own purse."[16] Early in our nation's history, presidents not only paid for all of their domestic staff but also underwrote all entertaining costs. President Washington started this unwritten rule, and it endured for more than a century after President James Buchanan left office. This custom partly explains why so many slaveholding presidents brought their enslaved cooks and personal servants with them — it was a lot cheaper than paying competitive wages for a professional cook in an open labor market. The custom finally came to an end during the Truman administration, when Congress made presidential residential staff and entertaining a regular line item in the federal budget.

PRESIDENTIAL PREROGATIVE

Few incoming presidents have started their presidencies as perfect specimens of health. They are usually older, sometimes overweight, and often on some physician-ordered diet. Add to that the overwhelming stress of

White House family dining room, circa 1901.
Mrs. John Logan, Thirty Years in Washington.

. . .

being president, and one has the sufficient conditions for an intense and persistent craving for junk food. Aside from their physicians, usually the only people who have saved the presidents from themselves have been their wives, who constantly and gently remind their husbands to watch what they eat. The First Ladies' efforts range from being antagonistic to engaging in a playful cat-and-mouse game. Presidents, like any spouse, are interested in promoting domestic tranquillity within their own household, so if they stray from their diet, they do it on the sly. To do so, presidents have enlisted the help of other family members, trusted aides, and the White House residence staff. White House maid Lillian Rogers Parks shared, "Every now and then we would get a chuckle out of hearing that someone had conspired with the staff to smuggle the President [Franklin D. Roosevelt] something he liked to eat. Usually it would be something that needed no cooking or just warming up."[17] In time, these surreptitious food acquisition schemes got fairly complex.

Second Ingredient: Others' Influences on Foodways

The second ingredient in the shaping of presidential foodways is the people who surround the commander in chief—namely, his family, friends, and staff. These folks, as we will learn, restrict the president's eating habits more often than one would think. It is not, however, accurate to think of this as a collection of people who want the president to be miserable. (That's the job of the opposition party in Congress.) No, these are people who love the commander in chief and are trying to maintain balance in his life and to keep him vibrant in the job and hopefully around long enough to enjoy a long ex-presidency.

THE FIRST LADY

Few people know a president better than the president's spouse. And while change is certain to come, through President Obama's administration our presidents have all been men, and so my research has uncovered a great deal of influence by First Ladies. The First Lady knows the president's aspirations, fears—and deepest food desires. Because of long-standing gender roles, the voting public, well into the twentieth century, expected most of our First Ladies to be model housewives. A First Lady had to be a good cook, keep her family healthy, maintain the household, and be a great hostess when called upon to entertain. Thus, First Ladies often supervised all of the culinary operations in the White House and became the "diet-enforcer-in-chief." The head cook would report directly to the First Lady to ensure that the president stayed on the right nutritional course. Knowing what presidents like and dislike, their wives have traditionally planned all of the private menus and consulted with the kitchen staff on what to make (and sometimes on how to make it). When the commander in chief is kept on a strict diet by his wife, cooks can feel caught in the middle between the president, who is their ultimate boss, and the First Lady, who is their immediate boss. When the two are together, the First Lady consistently wins. Take, for example, President Ronald Reagan, whose face, according to eyewitnesses, would light up like a little kid's when he boarded *Air Force One* and saw that Bavarian cream apple pie was on the menu. However, if his wife, Nancy, was with him, she anticipated what he would do, and according to one of the plane's crewmembers, "she would tell him, 'You're not having any of that,' and he would meekly acquiesce."[18]

In his memoirs, White House chief usher J. B. West wrote about the time First Lady Pat Nixon made a late-night impromptu food request:

Steaks we had—juicy, fresh, prime filets carefully selected by the meat wholesaler, waiting in the White House kitchen for a family who, we'd heard, loved steak. But cottage cheese? Chef [Henri] Haller called to request a White House limousine. "For two weeks we've laid in supplies in the kitchen," he wailed. "I think we could open a grocery store in the pantry. We've tried to find out every-thing they like. . . . But we don't have a spoonful of cottage cheese in the house. And what in the world would be open at this time of night—and Inauguration night to boot?" So the head butler, in a White House limousine, sped around the city of Washington until he found a delicatessen open with a good supply of cottage cheese. The kitchen never ran out, after that.[19]

West and his team were mortified, but they shouldn't have felt too bad after the yogurt episode with President Eisenhower. By coincidence, it was John Ficklin, Charles Ficklin's brother, who rode around town in a limousine to get Pat Nixon's cottage cheese. Who would have guessed that dairy products would cause the staff so much indigestion?

THE PRESIDENT'S PHYSICIAN

Surprisingly, the First Lady's powers of persuasion aren't always enough to keep a president healthy. Such was the case with First Lady Eleanor Roosevelt and President Franklin D. Roosevelt. Henrietta Nesbitt, the White House housekeeper during that administration, noted in her diary, "May 31, 1937—The President is cutting up an unusual tizzy-wizzy, as Mrs. R[oosevelt] calls it. She said he just never fussed over his food and this is most unexpected."[20] In such instances, Eleanor Roosevelt called for backup, and her call was typically answered by Navy vice admiral Dr. Ross McIntire,[21] the president's physician.

> "Call on me if you need help," [Dr. McIntire] said [to Mrs. Roose-velt] at the very start of the President's tizzies, and he co-operated on the menus and tried in every way to get the President's appetite back to normal. He sent to New York for specialists and finally he brought in doctors from the Naval Hospital, and a dietician arrived in uniform, and for a time the President ate everything he was told to eat, simply because it was "ordered by the Navy." The President's reducing diet came from the Navy and was the simplest on record: Cut out all fried foods.[22]

The president's own personal doctor from his private life often became the presidential physician, but in recent years, the physician tends to be a military doctor assigned to the White House. Like the First Lady, the presidential physician had veto power on anything the cooks planned to make and serve the chief executive. More times than not, the dynamic duo of the First Lady and the presidential physician formed a dieting alliance that even the president couldn't overcome, despite having several tricks up his sleeve.

WHITE HOUSE FOOD PROCUREMENT PROFESSIONALS

My blanket term for all of the people who shop for presidential groceries, once the parameters for the presidential diet have been set, is "White House food procurement professionals." Historically, presidential cooks have seldom shopped for food themselves. From the late 1700s until the late 1940s, the stewards, housekeepers, maître d', and food coordinators have discreetly bought the groceries. One of the presidential shopping hot spots during the nineteenth century was the Center Market, which opened on 15 December 1801, located where the National Archives Building now stands (700 Pennsylvania, NW). A few chief executives, notably Presidents Thomas Jefferson and William Henry Harrison, visited the Center Market themselves, which was demolished in 1931.[23] Only in the case of an emergency — such as a lack of dairy products — did a butler, a member of the Secret Service, or some other staffer purchase food. Today, due to security concerns, food procurement is outsourced to contractors who are vetted by the Secret Service (and sworn to secrecy), or the culinary staff shop anonymously at local grocery stores.[24] Regardless of who does the shopping, the procurers usually consult with the president's head chef to make sure any proposed menus fit presidential tastes. Still, one can't help but note that in this context, the people preparing the food are denied the joy of being at the market, getting to know the purveyors, and using their own discernment and senses to choose the ingredients with which they will cook — experiences that most personal cooks would have.

Some presidents have utilized the White House grounds for small-scale food production. President John Adams was troubled that the Executive Mansion didn't have a kitchen vegetable garden when he arrived. To him, "a house could not operate without a garden."[25] That was one of the first things he took care of when he moved into the Executive Mansion. President Jefferson expanded its cultivation and yield. During the Andrew Jackson administration, the kitchen garden was moved to the southwest portion of the grounds.[26] Historian William Seale argues, "It seems probable that the vegetable garden that spread southwest from the west wing supplied most of the needs of the table. The kitchen accounts of the various Presidents list few vegetables, and we know from the supplies purchased that through the summer and fall the cooks were much occupied with 'putting up' fruits and vegetables and otherwise making 'preserves' for the winter. These must have come from the garden."[27] The White House's kitchen garden took a quantum leap in recent years thanks to First Lady Michelle Obama's efforts (discussed in chapter 7).

There has been some small-scale husbandry over the years, mainly confined to a few dairy cows. Unlike many other households in nineteenth-century America, the White House grounds were not home to free-range chickens and pigs. Specific references to cows grazing on the White House grounds mark the Jefferson, John Quincy Adams, Jackson, William Henry Harrison, and Harding administrations.

Third Ingredient: White House Culture

The third ingredient that shapes presidential foodways is the culture, including the food culture, of the White House. The White House kitchen is a workplace just like any other professional kitchen, which brings an entire cast of people into the picture. I am sure that professional cooks everywhere will relate to how the food culture of their particular employer affects their ability to do their job.

THE WORKSPACE

Presidential chefs based in the Executive Residence have multiple workspaces. The starring attraction, of course, is the main kitchen, located in the White House's basement. If one stood in the current White House kitchen, one's first reaction might be, "That's it? It seems so small!" The first White House kitchen was located under the Entrance Hall, on the basement floor, where the Green Room is now. An early description indicates that the first White House kitchen "was about 43 feet long and 26 feet deep [wide], with two open fireplaces, whose hooks are still standing."[28] In the early days of the White House, its visitors could look down through the basement windows and into the kitchen and get a preview of what was cooking while they waited to get inside.[29] By the time of President Lincoln's administration, the kitchen had moved to the northwest corner of the basement and shrank a little to "40 feet in length and 25 feet wide. Leading out of it is a smaller apartment, known as the family kitchen, which is about half the size."[30] Servants ate their meals in the smaller space. Today, after more renovations, the White House kitchen is now a slightly smaller 30 by 26 feet in the 55,000-square-foot Executive Residence.[31]

Over time, First Families added cooking spaces to meet their needs. FDR added a kitchenette to the third floor solarium to accommodate the numerous relatives who dropped in for visits—and also to escape the horrible food he usually got (more on that later). President Truman added the White House Mess dining space and kitchen (further explained in chapter 5) during his administration to give his key aides a precious perk. In order to have a more intimate dining environment for her young family, Jacqueline Kennedy turned Margaret Truman's bedroom in the northwest corner of the second floor into a small kitchen, pantry, and dining space now known as the Family Dining Room. Given the space constraints of the existing White House, all of these additional cooking spaces are small and place a premium on functionality.

KITCHEN EQUIPMENT AND TECHNOLOGY

For most of its history, the White House kitchen has been on the cutting edge, being supplied with the finest and latest cooking equipment. Whenever the kitchen's equipment was upgraded, African American cooks stood as the expert practitioners of the old technology and were the first ones to try out the new technology. For the first fifty years, White House food was prepared in one of two large fireplaces. President Jefferson installed an iron range in one of the fireplaces that "burned coal, had spits, and was equipped with a crane. His 'stew holes,' or water heaters, also used coal. Presumably the fireplace at the opposite end of the room was fueled with wood and operated like any cooking fireplace of the day."[32] In the hearth, the cook expertly prepared all presidential meals, including state dinners for up to thirty-six people.[33]

In 1850, Millard Fillmore installed an updated cast-iron, coal-fired range in the kitchen. However, this was not a peaceful technological transition. Historical sources note that the new stove was immediately rejected by an unnamed African American woman who had been the head cook since the 1820s. According to a newspaper account of the new stove's installation,

its presence was first entirely ignored by the colored cook in charge, who continued to prepare the food served from her proprietary do-

White House kitchen, circa 1952. Courtesy Library of Congress.
. . .

main with the accoutrements with which she had been born and bred so to speak. Diplomatic pressure from Mrs. Fillmore in regard to the matter at first brought silent opposition and then incipient rebellion. The grapevine exchange in the kitchens of official Washington hummed with sympathy in the desecration of a great art that was involved before the altar of "dis contraption of de debil hiself which had done been unloaded on Marse Fillmore and his Missus."[34]

President Fillmore took a personal interest in the settling the matter, and he walked to the U.S. Patent Office, got the diagrams for the stove, learned how it worked, and made several demonstrations to the disgruntled cook. The stove's ease of use eventually won her over, and she, in time, became its fiercest advocate.[35]

The cast-iron range stayed a little more than a decade before it was moved to the new kitchen in the northwest corner. It soon developed mechanical problems that required Mary Todd Lincoln to call in the armed forces. A former soldier involved in the repair effort recalled in his memoirs, "Mrs. Lincoln told Colonel Butterfield [commanding officer of the Twelfth New York Militia guarding Washington] that the White House cook was in trouble — the 'waterback' of the range was out of order. . . . It certainly was a sight — four uniformed militiamen, with arms and accoutrements, marching into the White House kitchen, with an admiring group of colored servants looking on." President Lincoln thanked the soldiers in advance, saying, "Well, boys, I certainly am glad to see you. I hope you can fix that thing right off; for if you can't, the cook can't use the range, and I don't suppose that I'll get any 'grub' to-day!"[36] Once the range was working, it was a workhorse for decades. The earliest photograph of the White House kitchen shows that range as it existed during the Benjamin Harrison administration and with Dollie Johnson, his African American cook, nearby. We learn more about Chef Johnson in chapter 4.

By the twentieth century, the White House kitchen lost its status as the model kitchen of the United States. In the 1920s, Elizabeth Jaffray, the White House housekeeper of the time, observed, "The White House kitchens are . . . anything but modern. The only electric machine — with the exception of two or three small electric refrigerators — is an electric ice-cream freezer. There are really two White House kitchens — a very large one, and a reserve kitchen which is used only on the nights of special big dinners. Ordinarily the extra kitchen serves as a dining-room for the colored help. The dish-washing is done in the big kitchen by old-fashioned hand methods."[37] This slightly antiquated equipment managed to serve the presidential household well, but a decade later, the *Wall Street Journal* chided, "the executive mansion lacks many of the modern household appliances and equipment that new homes have today."[38]

A resourceful FDR figured out a way to modernize the White House kitchen while politically draping it as "putting people to work": he made the White House kitchen one of the federal Works Progress projects. As the press predicted, "the new stoves to be installed will mean learning new ways of cooking to the crack Negro staff, Ida Allen, chief cook, and her assistants, Catherine Smith, Elizabeth Moore and Elizabeth Blake."[39] When the work was completed, the revamped kitchen was shown off with much fanfare as First Lady Eleanor Roosevelt personally led the first tour: "The touring party was made up of newspaper reporters. They had come for the First Lady's press conference but before they were through they saw everything from a collection of electric waffle irons to the napkin rings of the domestic staff. . . . [Mrs. Roosevelt] announced with obvious relief that Ida Allen and Elizabeth Moore, first and second cooks, brought here from the Governor's mansion in Albany, approve of the new 'cook stove.'"[40] Once again, African Americans, as the first adopters of new cooking technology, given their status in the kitchen, had to approve the new equipment.

In addition to the new equipment, the renovation made the White House basement more functional. According to the *Baltimore Afro-American*, "The staff had been remembered in the renovation plans to the extent being provided, for the first time in [history], with locker rooms, a place in which to change their clothes and a rest room. Footmen, who in the past have been burdened with frequent trips up and down spiral stairs, leading from the kitchen to the main floor, also have some relief in store, through the installation of two large dumb waiters from the elaborate service pantry to another on the floor above."[41] Ultimately, the *New York Amsterdam News*, another African American newspaper, declared, "The new, most modern White House kitchens . . . have become the talk of the country, and [of] leading hotels, tea-rooms and dining rooms in Washington, Baltimore, Philadelphia, Atlantic City, New York, Ithaca and Boston."[42]

The next kitchen upgrade came in the early 1950s during the last years of the Truman administration. At that time, the White House was literally falling apart, and it had become too dangerous for the First Family to reside there. Though the structural quality of the residence was improved, the cooking appliances remained relatively the same. From that time until the early twenty-first century, the kitchen equipment has been updated as needed—for example, getting a microwave installed—but not necessarily with the latest gadgets. Today, the White House kitchen is adequately equipped and doesn't lag as far behind other professional kitchens as it has in the past.

COWORKERS

In his culinary memoir, former White House assistant chef John Moeller recalled a candid moment in the 1980s that he had with then White House executive chef Pierre Chambrin. Chef Chambrin "talked about the complex personalities you have to deal with [at the White House]. 'It's not so much the president or the first lady—it's all of the other characters who work in and around the White House. Cooking at the White House is different.' He made an important point: 'It's not a restaurant; it's not a hotel. You're cooking in somebody's home—and you're serving them almost every single day.'"[43] Yet, this is not just any home—it's a unique home, the most famous public housing in our country. Thus, the White House cooking crew is not a "dysfunctional, mercenary lot, fringe-dwellers motivated by money," as former restaurant chef and current television personality Anthony Bourdain once described the typical restaurant kitchen staff.[44] The U.S. Secret Service's screening process makes sure of that.

As with any workplace, an inordinate amount of White House cooks' happiness depends upon their relationship not only with their bosses but also with their coworkers. The presidential kitchen has been a multicultural workplace from the beginning, with people of different races, classes, sexes, legal status (enslaved or free), and countries of origin all working side by side. The earliest presidential kitchens were staffed by a five-person team: the steward or housekeeper, who purchased groceries and planned menus; a head cook in charge of all the meals involving the president; a second cook, who prepared meals for the residence staff; and two other workers who shared a variety of preparation and cleanup duties.[45] By the 1880s, the work dynamic changed when outside caterers and chefs were hired to handle the big entertainments like state dinners, congressional dinners, diplomatic corps dinners, and the U.S. Supreme Court dinners. The Taft administration ended this practice when, in a cost-saving move, all cooking operations were brought in-house.

As the White House staff, including political appointees and those who maintained the residence, grew in number over succeeding administrations, so did the culinary team. In the main White House kitchen, the team increased from five to eight people, including the first cook (what used to be called the "head cook" and would later be called the "executive chef"), two assistant chefs, a pastry chef, an assistant pastry chef, and three kitchen helpers to perform various kitchen duties.[46] Sometimes, the residence's culinary team grew to nine if a president wanted a private chef designated to cook meals solely for the First Family. For events with a large number of guests, like state dinners, extra chefs were temporarily hired after they passed an extensive security screening.

In such a high-stress environment as the presidential kitchen, it's no surprise that there always seems to be some interpersonal conflict simmering in the kitchen, but rarely have things boiled over to the point where it has been recorded for posterity. The cause of these disputes generally have involved the respect one feels one deserves, including how one feels about one's boss, how the boss feels about him or her, the cook's perceived status with the president, how one's salary compares with others', available perquisites ("perks"), and perceived slights based on race, seniority, or gender. Former White House housekeeper Henrietta Nesbitt probably put it best when she wrote, "There is something about working over a hot stove that brings out the best and worst in people."[47] At least some perks could help keep the worst in people at bay.

PERKS

Given their relatively low pay, presidential cooks constantly sought ways to supplement their income. As late as the twentieth century, White House residence staffers, including the kitchen staff, got tips from guests—that is, until First Lady Mamie Eisenhower banned the practice. Not surprisingly, her decision was not well received by the staff. As longtime White House maid Lillian Rogers Parks elaborated, "I know one kitchen worker at the White House who was widowed and supporting two children on about $48 a week before taxes. Losing the tips was hard for her and others like her. Many people think working at the White House is easy, because the work is divided among so many people, and those who work there have soft prestige jobs. Let me tell you that more people have ruined their health under the grueling strain of working at the White House than you would believe."[48] For people living on the margins, as White House staffers often did, the slightest changes in salary and supplemental income made a tremendous difference in their quality of life.

Living in the White House was another perk, but not always a pleasant one. Enslaved cooks were forced to live the majority of their lives in the White House's basement or attic, where the servant quarters were located. Jesse Holland, author of *The Invisibles*, helps us grasp the life circumstances of White House slaves:

The African-American slaves most often had rooms in the White House's basement, referred to as the ground floor today because it opens out onto the South Gardens and the National Mall. These were airy rooms directly beneath the principal floor of the house and on the north and south sides of the long groin-vaulted hall that ran from one end of the house to the other. . . . These rooms are now used as a Library, China Room, offices, and the formal oval Diplomatic Reception Room. However, this vaulted corridor once accessed a great kitchen forty feet long with large fireplaces at each end, a family kitchen, an oval servants hall, the steward's quarters, storage and workrooms, and the servant and slave bedrooms. This is where the presidents stashed their slaves, where enslaved Africans ate, slept, socialized and made the best of their imprisonment, all while making the lives of the president and his family as easy as possible so that the affairs of the household could be ignored for the more important affairs of state.[49]

This "live-in" job requirement continued even for free laborers well into the 1920s. White House housekeeper Elizabeth Jaffray wrote in the 1920s, "All of the servants, with the exception of the white maids, the four [African American] footmen, the firemen and the mechanic and the electrician, lived in the basement of the White House in rooms off the kitchens, and had their meals at a common table."[50] By the time of the FDR administration, African American cooks lived in their own homes off the White House grounds; however, the First Family's private cook lived in an apartment on the White House's second or third floor.

Presidential cooks also expected in-house meals. This was particularly important for African Americans on staff because in Jim Crow Washington, there wasn't a place for them to eat near the White House; they would be refused service. As Jaffray shared in her memoirs, "The White House help are fed much the same as the servants in any other large house. They are given staple vegetables that are served on the President's own table, but they are not given the same meats or expensive luxuries that necessarily grace the President's table. It is an invariable rule that on every Thursday chicken be served to the help, and this is always counted a great day by the colored servants."[51] The cooks did have some say in the staff meal menu. White House maid Parks observed,

> The cooks ate at their own table in the kitchen. Lunch was our big meal. We ate at twelve o'clock sharp because the family ate at one, and some of us would be needed to serve them. Again, we were sure that aside from state dinners, we servants have the best meals at the White House. Lunch might be roast beef, pork, stewed chicken, or baked ham. On Friday we always had fish. Every day we had hot vegetables and various cakes and ice creams for dessert. [In] summer we have watermelon, which I didn't eat. I would be accused of being prejudiced against Negroes—a little ethnic joke. One cook was a whiz at spoon bread, and she would frequently make it for us.[52]

Servants had autonomy over their in-house staff meals for several decades. This created a space for soul food to be the White House's everyday cuisine—at least for the majority black residence staff. As White House chief usher J. B. West observed, "Because Congress had permitted us to feed the servants since the beginning of the Trumans, [Johnson administration food coordinator] Mary [Kaltman] had $1,000 a month to spend for two meals a day (the servants worked on two shifts) for the thirty-two-person staff. They selected their own menus—not chili or pâté, but plain American Southern-style cooking: fried chicken, pork chops, pigs' feet, cornbread, black-eyed peas. They ate family style, in the help's dining room in the lower basement."[53] In some respects, the Executive Mansion operated as a daily "House of Soul," as the Carters soon discovered after they started living in the White House. When First Lady Betty Ford led her successor Rosalynn Carter on a White House kitchen tour shortly before Jimmy Carter's inauguration, Mrs. Carter overheard one chef say to another, "You know I really think that we're going to please the Carters with our Southern cooking—we cook like that every day for the help."[54]

Another plum food-related perk was getting the leftovers from the fancier White House meals. In the South, it had been customary for servants to take leftovers home, which was a great way to feed their families. This practice was called "to tote" or "toting"—a phrase derived from a West African word meaning "to carry." White House workers, however, were denied this privilege, which meant that leftovers had to be consumed on the spot. As White House housekeeper Henrietta Nesbitt explained,

> There was a rule that no "tote" be permitted from the White House kitchen. Nothing could be carried out as in other homes in Washington, where the Southern influence showed in letting the help "tote" home the leftover food. Mrs. Roosevelt and I had an understanding that red-letter day ice cream and cake should go to the charitable organizations, but we were overruled in this by an older, established White House tradition that decreed all the leftover specially made cakes, the specially made ice cream, and all the food left on the platters, or on the table, belonged to the help. They had to eat it then and there, since nothing could be carried out.[55]

Regardless of the amount of perks, the aura of working in the White House remains the best way to recruit and retain presidential employees. Jaffray summed it up best when she noted, "Naturally it is a great honor to any servant to be chief cook at the White House and the position carries considerable prestige with it. In some ways this offsets the disadvantage of the modest pay."[56] That same ethos survives to the present day.

As if cooking for and with humans doesn't cause enough drama, White House cooks have had to deal with presidential pets as well. For example, much like people, FDR's dogs had menus, meals of meats and vegetables, and they even had to go on periodic diets.[57] White House maid Parks relates,

> One day Eleanor returned from a trip to find an urgent message waiting for her at the White House to come to see the President in his bedroom. She had been worried about her husband's health and rushed there. The President looked very concerned. "I'm so glad you're here," he said. "I came right away. What's wrong, Franklin? Have you seen Dr. McIntire?" "No," he said, "I've seen Fala's vet. He left this special diet and says it's very important. So will you please give this to the cooks and see that this special medicine is added to it?"[58]

That's an interesting twist where the president, with respect to feeding his pets, acted much like a First Lady by keeping a beloved pet on a diet.

A president's concern for saving money can also get unleashed on pets, not just on humans. Former White House pet trainer Traphes Bryant wrote about his experiences with President Lyndon Johnson and his dogs, Him and Blanco:

> I'll never forget the day LBJ went on an economy kick, petwise. My diary records the date as July 22, 1965. It was the day the President discovered what dog food costs. It had been a day like so many others—the President gave a speech in the Rose Garden and afterwards took Him and Blanco to the south fence where tourists took pictures, shook hands, and formed quite a crowd. But at 9:00 P.M., the President suddenly blew his stack. He had just found out his monthly dog-food bill was $80. "Goddamn it," he said, "I'd be laughed out of Johnson City if anyone knew what I'm paying to feed a couple of dogs. Christ, a family could live on it." I told the President I would leave word for the ushers to stop buying hamburger. I did and Usher Carter asked me if the dogs were getting too fat. I said, "No, the President's pocketbook is getting too lean."[59]

Though LBJ's edicts had been in place for several years, he still sent mixed messages. Bryant's diary entry for 20 July 1968 reads, "I told the President that I took Yuki [another one of the president's dogs] to the second floor at 7:30 P.M. every night and Zephyr fed Yuki. But the Prez was still at it. The President said, 'You and Zephyr make a good salary. You all should put some weight on Yuki.' . . . He said maybe I was confused about his wanting to put some weight on Yuki but to take the fat *off* the beagles."[60] As one can see, when it came to feeding pets to keep both them and the president happy, the cooks often faced a "no-win" scenario.

Once in a blue moon, presidential pets have also interfered with the White House cooks' dining plans. One morning in March 1934, twelve plates of fried eggs and ham were set out for breakfast in the servants' dining room. After the cook stepped away to summon the staff to come eat, she returned to find the food missing from all of the plates! After an intense search, the culprit was identified as man's best friend, or in this case FDR's best friend—a Llewellin setter named Winks. President Roosevelt had picked up the dog during one of his sojourns to Warm Springs, Georgia. As much as Roosevelt loved that dog, Winks soon disappeared, leaving many to speculate whether or not he left the White House to "spend more time with his family." This event, along with others, cleared the way for FDR's more familiar dog, Fala.[61]

WHITE HOUSE WILDLIFE

This section doesn't refer to cute deer or fuzzy rabbits grazing on the White House lawn. No, it is about vermin, specifically the critters that one would expect to thrive in a swamp like the one where the White House is situated. During President Martin Van Buren's time, in the 1830s, the White House kitchen regularly flooded after rainstorms. By the 1890s, the basement was so overrun by insects, rats, and other vermin that one of the African American cooks allegedly killed rats by sitting on them.[62] As we'll see, some First Ladies were so exasperated that they wanted out of the White House altogether. The last known wildlife feed happened during the Lyndon Johnson administration when rats dragged an entire ham off the servants' dining room table. Only after an atrocious odor emerged months later did someone find a completely gnawed ham bone decaying behind a wall.[63] Don't be alarmed, gentle reader; the current White House is rumored to be quite immaculate.

RACIAL ATTITUDES

Until the civil rights movement in the 1960s, the social status of African Americans in general provides a strong subtext for their role as presidential cooks. As we'll see in this narrative, whites held a consensus that blacks were created for servitude. Most relevant to our story is the widely held belief that African Americans were "natural born cooks." Thus, many African Americans became cooks because it was one of the few occupations open to them. Race shaped how blacks, as a perceived servant class, got the job as a cook and influenced the expectations of how they should perform, what they got paid, and what they ate. Disappointingly, in this dysfunctional environment, African Americans internalized racial attitudes so much that it actually affected how they related to one another. Housekeeper Elizabeth Jaffray described how this intraracial dynamic played out in the 1910s and 1920s:

> Mrs. Taft and I had an embryo servants' revolt over the question of where the different servants should have their meals. For many years the servants had settled themselves into very distinct castes. At a special table the four of the five highest colored men of the staff would dine in state—the head steward, the head coachman and two or three others. At a table in the butler's pantry the dining-room staff would eat what was left over from the President's own table. Then the laundry-women and scrubwomen would eat at a table by themselves. I immediately ordered that all colored servants, regardless of rank or position, should eat at a single table and at a given hour. The white servants were to have their own table—but there was no other distinction of any kind. There were signs of sharp dissatisfaction, but when I promised dismissal the revolt died.[64]

In her memoir, Lillian Rogers Parks reported that this trend continued well into the twentieth century: "I must confess that backstairs, there is a little matter of a caste system among the help, based on position and seniority. For a time, we even took our positions at our long dining table according to the system. I sat 'high.'"[65] As one will see, before the 1960s, racial attitudes led many African Americans to the White House kitchen. During and after the 1960s, changing racial attitudes led African Americans not only away from the White House kitchen but also away from professional cooking in general.

Fourth Ingredient: Surprising Elements

Here we have arrived at the fourth and final ingredient in the shaping of presidential foodways: the always surprising elements that just simply extend beyond the president's control.

As noted earlier, during the Truman administration Congress began appropriating money for White House residence staff, food, and entertainment. Congress has frequently used its executive office appropriation as a check on any aristocratic indulgences by the chief executive. At other times, certain members of Congress used the appropriation as a political weapon to either exact revenge or embarrass the president. Such tendencies were on high display when the "Do Nothing Congress"—so named by President Truman—had say-so on his household budget.

In terms of figuring out the finances, the process works like this: Congress appropriates a sum of money that sets the budget parameters for presidential living expenses. When members of the First Family request anything involving food and drink, they are presented a bill for expenses, which is then settled out of their account on a weekly or monthly basis. Entertaining expenses are treated the same way. If the money runs out, the president must find funding from other sources or go back to Congress to ask for more money. The latter would be a public relations nightmare, so presidents have often "found" extra money by "borrowing" cooks from and/or charging expenses to other government agencies or outside parties. Aside from their salaries, this budgeting process has also had a direct impact on how the servants ate, but they were able to carve out some autonomy, as mentioned above. Because Congress is the repository of the people's power and sentiment, the next element is a fairly potent one.

PUBLIC PERCEPTION

This is the intangible element that worries presidents the most. A consistent narrative that the commander in chief is somehow out of touch with the average citizen can starve a president of the political capital needed to complete his political agenda—and can most certainly hurt his chances of getting reelected. In a democracy where everyone is theoretically equal, being perceived as a snob is a serious offense. The Founding Fathers' generation was very concerned about not aping the monarchy from which they had successfully rebelled. President Washington, knowing the very powerful precedent that his administration would set, remained very image-conscious during his presidency. But since he and the other Founding Fathers were doing things on the fly, they couldn't entirely shed the English customs they knew so well.

For European and American elites, French cuisine set the standard for elite dining. Accordingly, the American voting public has long been suspicious of a president who has a French cook, regularly dines on French food, and drinks French wines. For example, Patrick Henry heavily criticized Thomas Jefferson for celebrating Franco-southern fusion food and made him seem unpatriotic for doing so.[66] Because of the ease with which one could be charged with snobbery, presidents were frequently on the defensive if they indulged in French cuisine. The public disdain for "Frenchness" created the backdrop for an enduring rivalry: French chefs versus African American chefs. Time and time again, African American chefs and the food they prepared represented what was great in American cooking and supposedly lacking in French cuisine: comfort, informality, ingenuity, and simplicity. Many presidents went out of their way to reassure the public that they loved the homey dishes prepared by their African American cooks, though they rarely dignified these cooks by referring to them by their full names.

Thus, in the public imagination, the culinary competition between American and French food (and, by inference, between American and French cooks) ebbed and flowed with intensity from the time of Jefferson until LBJ. Since President Nixon, the White House has been pushed to be a strong advocate of American food and drink. The main difference of late is that such cooking is not expressly tied to the culinary genius of African American cooks. Sam Houston Johnson, LBJ's brother, underscored that point when he wrote in his autobiography, "The Kennedys had a fancy French chef who prepared all kinds of unpronounceable dishes, but I'm sure the White House has never had a better cook — or a more independent one — than Zephyr Wright. When she cooked her special roast with Pedernales River chili sauce or fried chicken with spoon bread, you started wishing you had two stomachs."[67]

FOOD GIFTS

As mentioned earlier, Americans feel a need to connect with their president. One way they have shown this desire is by sending great amounts of food to the Executive Residence by mail and special delivery. People dispatched food at the slightest impulse — a media report of the president's favorite food, congratulations for some achievement, wishing a speedy recovery from an illness, lobbying for a certain product, and many times just out of sheer admiration. It was definitely a different time, for past presidents would accept and actually eat these gifts! The U.S. Secret Service would never let that happen today, so the White House table is now provisioned by an array of security-checked food suppliers. If you feel motivated to send the president any food, you should eat it yourself or give it away, because it will be destroyed if it arrives at the White House.

CLIMATE

Cooking in the White House was seasonal employment until air conditioning was installed in the 1950s. Before then, presidents would regularly leave the Executive Residence for a milder climate because it got unbearably hot during the summer. Their travel destination was often an entirely different part of the country or their hometown. There were a few presidents who stayed in the D.C. area but just moved to higher elevations, as President Lincoln did at the Old Soldiers' Home in northwest D.C. or as Grover Cleveland did in the part of D.C. now known as Cleveland Park. The extended stays away from the Executive Mansion made a lot of sense because the threat of contracting a tropical disease like malaria was very real. After all, the White House kitchen was literally mired underneath a swamp. However, we'll see that, in some instances, the black cooks were forced to stay and cook for presidential staff, even though the president had left.

All four of the major ingredients in presidential foodways, as I've described above, are affected to one degree or another by a final, rather intangible ingredient—I call it the "White House Way." This means "tradition." It's astonishing, but understandable, how really closely presidents have stuck, through the years, to the way George Washington did things while he was in office.

It is the members of the Executive Residence staff—perhaps everyone except the head chef—who serve as the standard bearers for this sort of institutional memory. In short, staff members communicate to an incoming president, "It's *our* world, and you're just a visitor." Though many a First Family come to the White House with ideas of shaking things up, you would be surprised by how many acquiesce when the staff communicates how things have been done in the past.

In the midst of all of the potential and rich combinations of the ingredients considered above, each providing varying influences on and lending different flavors to a particular presidential administration, I note some trends that have emerged and have affected how African American presidential chefs have done their jobs. The first is a progressive trend, moving through time from slavery to freedom: chefs who were once forced to

The author (left) in the White House kitchen with presidential kitchen steward Adam Collick, 2015. Author's photograph.

. . .

cook became chefs who could choose their profession. The second trend is how the White House residence operation transitioned, under President Lincoln, from that of a "plantation big house" to that of a wealthy home (Lincoln to Hoover) and, since FDR, became like a hotel. The third and ongoing trend is the intensifying interest of the general public in presidential foodways.

To tell this diverse story over every presidential administration since George Washington's, I found it fascinating to shape *The President's Kitchen Cabinet* by large themes, exploring the wildly diverse daily duties and responsibilities, concerns, and often very entertaining realities of life for presidential cooks and food service staff. Chapter 2 begins with those responsible for hiring cooks, planning menus, and procuring the food. In chapter 3, we take a closer look at the different classes of cooks, some of whom worked side by side in the White House kitchen before the Civil War: slaves and independent culinary professionals. Chapter 4 chronicles how independent culinary professionals, military personnel, and personal servants shaped the White House food story after Emancipation. We then see, in chapter 5, what happens to food operations when the president travels away from the White House. Chapter 6 closely explores what beverages our presidents have used to wash down their food and, sometimes, their cares. We will finish up with some divining on my part about the future prospects of African American chefs.

Chefs and cooks predominate these pages, but there will be times when non-chefs, airplane crews, butlers, maids, maître d's, and wait staff join the story. And throughout, marveling at all these personalities and their stories, I strive to answer these essential questions about the presidential cook staff: How did they learn to become a cook? What was their path to cooking for a president? What type of food did they make? Over the course of American history, we will see how African American presidential chefs stood at a unique intersection of class, personal relationship, race, and power. Though they primarily related to the president and First Families through the excellent and comforting food they prepared, we'll see how these culinary professionals used their positions to illuminate race relations, advocate for civil rights, gain trust as a confidante, become part of the First Family, and sometimes become close friends with the presidents they served.

During the presidency of Andrew Jackson, much ink (positive and negative) was spilled in newspaper editorials over the creation of an informal group of presidential advisers who were often unnamed and unaccountable to the public but highly trusted by the president. Because they reportedly met with the president in the White House kitchen in order to avoid scrutiny, this group of advisers was nicknamed the "Kitchen Cabinet."[68] Speaking of these informal advisers, presidential historian Michael Nelson quoted President Franklin Roosevelt as once saying, "The president 'needs someone who asks for nothing but to serve [the president].'"[69] Many presidents found such individuals among the African Americans who prepared and served their meals. These are their stories.

Recipes

HOW TO ROAST DUCKS

Since the beginning of the presidency, journalists have often failed to record the names of those working in the White House kitchen. I stumbled upon this recipe credited to one of President McKinley's African American cooks while flipping through a dusty, old cookbook. In *Cooking in Old Creole Days*, author Celestine Eustis lists several recipes attributed to Katie Seabrook, whom she identifies as "Pres. McKinley's Colored Cook." I love this recipe because it shows a complex melding of flavors despite the recipe's simplicity.

Don't wash your ducks, but wipe them thoroughly with a clean cloth, inside and outside. Rub the back (inside and outside) with a small piece of onion. Salt and pepper them the same way. Tie them up tightly so the juice does not escape. Rub the breast of each duck with a spoonful of olive oil. Lay in your dripping-pan a slice or two of bacon, one carrot, one leek, two bay leaves, a piece of celery. Place the ducks on this, and let them cook in a moderate oven twenty-five minutes. Put in any dressing you would make for a roast chicken. With all your roast meats put in the bottom of your roast-pan a carrot cut in half, a piece of onion, celery and parsley. The same with boiled meats or fish, to give foundation taste to your food.

ZEPHYR WRIGHT'S POPOVERS

Lynda Bird Johnson Robb, Lyndon and Lady Bird Johnson's elder daughter, graciously reminisced over the phone with me about Zephyr Wright. I asked her about her fondest culinary memories, and these popovers were foremost in her mind. The recipe is credited to Lady Bird Johnson, but it was Zephyr Wright's cooking of the popovers that brought back the memories.

Makes 6 popovers

1 cup sifted all-purpose flour
1/4 teaspoon salt
2 eggs, beaten
1 cup milk
2 tablespoons shortening, melted (or 1 tablespoon butter and
  1 tablespoon shortening, melted)

1. Preheat the oven to 450°F. Generously grease a 6-cup popover pan and place it in the oven while it preheats.
2. Sift the flour and salt into a large bowl.
3. In a separate bowl, combine the eggs, milk, and shortening.
4. Gradually whisk the liquid into the flour mixture.
5. Beat the mixture for one minute or until the batter is smooth.
6. Carefully remove the pan from the oven and fill the cups three-quarters full with the batter.
7. Bake for 20 minutes.
8. Reduce the heat to 350°F and continue baking for an additional 15–20 minutes.

Chef Sonya Jones grew up in Atlanta, Georgia, and, when she was ten years old, began helping her mother prepare food sold in the family café. Chef Jones coupled that early culinary education with professional training at the Culinary Institute of America in Hyde Park, New York. She now runs the Sweet Auburn Bread Company in Atlanta, Georgia, not far from where she grew up. In 1999, President Clinton took one bite of Chef Jones's rich riff on a traditional cheesecake and loved it. Sweet potatoes are the magic ingredient for this cheesecake, and the "crust" is made of thin slices of southern pound cake.

Makes 10–12 servings

For the pound cake crust
  1 1/2 cups (3 sticks) butter
  1 (8-ounce) package cream cheese
  3 cups sugar
  6 eggs
  2 teaspoons pure vanilla extract
  2 teaspoons pure lemon extract
  3 cups unbleached all-purpose flour, sifted

For the cheesecake
  About 1 pound sweet potatoes
  3 (8-ounce) packages cream cheese
  1 1/2 cups sugar
  3 large eggs
  1 cup half-and-half
  1 teaspoon pure vanilla extract
  1 teaspoon freshly grated nutmeg
  Fresh berries to taste

To make the pound cake:
  1. Grease and flour a 10-inch tube pan.
  2. Using a mixer, cream together the butter, cream cheese, and sugar until the mixture is light and fluffy.
  3. Add the eggs one at a time, beating well after each addition.
  4. Blend in the vanilla and lemon extracts.
  5. With the mixer set to low speed, gradually add the flour and beat just until incorporated.
  6. Pour the batter into the prepared pan.

7. Place the pan in a cold oven and turn the temperature to 325°F; bake for 1 1/2 hours, or until a toothpick inserted in the center comes out clean.
8. Remove the cake from the oven and allow it to cool in the pan for 10 minutes before turning out onto a wire rack.
9. Cool completely before slicing.

To make the cheesecake:
1. Boil the sweet potatoes for 40–50 minutes, or until tender.
2. Drain the potatoes and run them under cold water to remove the skin.
3. Mash the sweet potatoes in a bowl; you should have 2 cups. Set them aside and allow to cool completely.
4. Preheat the oven to 350°F.
5. Line the bottom of a 9-inch round cake pan with parchment paper and spray the sides of the pan with nonstick cooking spray.
6. Lay flat six or seven 1/4-inch slices of the pound cake in the bottom of the pan (they should not overlap). Set aside.
7. Using a mixer, beat the cream cheese until fluffy, then gradually add the sugar until it is well blended.
8. Add the eggs, one at a time, beating well after each addition.
9. Stir in the mashed sweet potatoes.
10. Add the half-and-half, vanilla, and nutmeg and mix well.
11. Pour the mixture into the prepared pan and bake for 1 hour, or until the center is almost set.
12. Remove from the oven and allow the cheesecake to cool.
13. When the cake is cool, run a knife along the edges and remove it from the pan by inverting it onto a plate.
14. Transfer the cheesecake to a serving platter, crust-side-down, and refrigerate until ready to serve.
15. Garnish with fresh berries.

2
Feeling at Home
THE WHITE HOUSE STEWARD AND
THE EVOLUTION OF PRESIDENTIAL
PROVISIONING

The White House steward, in exercising his prerogative
of selecting candidates for office in the President's household,
enjoys a political patronage somewhat less than a Member of Congress,
but still considerable. He also administers extensive commercial patronage.
He purchases all of the supplies for the President's table, and replenishes
all household stores, such as table and bed linen,
cooking utensils and crockery.
FLORA MCDONALD THOMPSON,
"Housekeeping in the White House," *Junior Munsey*, 1901

For thousands of years, stewards have served as the ultimate arbiter of good taste. In the Christian tradition, Jesus Christ performed his first miracle by turning water into wine at a wedding at Cana in Galilee. After the miracle was performed, the wedding's steward (translated as the "master of the feast") tasted the miraculous wine and immediately asked, "Why are you putting out the good stuff *at the end* of the wedding?"[1] Presidential stewards have long accomplished roles as both tastemaker and miracle worker, usually under difficult circumstances. Though the proper title and responsibilities of the steward position have shifted over time, presidents have frequently called upon African Americans to oversee the Executive Mansion's domestic operations, which include the culinary department. This chapter focuses on the White House experiences of six representative presidential stewards: Samuel Fraunces, William T. Crump, Henry Pinckney, Alonzo Fields, Stephen Rochon, and Angella Reid.

During the eighteenth and nineteenth centuries, a "steward" was generally defined as "an official who controls the domestic affairs of a household, supervising the service of his master's table, directing the domestics, and regulating household expenditure."[2] Accordingly, presidential stewards have performed the same duties for the presidential household: hiring and supervising all of the residence employees, administering all public and private dining, and ultimately being responsible for purchasing and safeguarding all White House property. Stewards answered solely to the First Family. Presidents have looked for a handful of key attributes in their stewards: trustworthiness, a demonstrated ability to do the job well (usually based on prior servitude in private life to the individual who became president), and African ancestry.

An overwhelming number of the African Americans who have held the presidential steward position have been biracial men, and this fact fed into a persistent stereotype from antebellum America: that enslaved biracial people (usually African and European) worked primarily as servants for the plantation master's family in the "big house" while the darker-skinned enslaved African Americans labored in the plantation's fields. In addition, it is believed that the legacy of this purposeful separation and differing status based on skin color has been a major stumbling block to collective black progress to this day. Yet slavery scholar Eugene D. Genovese, among others, has argued that this idea of a sharp color-based division of plantation labor is more myth than reality: "As often as not, southern slaveholders . . . enjoyed being served by blacks— the blacker the better—as well as by light-skinned Negroes. Even during the colonial period, whites did not show any great partiality to mulattoes, except when they were blood relatives."[3]

Genovese's conclusion became the conventional wisdom in scholarly circles, but Howard Bodenhorn, an economic historian at Clemson University, has recently called for a reassessment: "Eugene Genovese downplayed or dismissed mixed race preferences, but contemporary observations and modern statistical analysis point toward modestly favored treatment [for mixed race slaves]. Planters preferred mixed-race men and women as house servants, and gave them more skill training. Mixed-race slaves were more likely than blacks to receive some education, to eat from the Big House's kitchen, to be better clothed and shod, and have greater freedom of movement on and off the plantation."[4] With this advantage in skills and training, biracial men were well positioned to get domestic household jobs or to start their own businesses (caterers, hoteliers, and restaurateurs). With this historical context, then, it is not surprising that our first president, a slave owner, put a biracial man—one who had run several successful businesses and one whom he knew very well—in charge of his household affairs.

President George Washington, it turns out, set a high standard for all presidential stewards who followed when he chose Samuel Fraunces to be the first. Before delving into Fraunces's story, though, we must address a simmering-for-centuries controversy over his race. Some historians have strongly argued that Fraunces was white. In his painted portrait he looks white, and while this is not dispositive of African heritage, the image raises doubts. We know that Fraunces hailed from the West Indies, probably from Jamaica or Saint Domingue (present-day Haiti), but again, that fact in and of itself is not determinative of his race. Alexander Hamilton, a well-known Caucasian, was from the same place. Yet there are other qualities about Fraunces that would have been highly unusual for someone of African heritage—who was not passing for white—to possess in eighteenth-century New York City. First, Fraunces owned white indentured servants, and when they escaped he advertised rewards for their recapture in local newspapers.[5] Additionally, he was listed as "white" in the 1790 federal census, he was a member of the Freemason secret society, he was a registered voter, and he attended Trinity Church in New York City.[6]

The most compelling positive case for his African heritage is that his contemporaries nicknamed him "Black Sam." In those days, one would be called "black" for one of two reasons: having a villainous disposition or having a dark-complexioned skin tone. The first attribute is highly unlikely, given that General Washington thought so highly of him and trusted him. In a letter to Fraunces, Washington wrote, "You have invariably through the most trying times maintained a constant friendship and attention to the cause of our country and its independence and freedom."[7]

The second reason, a darker skin tone, hasn't always led to the assumption that one had African ancestry; there are whites who have been described as having a "swarthy" complexion without any further speculation about their race. But that's not the case with Fraunces, who has generated a great deal of curiosity and controversy about his racial background, mainly due to the dogged efforts of journalists and (primarily) amateur historians.[8] Supposedly, a birth certificate existed indicating that Fraunces had a white father and an African mother.[9] Other "reputable class publications" and contemporaneous media accounts also describe Fraunces as a "mulatto," the term of that time for biracial people.[10] Fraunces biographer Charles Blockson adds, "While researching the story of his life, it was discovered that Fraunces' racial identity was recorded as Negro, colored, Haitian Negro, Mulatto, 'fastidious old Negro' and swarthy."[11] Given the above, Fraunces arguably had African DNA—

a conclusion embraced by some of his descendants—and I proceed on that assumption.[12]

Born in 1722, Fraunces arrived in New York City sometime in the early to mid-1750s, probably as a stowaway on a ship from the West Indies. He had an entrepreneurial spirit and opened his first business selling pickles and preserves. Thanks to his business success, he established his reputation as a dandy, often wearing a heavy watch chain and an elaborate wig. In 1762 he purchased the DeLancey Mansion for £2,000 and renamed it Queen Charlotte's Head Tavern, which became Queen's Tavern and then ultimately Fraunces Tavern. A replica of the original building currently stands at its original location of 54 Pearl Street (intersecting Broad Street) in the Wall Street district of New York City.[13] Food-and-drink-loving people who were increasingly disenchanted with the British government gravitated to Fraunces Tavern. The British saw the tavern as a dangerous gathering place, and on 23 August 1775 the British warship *Asia*, patrolling in New York Harbor, shelled the tavern, hoping to kill a group of the revolutionaries in one fell swoop.[14] That attempt was unsuccessful, and despite the physical damage to the building, the rebellion, Fraunces, and the tavern soldiered on.

General Washington began frequenting Fraunces Tavern in the 1770s and almost lost his life in what some call the "Poisoned Pea Plot of 1776." One day Washington dined at the tavern, and Fraunces, knowing what the general liked, prepared a meal that included Washington's favorite—green peas. Fraunces's daughter Phoebe, as she had done countless times before, helped cook the meal. Enter Thomas Hickey, who was part of General Washington's personal security detail but not really on "Team Washington." Hickey was loyal to the British Empire and increasingly perceived the general as a growing threat to the crown. Hickey concluded that Washington should be assassinated, an event that would certainly have pleased King George III, and he waited for an opportune time to act.

Hickey first sought access to the general via the kitchen at the tavern, and he thought his best chance at that was to win Phoebe's heart. Hickey started hanging around the kitchen, sweet-talking Phoebe in order to seduce her and gain her trust. When the opportunity presented itself, he distracted Phoebe long enough to add some "special seasoning" to General Washington's peas. Phoebe suspected that something was up and alerted her father. There was only one problem—the plate had already been sent out to the general's table. The moment he got word, Fraunces sprang into action, ran to Washington's table, grabbed the plate of food

Feeling at Home

before the general could take a bite, and threw it out of a window. At that precise moment, a chicken walked by the open window, spotted the providential peas, and started pecking at them. Within moments, the chicken died. Thanks to this instance of animal testing, everyone knew what Fraunces had already surmised: the peas had been poisoned with arsenic, a naturally occurring mineral that is deadly when ingested. Hickey was arrested for treason, jailed, court-martialed, and publicly hanged on 28 June 1776 before a crowd of 20,000 people in a New York public square near the present-day location of the Old Bowery.[15] We might call this the first act of culinary homeland security in our great nation.

It's a fantastic story but probably untrue for several reasons. Fraunces had children, but none of them were named Phoebe, though that could have been a family nickname. Second, Hickey was arrested and hanged, but his crime was counterfeiting (he falsified papers that would have allowed assassins to be in close proximity to General Washington), not attempted murder. Third, it's not entirely clear that Fraunces was operating the tavern in 1776. Things were getting hectic for revolutionaries, and as British ground troops occupied the city, he escaped from New York to Elizabeth, New Jersey, in 1775 and turned the business over to someone else to manage in his absence. While in New Jersey, he was captured by British forces. Fortunately for Fraunces, his culinary reputation earned him a "get out of jail free" card: instead of imprisoning him, the British general overseeing military operations in the area made the curious and potentially dangerous decision to install Fraunces (an enemy of the British crown) as his personal cook.[16] Regardless, Fraunces earned and retained enough of a hero status—through this and other exploits— to later successfully lobby Congress to compensate him $2,000 for his patriotic services to the country.[17]

Fraunces returned to operate the tavern by 1783, and General Washington continued to patronize the business. The tavern held such a special place in Washington's heart that he gave his farewell to his Continental army troops in the tavern's upper room on 4 December 1783. This event caused the tavern to be inaccurately nicknamed "Washington's Headquarters."[18] General Washington had hoped that it would be a true farewell and that he could quietly retire to his plantation at Mount Vernon, Virginia. Yet the public clamoring for his return was so great that Washington was forced to come out of retirement. He reluctantly agreed to be the first president of the United States.

President Washington was keenly aware that everything he did would

> WHEREAS, all Servants and others, employed to procure Provifions, or fupplies, for the Houfehold of *The Prefident* of the *United States*, will be furnifhed with monies for thofe purpofes. *Notice is therefore given,* That no Accounts, for the payment of which the Pub-lic might be confidered as refponfible, are to be opened with any of them.
>
> SAMUEL FRAUNCES, *Steward of the Houfehold.*
> *May 4th,* 1789.

Fraunces newspaper advertisement.
Connecticut Courant and Weekly Intelligencer, *11 May 1789.*

. . .

be heavily scrutinized and would set precedent for future presidents. How he dined and entertained was no exception. President Washington did not want to act, or even appear to act, as a monarch. Yet, he wanted the best for his table. In May 1789 he hired Fraunces to serve as the steward for the first Executive Mansion, which was the Osgood Residence at 1-3 Cherry Street (intersecting Pearl Street) in New York City.[19]

Once installed as steward, Fraunces quickly let everyone know that he was "in charge." He anticipated that merchants would try to capitalize on any business relationships they had with President Washington and therefore published a bill of notice in local newspapers that left no doubt that all household business matters went through him.[20] Fraunces served a very short stint in New York City before the nation's capital was moved to Philadelphia in 1790. There, the new Executive Mansion was the Robert Morris House at 190 High Street, one block from Independence Hall. The culinary team that Fraunces put together, subject to President Washington's approval, included a mix of free whites (hired on the open labor market) and enslaved blacks whom Washington relocated from Mount Vernon. With the team in place, Fraunces began the difficult task of running the presidential household.

Fraunces set a fantastic table for President Washington. In a glowing letter to Tobias Lear, Washington wrote about one meal, "Fraunces, besides being an excellent cook, knowing how to provide genteel dinners, and giving aid in dressing them, prepared the dessert and made the cake."[21] Lear must have agreed. A Washington biographer wrote, "Tobias Lear stared agog at the heaps of lobster, oysters, and other dishes, saying

Feeling at Home

Fraunces, 'tossed up such a number of fine dishes that we are distracted in our choice when we sit down to table and obliged to hold a long consultation upon the subject, before we can determine what to attack."[22] Fortunately, one of the president's dinner guests, U.S. senator William Maclay from Pennsylvania, wrote in detail about one of the "genteel dinners" that Fraunces supervised:

> In his diary, Maclay described a dinner on August 27, 1789 in which George and Martha Washington sat in the middle of the table, facing each other, while Tobias Lear and Robert Lewis sat on either end. John Adams, John Jay and George Clinton were among the assembled guests. Maclay described a table bursting with a rich assortment of dishes — roasted fish, boiled meat, bacon and poultry for the main course, followed by ice cream, jellies, pies, puddings and melons for dessert. Washington usually downed a pint of beer and two or three glasses of wine, and his demeanor grew livelier once he had consumed them.[23]

According to one presidential food historian, "At dinner parties [Fraunces] cut quite a figure in his silk knee breeches, white ruffled shirt, and carefully powdered black hair as he stood at the sideboard throughout the meal, watching to be sure the footmen attended all of the guests properly."[24]

Though President Washington relished Fraunces's meals, he was troubled by what he saw as his steward's reckless spending. This dynamic set up a repeated back-and-forth that strained their relationship. The most celebrated example of such is a bad fish tale that President Washington's stepgrandson, George Washington Parke Custis, shared in his memoirs:

> President Washington was remarkably fond of fish. . . . It happened that a single shad was caught in the Delaware in February, and brought to the Philadelphia market for sale. Fraunces pounced upon it with the speed of an osprey, regardless of price, but charmed that he had secured a delicacy that, above all others, he knew would be agreeable to the plate of his chief. When the fish was served, Washington suspected a departure from his orders touching the provision to be made for his table, and said to Fraunces, who stood at his post at the sideboard, "What fish is this?" — "A shad, a very fine shad," was the reply; "I knew your excellency was particularly fond of this fish, and was so fortunate as to procure this

one in market—a solitary one, and the first of the season"—"The price, sir; the price!" continued Washington, in a stern commanding tone; "the price, sir?"—"Three—three—three dollars," stammered out the conscience-stricken steward. "Take it away," thundered the chief; "take it away, sir; it shall never be said that my table set such an example of luxury and extravagance." Poor Fraunces tremblingly obeyed, and the first shad of the season was removed untouched, to be speedily devoured by the gourmands of the servants' hall.[25]

I'm sure Fraunces went into that situation thinking that his accomplishment was "off the hook," but he seriously jeopardized his continued status as Washington's steward. Before this incident, President Washington had frequently lectured Fraunces about controlling costs. In addition to worrying about providing fodder to his political enemies, Washington had a very real concern about frivolous spending. In response, a chastised Fraunces promised to do better but reportedly said, "Well, he may discharge me if he will, but while he is the President and I am his steward his establishment shall be supplied with the best the whole country can afford."[26] President Washington eventually had enough and fired Fraunces in 1790. He experimented with another steward, but that didn't last long. Washington rehired Fraunces six months later.[27]

Thanks again to Custis, we have some glimpses of Fraunces's culinary duties for the Washington household. The president typically ate a light breakfast of corn cakes or buckwheat cakes, but all other meals were top-notch. Every Tuesday afternoon, Washington hosted a social hour called a "levee" where invited guests could interact with him (I am purposefully avoiding the word "socialize" because there appeared to be very little talking at these events). When he hosted members of Congress for dinner, the meals started promptly at 4 P.M., and as noted earlier, punctuality was a must. With Fraunces's help, the Washingtons earned a solid reputation for their presidential entertaining, and guests looked forward to being at their table. Fraunces managed to stay in President Washington's good graces until 1794, when he left of his own volition to open a tavern in Philadelphia that he ran with his wife, Elizabeth.[28] Fraunces died in 1795 and is buried in an unmarked grave in the cemetery at St. Peter's Episcopal Church in Philadelphia.[29] In remembrance of Fraunces's life, a tribute obelisk has been placed at the cemetery's entrance.

Though the Robert Morris House had long been demolished, the site of this early presidential household made headlines in 2002. The National

Feeling at Home

Park Service, during a planned expansion of the Liberty Bell Center, unearthed the remains of the house's slave quarters. Inexplicably, the National Park Service initially planned to ignore the discovery, but a band of local citizens created enough of a stir to persuade the agency to honor the site's historical significance.[30] Today, visitors to the Liberty Bell complex will see an open-air re-creation of the Robert Morris House with just the building's frame and walls in their original locations. Through a self-guided tour, visitors may go from room to room and watch an interactive video that explains what daily life was like in that specific part of the house, particularly from the viewpoint of the enslaved workforce.

From President Washington's time until the Civil War, white U.S. citizens and white foreign nationals were regularly employed as presidential stewards. Yet there were some notable African American exceptions: George DeBaptiste, a leading Detroit caterer, who served during the very brief administration of President William Henry Harrison; William Slade, a messenger in the Lincoln White House whom President Andrew Johnson elevated during his administration;[31] and John A. Simms, who served for part of President Rutherford B. Hayes's administration. These individuals avoided public attention, but one presidential steward loved the limelight: William T. Crump, who served as steward for President Hayes.

Crump was born circa 1840, and though relatively little is known about his early life, we know that he met Hayes during the Civil War when Crump served as Hayes's Union army orderly. Crump must have made a good impression upon Hayes, which paved the way for his eventual hire as presidential steward. In that role, Crump earned a reputation for being a "faithful and efficient man."[32] For Crump, the steward's duties were essentially the same as they were in Fraunces's day: procure the food, supervise the domestic staff, get outside caterers, hire extra help for large events, and have the ultimate responsibility for all government property at the White House.[33] Yet, a steward's duties could vary from administration to administration based on the personality quirks of a particular president. For example, President Hayes directed Crump to shop at the local markets, in contrast to his immediate predecessor, President Ulysses S. Grant, who had his steward economize by getting food from the Army commissary at a marked discount. The difference in these approaches is that President Hayes probably didn't care about cost because he was wealthy and paid for everything out of his own pocket, while President Grant was a man of limited means.[34] Crump's life as the White House steward was pretty routine, except for two events — one (allegedly) caused by a bottle of liquor and the other by an assassin's bullet. The former involved a controversial state dinner given by the Hayeses where alcoholic drinks may or may not have been served. While that state dinner (discussed in chapter 6) got on the public's nerves, the attempted assassination of Hayes's successor, President James Garfield, truly put the nation on edge.

When Charles J. Guiteau shot President Garfield at the Baltimore & Potomac Depot in Washington, D.C., on 2 July 1881, he retraumatized a nation still healing from President Lincoln's assassination. By all accounts, Garfield suffered immensely during his unsuccessful convalescence, and not only from the bullet wound. His doctors, equipped with nineteenth-century medical practices and devices, tried a variety of treatments that hastened his death rather than saved his life. Newspaper readers received daily progress reports on President Garfield's condition, often directly from Crump, who was the only one who had access to the president besides Mrs. Garfield, General David Swain, Dr. Willard Bliss, Dr. S. E. Boynton, and Colonel A. F. Rockwell (a close friend).[35]

As a frequent source of news on Garfield's condition, Crump inadvertently and informally became the White House's first press secretary a half century before the position became official. Crump knew Garfield's condition was terminal, but he chose to be upbeat. The *Critic* reported that "Mr. Crump has every confidence in the President's recovery, and says he is willing to bet that he will be able to take a drive inside of a month. The speaker grew more enthusiastic as he [warmed] up to his subject, and said, 'Wait till the President gets well, and then we'll have a Fourth of July worth talking about.'"[36] Crump's reports boosted the nation's hopes for the ailing president as well as its economy much more than the reports from Dr. Bliss.[37]

During President Garfield's attempted convalescence, Crump tried to provide every comfort, and the nation saw the president's appetite for food as the strongest indicator of his appetite for life. Folks were downright gleeful to hear that Garfield had graduated from drinking only water, beef broth, or chicken broth to eating a piece of toast that Crump drenched with the juice of a cooked steak followed by a small piece of the steak itself.[38]

The good news didn't last long. Though there were flashes of improvement, President Garfield's health continued to deteriorate. And in response to reports of the president's poor appetite, an empathetic American public responded to the jarring turn of events with an outpouring of concern, grief, and booze. Much to the dismay of temperance advocates, the White House overflowed with alcohol. As one newspaper of the day reported, "During the first month following the wound of the assassin, when brandies, whiskies, champagnes, sherries, tokay, madeiras, gins, cordials, bitters and stimulants of every description, sent by kindly hands to the sick man, blocked the corridors, rooms and ante-chambers of the White House, Crump, like the skipper of a fast ship in a fair breeze, was always on deck chirpy and cheerful."[39] But the president could not enjoy the flood of libations. He could barely keep down anything but water in his weakened condition.

Crump rose to semicelebrity status, but the glow of his limelight faded after President Garfield died on 19 September 1881. He continued on as presidential steward to Garfield's successor, President Chester A. Arthur, but Crump didn't thrive under the new administration and resigned from his White House position in May 1882 for health reasons. After a White House farewell party, where he was presented with a gold-headed cane, Crump reportedly sailed to Liverpool, England, to visit friends.[40] Yet he was back at the White House a couple of years later, working for President Arthur again.

President Arthur was generally regarded as a bon vivant and the most accomplished gourmet to entertain in the White House since Jefferson.[41] In a newspaper interview, Crump complained about the long hours he and the staff worked due to President Arthur's late-night entertaining. The interviewer asked him, "Is the position of steward a desirable one?" Crump responded, "Not very at this time. The work is very hard. In addition to the catering and seeing that the house is kept in order, the steward has to watch the relic-hunters."[42] The last part of that sentence referred to guests at White House functions who were compelled to steal—I mean, "take home a souvenir"—from their White House experience.

By 1886, Crump had left the White House to operate a hotel in suburban Washington that was "filled with ghastly mementoes of Garfield's untimely taking off. He has a part of the shirt which the martyred President wore when shot, the easy reclining chair to which he was transferred from the bed at Elberon [the place in New Jersey where President Garfield died], his ink stands, whisp-broom and many other relics." He also kept a record of all who were guests at President Garfield's table when they ate at the White House and a list of those who called on Mrs. Garfield. Included in this list was Charles J. Guiteau, the assassin.[43] Evidently the public agreed that the hotel was in poor taste. It was lightly patron-

William T. Crump, presidential steward. Philadelphia Inquirer, *25 December 1892.*
. . .

STEWARD CRUMP.

ized with their business, and it soon closed. Crump fell on hard times and took a page from the playbook of previous presidential steward Samuel Fraunces—he appealed directly to Congress for money. Though he had been paid $1,800 a year in salary as a presidential steward, he asked for an additional $3,000 for rendering additional services under extraordinary circumstances, since caring for President Garfield had been difficult and had adversely affected his own health. His arduous duties had included lifting the ailing president up several times a day for bathing and other care. The controversial appeal led to a prolonged and raucous debate in the halls of Congress and in newspaper editorial pages across the country. In 1888, the U.S. Senate finally approved legislation to pay Crump, and he got $5,000 instead of the $3,000 he initially requested. Crump owed his big payday to the best lobbying effort that he could have had at the time— a letter of support from President Garfield's widow.[44]

Crump later figuratively threw his weight around in public as a celebrity pitchman who played on his White House tenure. Crump had entered the White House weighing a spry 225 pounds, but by the time he retired he had gained another 100 pounds. For the sake of his health, he had to do something about his weight. Since losing weight was slow going, Crump adopted a strategy of shifting how his stomach was supported: he got a girdle made for men. Who knows why Crump made the short list, but the marketing people promoting "Dr. Edison's Obesity and Supporting Band" chose Crump as its spokesperson. Dr. Edison's marketing team went big with their advertising campaign. Not only did they communicate Crump's personal experience with excessive weight, but they also highlighted his past presidential staff experience as well as his future prospects. The pun-heavy top line blared, "M'Kinley's Possible Steward REDUCED."[45] Crump, true to form, showed his confidence in future White House employment by expressing in the ad, "[I]f Major McKinley is elected President, [Crump] will again become a steward in the White House."[46] No one knows if William McKinley ever read this advertisement, but whatever slim opportunity Crump had to regain his old position, it never worked out. McKinley chose another African American man, William Sinclair, to serve as his steward. Crump faded into obscurity and died in 1909. Sinclair resigned when Theodore Roosevelt became president, and that led to the hiring of Henry Pinckney, the last of the great African American White House stewards.

Like so many before him, Pinckney began his path to the White House when he became the personal servant of a future president. Pinckney, born in 1857, grew up in Charleston, South Carolina, and was eventually employed as a messenger for several New York governors, including Theodore Roosevelt.[47] Unlike many of his predecessors, Pinckney was not a biracial man; rather, he was described as "an undersized negro, black as night."[48] Though his skin color differed, Pinckney shared an important trait with his biracial predecessors—he was extremely trustworthy. Pinckney left his state government job to work for Governor Roosevelt at his private residence in Oyster Bay, New York, before turning to federal employment when Roosevelt became vice president and then president of the United States.[49] Pinckney became the presidential steward in October 1901. He and his wife were certainly appreciative, for later that same month they named their newborn son Theodore Roosevelt Pinckney.[50]

By Pinckney's time, the White House steward's power was formidable. The *Evening Star* reported, "The whole domestic distribution of the White House is under control of the steward. The President's wife is little more than a distinguished figurehead."[51] In addition to the various butlers, clerks, maids, messengers, and police, Pinckney supervised "five negro women—a cook, assistant cook, scullion and two laundresses—[who] have long been carried on the White House pay roll at $1 a day each."[52] However, the racial makeup of the kitchen staff changed as more ethnic white European immigrant women were hired into the Roosevelt kitchen.[53] Even with the changing racial dynamics, Pinckney was good at what he did, and outside observers lauded his professionalism. "He is very quiet and unassuming in manner, but thoroughly trustworthy," the *Hartford Courant* related. "Every morning he goes to the markets, and the way in which he conducts these expeditions would do credit to a diplomatist."[54]

In terms of marketing, Pinckney continued a longtime practice (since Crump's time) of procuring provisions under a low profile. One newspaper reported, "The majority of the purchases are even sent to the White House in an unlettered wagon. This wagon comes in at the south entrance and drives through the west colonnade to the kitchen door. . . . Any passer-by looking over the railing could see it, but he would never be able to guess from anything about its appearance what grocery house or market feed which it contains comes from."[55] One big difference between Pinckney and his predecessors was that every day he made a special delivery before picking up groceries. The *Washington Times* informed its readers that "Archibald Roosevelt goes to school every morning in the White House wagon, which is considered a good enough vehicle for the transportation of a President's son. Every morning Archibald is loaded aboard the cart, bound for the educational establishment at which he is acquiring large chunks of learning. This wagon belongs, officially speaking, to the steward of the White House, and he is employed ordinarily for bringing provisions to the Executive Mansion."[56]

After dropping off Archibald, Pinckney routinely purchased big pieces of meat at the market, which eventually resulted in the first of several press scrutiny headaches he would suffer—and help manage. It began with Pinckney consenting to what he thought would be a harmless *Washington Post* interview on President Roosevelt's food habits. The White House immediately went into spin control mode when the following headline appeared: "White House Table Supplied with Best Market Affords, but Wholesomeness First Considered."[57] Much like his predecessor Fraunces, Pinckney wanted the best for the president's table, but he made the mistake of boasting about it to the press. Pinckney had enthusiastically painted an epicurean image that smacked too much of elitism for a president who purported to be a "man of the people." President Roosevelt asked the newspaper to print a correction story that extensively clarified that the First Family didn't regularly consume "fancy dishes" and ate like other typical American families.[58] With the follow-up article, President Roosevelt managed to get a "clean plate" with the public.

Another controversy, albeit a much smaller one, came during the holi-

White House market wagon, circa 1909.
Courtesy Library of Congress.

· · ·

days. For most people, Thanksgiving is the official kickoff to a holiday season that promises to be full of family, food, and fun. But for Pinckney, the holiday brought another headache that could not be solely blamed on tryptophan. Since the Grant administration, wealthy turkey ranchers vied to have their bird served as the official White House Thanksgiving turkey. Most years, that honor went to Horace Vose of Rhode Island.[59] Trouble came when more than one turkey was delivered to the White House.[60] Most times, Pinckney would choose among the turkeys, and Vose's bird was usually preferred because of its high quality. However, the selection process became political as the wealthy donors who were left out were miffed that they were unable to publicize that the president preferred their turkey above all others. In order to keep the wealthy donors happy, Pinckney's solution was to cook all of the turkeys they received, carve them up, and then mix up all of the meat before serving. This gave President Roosevelt something all presidents covet — plausible deniability. When asked by one of the donors, President Roosevelt could honestly say, "I ate your turkey." Given his wise resolution of the potential conflict, I truly hope that to "pull a Pinckney" or "mix your turkeys" will enter our lexicon as an alternative to "split the baby."

Feeling at Home ★ 47

Things got easier for Pinckney by Christmastime when he oversaw the annual turkey distribution to White House employees—a perk that Roosevelt instituted during his first term. As reported in 1904,

> [Pinckney] made a trip to the market early this morning and selected thirty-five of the fattest birds he could find. These he brought back to the White House in the big covered market wagon, and piled them in a tempting array on a table in the basement kitchen. As soon as the word was given out, shortly after 3 P.M., that the turkeys were ready to be distributed, there was a general rush in the direction of "Pinckneyville," as some of the employes [*sic*] term the steward's domain. It was first come, first served, and Pinckney was not charged with favoritism. The unmarried employes [*sic*] of the White House, who did not share in the distribution, watched the proceedings with envious eyes. "To the benedicts belong the spoils," remarked Secretary [William] Loeb [Jr.] to one of the bachelor clerks who asked about his turkey. "You may get one next year if you continue to stand in the favor of a certain young woman out in the Northwest."[61]

A few years later, the distribution increased to 125 turkeys, and Pinckney created an elaborate tagging and numbering system. The unmarried employees, however, were still left out.[62] The turkey distribution scheme may have created an incentive to get married, but it's unclear if anyone took that step.

It wasn't until after his presidency that Roosevelt would again have egg on his face for White House food operations. In 1910, newspaper editors who were not fans of the former commander in chief salivated at the opportunity of a lifetime. Roosevelt, the very man who had crusaded for food protection laws, allegedly ate and approved of the tainted meat while in the White House. One newspaper gleefully reported,

> At the White House dinners during the last Administration the meat was often so unwholesome that it was ready to fall to pieces, according to the testimony given to-day by Food Inspector Dodge of the District Health Department before the Moore special committee of the House investigating the food cost question. He said that while Mr. Roosevelt was President the steward at the Executive Mansion used to hang up his beef and keep it there until he could stick his finger into it in order to allow it to get "ripe." When it was ready to fall to pieces, the food inspector declared, it was taken down and

served, and not before. But the testimony continued with the statement that the practice of using unduly aged meat was well established in many wealthy homes and that dealers who catered to a fashionable trade had to keep old meat on hand because some of their customers would take no other.[63]

A seriously offended Pinckney quickly rebutted the allegations, using with some irony the same sentiment that had gotten him in hot water four years prior—the excellence of White House food. Decrying the article's lies, Pinckney emphatically stated that all meat procured by the White House was fresh as ordered by the cook and that he never hanged such up in the White House. On top of that, he said no health inspector ever went to the White House during his tenure and shouldn't be there, since it is a private residence. He concluded by restating that Inspector Dodge's testimony was "a falsehood from beginning to end."[64]

Pinckney went on to serve as steward in the William Howard Taft administration, but he died in April 1911, a little more than two years into the job, and along with him died the long reign of African American stewards. The not-so-wealthy Tafts, in a cost-saving move, eliminated the position of White House steward and put all domestic operations under the control of Elizabeth Jaffray, a white woman who served as the White House housekeeper. This was a significant change, because the White House's food operations, which had functioned as a hybrid between how food service happens at a hotel and how it happens at a wealthy residence, made a full transition to mimicking that of a wealthy home: all cooking was done on site with no meals outsourced to caterers. The White House housekeeper position would reign supreme in the residence for the next three decades. The housekeeper had the same duties as the steward, minus the responsibility for White House property. That responsibility was charged to another White House employee, typically an African American. With the ascendancy of a powerful white housekeeper, it would be several decades until an African American again played an important role in presidential food operations. That person was Alonzo Fields.

Alonzo Fields was born in 1901 in the all-black community of Lyles, Indiana. He was the son of two entrepreneurs: his father ran a general store, and his mother operated a boardinghouse for railroad workers. His father was also musically inclined and directed a large and popular brass band that he had formed. Fields, who could play instruments and sing, loved music as well and planned a career in that field. His journey led him all the way to the New England Conservatory of Music in Boston, but he soon ran out of money. A friend offered to help Fields get a job as a butler for Dr. Samuel W. Stratton, who was president of the Massachusetts Institute of Technology. Fields wasn't keen for such a position, but he was persuaded that it was just a job and would help him observe how people of good breeding and connoisseurs of good taste like Stratton behaved. That, in turn, could be of use when he resumed his classical music career. So Fields agreed, and while in the Stratton household he soon met a lot of notable people who would eventually help him out in a pinch.[65]

Fields wrote in his memoirs about how various personal connections helped him get a job at the White House:

> When I went to the White House through Mrs. Hoover's [the First Lady] invitation, Dr. Stratton had died suddenly. I was at the time trying to follow a musical career as a concert singer. That was the height of the Depression. My wife lost her health. Mrs. Hoover had Lieutenant [Frederick] Butler call me and ask me what I was going to do. I said I didn't know what I was going to do. So he said that Mrs. Hoover thinks that you ought to come down here [to the White House] for the winter. And I went down for the winter. And, of course, Ike Hoover [the chief usher] didn't know of my coming whatsoever. This was all above him. You see, when I went on the job, of course, as I say, he was always very kind to me. But I think he interpreted the fact that Mrs. Hoover had invited me there. I didn't give him any reason, and I wouldn't give him any reason. But he was always very kind to me.[66]

Fields began his lengthy White House career in 1931. At six foot one and 240 pounds, he was a memorable figure in the Executive Residence. By some accounts, the first floor ceiling creaked as he walked on the second floor (this was an early warning sign of the sad state of the White House's deteriorating physical condition), and dishes rattled when he entered and exited the pantry.[67] When he was first hired, he was in charge of President Herbert Hoover's "medicine ball breakfast" table — so called because Hoover would meet with his staff early in the morning and pass a medicine ball around for exercise while they discussed the day's topics.[68]

Early in the Franklin Roosevelt administration, Fields rose in the ranks, though he apparently wasn't angling for a promotion. In his memoir, Fields described how "accidental" his promotion was with this sequence of events, chiefly involving then chief usher Ike Hoover and a butler named Incarnation Rodriquez:

> And when the Hoovers went out, he [Ike Hoover] and Lieutenant [Frederick] Butler got together, I'm sure, and a man by the name of Incarnation Rodriquez was in line to be the head man. Ike Hoover just came into the dining room and took it all over. Ike Hoover came into the dining room and said to call all of the butlers together. He said, "Rodriquez, you're the second man here." He said, "Yes." He said, "Well, you'll still be the second man." And he pointed to me and he said, "Fields, you take charge." That's all the information that I got. And I took charge.[69]

Fields got his next promotion while the Trumans lived in the Blair House during the White House renovation that took place in the early 1950s: "I went to the Chief Butler during the Truman administration. Then, President Truman decided that I should be in complete charge, plan all of the menus, and so forth, and so I was the maître d'hôtel in the Truman administration."[70] With Fields's new title and redistributed responsibilities, we see the White House transitioning from being run like a wealthy residence back to being run like a hotel.

Fields described his duties as the maître d'hôtel during the Truman administration in ways that were not far off from those of a nineteenth-century steward: "For more than twenty-one years I served the White House as butler, chief butler and maître d'hôtel. . . . I planned and directed all of the family, state, and social functions of four Presidents and kept the inventories of china, glassware, table linens, and silverware. . . . As the maître d'hôtel, I was further required to plan all the menus and direct the activities of the butlers and the kitchen."[71] Here, Fields is really describing what he did toward the end of his career, for while he worked in the Roosevelt administration, Henrietta Nesbitt supervised all culinary operations in her capacity as White House housekeeper. Fields took over after Mrs. Truman fired Nesbitt for refusing to let the First Lady take a stick of butter from the White House kitchen to a potluck luncheon hosted by one of her friends.[72]

Consciously or inadvertently, members of the First Family often put a lot of pressure on the culinary staff, who have to make sure that they get the food they like and that it meets any dietary restrictions they may have. Reflecting on the Trumans, Fields wrote,

Preparing menus for the Trumans was not too easy. Not that they were difficult to please or fussy, but Mrs. Truman was on a salt-free diet, the President required a low-calorie and high protein diet, and Mrs. Wallace [President Truman's mother-in-law] needed all the calories that she could get. Miss Margaret was away most of the time, working at her career of singing and the stage. Only when she was home could we go overboard. The family meals were simple three-course affairs except for Sundays or when guests had been invited.[73]

Chief usher J. B. West added, "We even had to remove the water-softening system from the cold-water plumbing, because it contained sodium."[74]

Fields's next concern was making sure that there was enough food to go around, given budgetary restraints. This hasn't been a problem for most First Families because few presidents have had large families living with them in the White House, and even fewer entertained extended family. One big exception was President Franklin and First Lady Eleanor Roosevelt. "The Roosevelt grandchildren and nurses added many problems to the duties of serving meals on trays," Fields noted. "Finally a kitchen was built on the third floor which also served as a diet kitchen for the President. When all the grandchildren were present, meals could be prepared there and served in the sun parlor or hall."[75]

The new kitchen meant the Roosevelts needed another cook, and that process took an interesting turn for the Fields family. Fields recalled,

My wife, Edna, was hired by Mrs. Nesbitt to cook for the grandchildren. I protested, for as I told her, my wife was not a cook. Nevertheless, she went to work and I must say she surprised me, for she certainly cooked much better for them than she had for me. My wife still tells me off about the time I told people at the White House that she couldn't cook. I am not sure whether she has forgiven me, but she certainly hasn't forgotten about it. She happened to cook a few meals there for the President when the grandchildren were there, so now I dare not go into the kitchen at home when a meal is being prepared.[76]

Fortunately, Fields lived to see another day.

As maître d', Fields also knew the importance of building a sense of camaraderie with the White House staff. He often looked for opportunities to lighten things up around the workplace and to build a rapport with those he supervised. In his memoirs, he shared this story about how his joking put one of the black cooks on edge:

> The Trumans moved into the White House in time for the President's birthday, May 8, 1945, and Elizabeth Moore, who was then the head cook, baked a cake for the President. It was rather funny, for the kitchen had never baked a birthday cake in twelve years; for that matter, no hot rolls, doughnuts, coffee cake, or breads either. Sometimes they made popovers for breakfast. Otherwise a local bakery supplied all of the breads; hot rolls at the White House meant warmed-over bakery rolls. President Truman was so pleased with his birthday cake that after dinner he wanted to see the cook and personally thank her. But Elizabeth and her crew had cleared out as soon as the cake had been set up. Next morning I told her, with a long face, that the President had wanted to see her the night before about the cake she had baked. She said, "Oh, Fields! What happened? What was wrong with it?" "You baked it," I said. "Don't you know?" Then I pulled up a chair and said, "Girl, take this seat before you faint. The President was so pleased that he merely wanted to thank you personally." She found it harder to believe that the President wanted to thank her than that something was wrong with the cake. So on his way to the office the next morning the President did stop by the kitchen and met the whole crew.[77]

Dispensing compliments about the food was not always left to Fields. White House history is full of anecdotes where presidents paused a moment to praise their cooks. Despite Moore's reaction, President Truman was known to do so regularly. Such a small act meant the world to these cooks and made up for the long hours they spent in a frequently high-stress environment.

Fields was in a privileged position to observe some amazing scenes in the private White House, including experimentation and consumption of unusual foods. In the 1920s, Franklin Roosevelt spent time in Warm Springs, Georgia, to get treatment for his polio. While there, many of his meals were cooked by a woman named Daisy Bonner (who is further discussed in chapter 5). Bonner introduced FDR to a lot of southern delicacies, and he took a liking to one you might not expect—pigs' feet! In no time, FDR was grubbing on pigs' feet in a variety of ways and was eager to share this culinary delight with others—including "Very Important People." One day, Fields was an eyewitness to President Roosevelt sharing his love of sweet and sour pigs' feet with a favorite VIP:

It was this type of pigs' feet that he requested to be served at a luncheon for just the Prime Minister, Winston Churchill, and himself. Princess Martha of Norway, who lived at Pookshill, Maryland, during the war, had a cook who often prepared pigs' feet in this style and she had brought the President this dish. He had a twinkle in his eye when he said, "Let's have them for the luncheon tomorrow for the Prime Minister." When the luncheon was served and the Prime Minister started to help himself, he inquired, "What is this?" He was told, "Sir, this is pigs' feet." He said, "Pigs' feet? I never heard of them," and then heartily helped himself. After tasting them he said, "Very good, but sort of slimy." The President laughed and said, "Yes, they are a bit, but I am fond of them. Sometime we will have some of them fried." Whereupon the Prime Minister replied, "No, thank you. I do not believe I would care for them fried." Then they both had a hearty laugh.[78]

This may have been one of the top soul food moments in White House history. Still unconvinced as to President Roosevelt's pigs' feet habit? In 2011 I visited the "Little White House" site in Warm Springs, Georgia, and saw on display the shopping list written in advance of what would be FDR's last week of life. It lists "4 hog's feet."

Once Fields retired in 1953, he passed the white gloves to Charles Ficklin, an African American who served as the maître d'hôtel until 1965, and then Charles's brother John (profiled in chapter 6) assumed the position and served for several decades. During the Ficklins' stint, the nature of the maître d'hôtel job changed when First Lady Jacqueline Kennedy created the position of White House executive chef in 1961. From that point on, the executive chef has handled most of the culinary duties and directly consulted with the First Lady. As we'll also see in chapter 6, the maître d' became the White House sommelier during John Ficklin's tenure. Otherwise, the maître d' position is essentially that of chief butler or headwaiter. Though a diminished role from the presidential stewards of yore, the maître d'hôtel job was still a very important one in White House food operations.

It would be decades before an African American once again held total responsibility for the operation of the Executive Residence, and that happened on 27 February 2007, when President George W. Bush tapped

Rear Admiral Stephen W. Rochon, USCG (Ret.), to be the eighth White House chief usher in history. Admiral Rochon's distinguished naval career began in the Coast Guard in 1970. According to the White House press release about his hiring, "With 36 years in public service, Admiral Rochon has an extensive background in personnel management, strategic planning, and effective interagency coordination."[79] Rochon caught President Bush's attention because he was the Coast Guard's head person in charge of the Port of New Orleans during a devastating oil spill in 2000 and during the aftermath of Hurricane Katrina in 2005.[80] Rochon's ability to handle crisis situations involving a lot of moving parts made him a great candidate for the usher's job. Who better to run a tight ship like the White House than a former admiral? Again, with the executive chef in the mix, Rochon had little to do with culinary operations other than hiring kitchen staff, but he had to manage what many describe as "an invisible army."[81] Although Rochon was the first African American to serve as a chief usher in a technical sense, the duties that came with the position put Rochon squarely within the legacy left by African American stewards a century earlier.

Rochon, with a strong appreciation for history, was acutely aware of the honor bestowed upon him. In 1996, as a coast commander stationed in Baltimore, he hosted a ceremony to posthumously award the "Gold Life Saving Medal" to seven African American men who had performed a "daring rescue off North Carolina's Outer Banks in 1896" by saving the lives of several people on a sinking ship while a hurricane raged around them.[82] With the essential help of some outside researchers, Rochon was able to right a wrong and shine a light on bravery and skill that had been overlooked due to racism. Rochon was the first person besides former president and Mrs. Bush to greet President and Mrs. Obama in the White House. President Obama would soon be needling him about installing a basketball court on the White House grounds. In a final example of history coming full circle, Rochon, in one of his last public events as White House chief usher, attended the U.S. Coast Guard Academy graduation ceremony of Patrick George Bennett III, his grandson, held in May 2011. The commencement speaker that day was none other than President Barack Obama.[83]

When Admiral Rochon left the White House to work in the U.S. Department of Homeland Security, President Obama also broke the mold when he selected Angella Reid to be the first African American woman (and first woman, period) to serve as chief usher. Reid is a Jamaican national who earned her chops in the hotel management industry. Before the White House, Reid was in an upper management position at the Ritz-Carlton properties in Pentagon City, Virginia; Miami, Florida; and Washington, D.C. Prior to her tenure with the Ritz-Carlton, which began in 2008, Reid was general manager at the Hartford Marriott Rocky Hill Hotel in Connecticut and director of operations at the Renaissance New York Hotel in New York City. Reid holds a degree in hospitality management from the Carl Duisberg Gesellschaft School in Munich, Germany, and is conversational in German and basic Spanish.[84]

When the Obama White House announced Reid's hire, they elaborated on her duties in a way that gives much more clarity to what the current job entails. As chief usher, Reid would be responsible for overseeing all aspects of the operations and activities within the Executive Residence and on the Executive Residence grounds. Among her many concerns, Reid would oversee management of the Executive Residence to ensure activities and resources are used efficiently and effectively. In addition, she would maintain close liaison with the White House Historical Association, the Committee for the Preservation of the White House, the U.S. Commission of Fine Arts, and other related entities to maintain and preserve the historic People's House. Reid would also oversee "the annual inventory of White House property, conducted by the Office of the Curator and the National Park Service."[85] Reid believes that "genuinely caring for people" is the secret to success.[86] Mindful of the same concerns that had plagued George Washington and Samuel Fraunces more than two centuries earlier, the *New York Times* reported that Reid was "not [hired] to make the house more luxurious . . . but simply to bring its various functions a bit more up to date."[87]

Over the span of roughly 150 years, two-thirds of presidential history, African Americans have had the awesome responsibility of making sure that things ran smoothly wherever the president lived, especially concerning the food operations. In the nineteenth century, the White House operated as its creators first contemplated, akin to the big house on a plantation. With the increase of staff, the Executive Residence has morphed to the point where it operates like a high-end hotel. In that context, it makes perfect sense that a hotel industry person currently runs the residence's operations. As the steward, maître d'hôtel, or chief usher, these powerful people literally and figuratively set the table for the presidential culinary story. As we'll see next, it was the personal chefs, whether enslaved or free, who ultimately translated the president's culinary hopes and dreams into an edible reality.

Recipes

MINTED GREEN PEA SOUP

This is a culinary shout-out to one of George Washington's favorite foods, sans arsenic. White House executive chef Walter Scheib developed this recipe, and it quickly became a favorite for First Lady Laura Bush. The soup is regularly served at the George W. Bush Presidential Library's restaurant in Dallas, Texas, where I first savored it.

Makes 4 servings

1 1/2 cups freshly shucked or frozen peas
1 tablespoon butter
1/3 cup julienned leek whites
1/4 cup diced onions
4 cups chicken or vegetable stock
1/4 cup chopped mint
1/2 cup heavy cream
1 tablespoon fresh lemon juice
4 mint sprigs

1. Blanch and cool the peas; reserve 2–3 tablespoons for garnish.
2. In a soup pot over medium heat, cook the leeks and onions in the butter until tender, 3–4 minutes.
3. Add the stock and simmer for 4 minutes.
4. Add the peas and mint and cook for 2–3 minutes, or until the peas are tender.
5. In a blender or with an immersion blender, purée the soup until very smooth; strain the soup into a bowl through a fine-mesh sieve and discard the solids.
6. If the soup is to be served hot, return the soup to the soup pot and add the cream and lemon juice and reheat gently. If the soup is to be served chilled, cool it quickly by placing the bowl in an ice bath and then add the cream and lemon juice.
7. Garnish with reserved peas and the mint sprigs.

Few of Samuel Fraunces's recipes survive, but one of the more famous ones that do was his "onions done in the Brazilian way," which was served at his tavern that future president George Washington frequented. The original recipe appears in *Martha Washington's Rules for Cooking used everyday at Mt. Vernon; those of her neighbors, Mrs. Jefferson, Mrs. Madison and Mrs. Monroe,* by Ann Parks Marshall in 1931. Here, with the help of Ramin Ganeshram, I developed a healthier version using seasoned bison, sweet onion, egg whites, and olive oil instead of the beef mincemeat and egg yolks called for in the original recipe.

Makes 4 servings

4 medium-sized sweet onions (like Vidalia or Walla Walla)
1/2 pound ground bison meat
1 green bell pepper, chopped
1 garlic clove, minced
1/4 cup beef stock
1/4 teaspoon dried sage
1/4 teaspoon dried oregano
Salt and pepper to taste
2 egg whites, lightly beaten
1/2 cup olive oil

1. Peel and halve the onions and parboil for 5 minutes.
2. Remove the inner core of the onions to create cups and set them aside. Discard the cores.
3. In a large bowl, combine the meat, bell peppers, garlic, stock, sage, and oregano and season with salt and pepper.
4. Fill the onion cups up with the meat mixture, packing them just enough to ensure that the mixture doesn't fall out.
5. Brush the tops of the meat mixture with the egg white wash.
6. In a large frying pan, heat the olive oil over medium heat. Invert the meat-packed onions into the pan and cook for 5 minutes, or until the meat mixture is cooked through.

3

Bittersweet

AFRICAN AMERICAN
PRESIDENTIAL COOKS IN
ANTEBELLUM AMERICA

"You know, the White House is really modeled after a plantation big house." Chef Walter Scheib startled me when he said this during our first telephone conversation on 12 October 2010. It wasn't because of concerns over the accuracy and clarity of his statement but because he said it to someone he really didn't know. That's just one of the reasons why, since his tragic death, I really miss the chance to delve more deeply with him into the complicated racial history of the presidential kitchen. Just like the white paint that is periodically applied to the White House exterior to cover up the scorch marks left when the British set the building afire in late August 1814, the retelling of White House history frequently masks the stain of slavery. This is maddening stuff given how deeply the legacy of slavery permeates the building, its grounds, and the entire city. Washington, D.C., was carved out of swampland from two slaving states (Maryland and Virginia), the land was donated by planters who were enriched by tobacco slave labor, slave labor was used to construct the building, and slaveholding presidents and enslaved people lived and worked there.[1]

Before we focus on what happened within the White House's walls, it helps to understand what antebellum black life was like in our nation's capital during the nineteenth century. For most African Americans, it was miserable. Washington, D.C., was a slaving city, and the incidents and badges of slavery were omnipresent: enslaved people were sold at spots throughout the city, slave coffles moved regularly about the streets, slave pens dotted the cityscape, and enslaved people busily constructed many of the city's buildings and much of its infrastructure and did a wide range of activities associated with forced servitude. D.C. operated under its own set of "Black Codes." Such laws constrained the liberty of both enslaved and free African Americans. For example, the city's 1808 Black Code enforced a 10 P.M. curfew on all African Americans that, if violated, was punishable by a fine. In the 1812 iteration of that particular code, enslaved people who violated the curfew were whipped with forty lashes. Free black people were also fined and could be jailed for up to six months if fines went unpaid. During this time, no black person could step on the grounds of the U.S. Capitol unless they had documented official business.[2]

Black Codes were designed to preserve a racial social order and, at first, were slowly enacted after enslaved Africans arrived in Virginia in 1619. As the number of enslaved Africans dramatically increased in the eighteenth century, Black Codes proliferated in slaving states. The Black Codes, white racism, and white resistance to black progress combined with a cruel efficiency to constantly remind African Americans of their second-class status. In fact, it's hard to imagine any social event in nineteenth-century Washington, D.C., that didn't have an African American somehow involved in every aspect from start to finish. This included buying supplies at the market and preparing and serving the food and drinks. As one historian noted of the time period, "Nearly every distinguished family in Washington had colored servants, butlers and cooks and entertained lavishly. White servants and cooks came later."[3] Black hands—enslaved and free—wove the fabric of social life in the nation's capital, and black people, widely considered by whites as inherently bred for servitude, were integral to cementing a white family's social status as an elite household. Our presidential families were no exception, and this chapter delves into how slave labor powered the White House kitchen and nourished our presidents and, in one case, a future president. We'll peer into the lives of people we can name (Hercules, James Hemings, and Mary Dines) and many whom white society didn't feel obligated to identify by name in documented accounts of daily life at the White House.

We begin with Hercules (nicknamed "Uncle Harkles"), the enslaved cook for President George Washington. After experimenting with a couple of white cooks—a woman named Mrs. Read was one—President Washington summoned Hercules from Mount Vernon and installed him as his presidential cook in Philadelphia. George Washington's stepgrandson, George Washington Parke Custis, did history a great service by paying some attention to Hercules's culinary skill, professionalism, resourcefulness, and personality at a time when enslaved people were generally ignored. Some researchers and writers, most recently and notably Craig LaBan of the *Philadelphia Inquirer*, use Custis's historical sketch as a starting point and have provided additional details to paint a more complete picture of Hercules's life.

Hercules, because of his name, may have been a big child when he was born circa 1753. Custis wrote of Hercules in his memoirs, "He was a dark brown man, little, if any, above the usual size, yet possessed of such great muscular power as to entitle him to be compared with his name-sake of fabulous history."[4] Being named after the strong man in the center of Greek and Roman mythology wasn't unusual for the times because American elites were going through a deep wave of neoclassical nostalgia for ancient Rome and Athens. They fancied themselves as the true heirs of the classical period, and they evidenced this sentiment in a number of ways: places in the United States were given Roman- and Greek-inspired names (for example, Athens, Georgia, and Rome, New York), buildings evoked classical architecture, and prestigious kitchens replicated menus and prepared food straight out of old Roman cookbooks. There's another interesting cultural confluence as well. As slavery historian Peter H. Wood explains, "The most frequent biblical and classical names accepted among slaves will reveal that they often resemble African words. . . . One reason that the name *Hercules*—often pronounced and spelled *Hekles*—was applied to strong slaves may well be the fact that *heke* in Sierra Leone was the Mende noun meaning 'a large wild animal.'"[5] Thus, the "Uncle Harkles" nickname could have been less a bad pronunciation of the name Hercules and more about the appropriation of an African word.

Washington purchased a teenage Hercules in 1767 while the latter worked as a ferryman.[6] When Hercules arrived at Mount Vernon, Washington had several home improvement projects underway: "Between 1759 and his death in 1799, [Washington] expanded upon the original farmhouse his father had built to create a two-and-a-half-story, twenty-room mansion, complete with several kitchens and dining rooms, and he designed and erected the twelve outbuildings that stand today. He also increased the plantation's size from twenty-one hundred to eight thousand acres."[7] Washington added Hercules to his workforce that included slaves he had inherited from his father, slaves he had acquired when he married Martha Dandridge, slaves he had purchased, and slaves loaned to him from neighboring slave owners. At some point, Washington transferred Hercules from ferrying boats to cooking in the Mount Vernon kitchen under the direction of Old Doll, the plantation's chief cook, a slave whom he had acquired when he married Martha.[8]

Though the timing isn't clear, Hercules eventually took Old Doll's place in the kitchen. Washington's slave inventory from February 1786 listed Hercules and Nathan as the cooks in the "House Home," and Old Doll was listed as "almost past Service," indicating her advancing age.[9] By the time that Hercules took over, the kitchen had been fully renovated and updated. As the Mount Vernon website indicates,

> The new kitchen was larger and more architecturally detailed than the original, matching the Mansion in many aspects. Most notably, the siding boards on the facade facing the circle were beveled and sanded to create the appearance of stone blocks. Covered walkways called colonnades were built to connect each of the new structures to the Mansion. Workers carrying food back and forth between the kitchen and the Mansion did so along a protected passageway.
>
> The updated kitchen included three workrooms on the first floor and a loft above, which served as the residence of the cook or housekeeper. The largest of the three workrooms included a fireplace and attached oven. The other workrooms were a scullery where food was prepared and dishes were washed, and a larder with a subterranean cooling floor to store food. According to the inventory of the kitchen completed after George Washington's death, the kitchen contained a wide variety of cooking equipment, including pots and pans, skillets, a griddle, a toaster, a boiler, spits, chafing dishes, tin and pewter "Ice Cream Pots," coffeepots, and strainers.[10]

Using what appeared to be the latest cooking equipment and technology and an abundant larder from the surrounding countryside, Hercules honed his culinary skills and unwittingly prepared for his presidential moment.

Hercules was thirty-six years old when he arrived in Philadelphia to cook in the Executive Mansion. He experienced a food scene more cosmopolitan than that of other cities. A Philadelphia historian wistfully remembered in an 1860 memoir,

> There was a time, in the end of the last and beginning of the present century, when the "Carrying Trade" between the United States and the West India Islands, was a fruitful source of life to the commercial interest of Philadelphia. . . . Our intercourse with the West Indies was active, spirited, and rich in results; for whilst our Beef and Pork, Flour, Apples, Onions, Butter, Lard, and any other product of our fields or farms, were toothsome and desirable to the planter there, the issues of their soil, of Sugar, Coffee, Oranges, Lemons, Pine-Apples, etc., paid much better here, and laid the foundation of ease and comfort to very many of the retired dealers of that day.[11]

Because of this extensive exotic food trade, noted African American food-ways scholar Jessica B. Harris urges readers of her book *Beyond Gumbo* to reimagine Philadelphia as "a Creole city."[12]

Though President Washington was the ultimate boss, Samuel Fraunces—now starting his second stint as presidential steward—was the one who would decide whether or not Hercules's culinary skills were up to snuff. Tobias Lear, President Washington's private secretary, informed the president of this fact in a letter dated 15 May 1791:

> Fraunces arrived here on Wednesday, and after signing his Articles of Agreement—going over the things in the house & signing an inventory thereof, entered upon the duties of his station. I think I have made the agreement as full, explicit & binding as any thing of the kind can be. In the Articles prohibiting the use of wine at his table—and obliging him to be particular in the discharge of his duty in the Kitchen & to perform the Cooking with Hercules—I have been peculiarly pointed.
>
> He readily assented to them all (except that respecting Hercules, upon which he made the following observation—"I must first learn Hercules' abilities & readiness to do things, which if good, *(as good as Mrs. Read's)* will enable me to do the Cooking without any other *professional* assistance in the Kitchen; but this experiment cannot be made until the return of the President when there may be occasion for him to exert his talents"—) and made the strongest professions of attachment to the family, & his full determination to conduct in such a manner as to leave no room for impeachment either on the score of extravagance or integrity. All these things I hope he will perform.[13]

History has not recorded how Washington reacted, but future president Ronald Reagan would surely have approved of Fraunces's effort to "trust, but verify" Hercules's culinary skill level. Coincidentally, the exotic food trade was disrupted in 1792–93 by the successful revolution happening in Fraunces's birthplace: Haiti.

In the Philadelphia Executive Residence's kitchen, Hercules worked with a team of eight people: Fraunces the steward, some assistant cooks (including his own enslaved teenage son Richmond), and several waiters. He cooked in a large fireplace filled with cooking equipment. This type of cooking is also known as "hearth" or "hearthside" cooking. It involves starting and tending a fire, operating numerous gadgets and cooking equipment that are either suspended over the fire or on the floor in front of the fire, or sometimes cooking food in the ashes of the fire.[14] Such hearth cooking is difficult and dangerous, but, according to Custis, Hercules excelled at it:

> The chief cook would have been termed in modern parlance, a celebrated *artiste*. He was named Hercules, and familiarly termed Uncle Harkless. . . . [He] was, at the period of the first presidency, as highly accomplished a proficient in the culinary art as could be found in the United States. . . .
>
> The steward, and indeed the whole household, treated the chief cook with much respect, as well for his valuable services as for his general good character and pleasing manners.
>
> It was while preparing the Thursday or Congress dinner that Uncle Harkless shone in all his splendor. During his labors upon this banquet he required some half-dozen aprons, and napkins out of number. It was surprising the order and discipline that was observed in so bustling a scene.[15]

No recipes known to be attributable to Hercules survive to this day, and there are few descriptions of the meals that he made for President Washington during his time in Philadelphia from 1791 to 1797—a curious fact given President Washington's celebrity status. Fortunately, one Washington biographer found this reference to one of those meals: "Bradbury gives the menu of a dinner at which he was, where 'there was an elegant variety of roast beef, veal, turkey, ducks, fowls, hams, &c.; puddings, jellies, oranges, apples, nuts, almonds, figs, raisins, and a variety of wines and punches.'"[16] If one needs further evidence of culinary prowess, note that President Washington allowed Hercules a unique opportunity to earn additional income. As Craig LaBan notes, "Most telling . . . was allowing Hercules the right to sell the kitchen 'slops'—the remaining animal skins, used tea leaves, and rendered tallow that would have been compost on the plantation. In the city, these were lucrative leftovers, an income-producing perk traditionally bestowed on top chefs. . . . For Hercules that meant annual earnings of up to $200, if Custis is accurate, as much as the Washingtons paid hired chefs."[17] Thus, Hercules earned upwards of $5,000 (in 2015 dollars) in extra income.[18] Hercules used some of the money to acquire a spectacular wardrobe, and almost every day he walked the Philadelphia streets wearing "a blue coat with a velvet collar, a pair of fancy knee-breeches, and shoes with extravagant silver buckles.

Thus attired, with a cocked hat upon his head and a gold-headed cane in his hand, he strutted up and down among the beaux and belles until the stroke of the clock reminded him that he must hurry off to the kitchen and prepare the evening meal."[19] He was quite the fashionable figure for his time.

Those who watch cooking competition shows and reality shows about restaurants on television probably think of a professional kitchen as a place where arrogant, self-absorbed chefs terrorize line cooks with abusive language and impossible demands. It appears that Hercules was that kind of chef. Custis observed, "The chief cook gloried in the cleanliness and nicety of his kitchen. Under his discipline, wo [sic] to his underlings if a speck or spot could be discovered on the tables or dressers, or if the utensils did not shine like polished silver. With the luckless wights who had offended in these particulars there was no arrest of punishment, for judgment and execution went hand in hand."[20] Evidently, Hercules ran a very tight ship: "His underlings flew in all directions to execute his orders, while he, the great master-spirit, seemed to posses the power of ubiquity, and to be everywhere at the same time."[21] What made Hercules so demanding? Was it his natural temperament? Was he reacting to a stressful environment? Perhaps it was just learned behavior from President Washington, who had a very bad temper, or a combination of all of the above. Whatever the reason, Hercules possessed a personality well-suited to being a demanding chef.

Though the Washingtons were pleased with Hercules's cooking, having an enslaved chef in Pennsylvania created political and logistical headaches as well as a potential public relations nightmare for them. Annoyingly for President Washington, prior to him taking residence in Philadelphia, the Pennsylvania state legislature had enacted the Gradual Abolition Act of 1780. This law freed any enslaved person who stayed on Pennsylvania soil for longer than six continuous months. To skirt the law, President Washington decided, after considerable research and consultation, that the best course of action would be to send all of his slaves back to Mount Vernon every time the six-month deadline was about to toll. They would stay at the plantation for a few weeks and then return to Philadelphia to restart the "freedom clock." President Washington surmised that his slaves, especially Hercules, were well aware of the law, and at one point late in his second presidential term, he accused Hercules of plotting to escape. According to Tobias Lear, Hercules was visibly upset that President Washington would even suspect him of such betrayal.[22]

It's puzzling that President Washington would be concerned about Hercules's possible flight, since he had previously granted him some limited freedoms. In addition to Hercules's off-the-clock excursions, the president's expense reports also show that Hercules and other slaves were allowed to go to the circus and the theater by themselves.[23] Hercules certainly could have attempted to get away at any point during these activities but chose not to. Perhaps he refrained because he was aware that the president had signed the Fugitive Slave Act of 1793, which would have forced his return to President Washington if he escaped and were recaptured anywhere on American soil. Hercules knew he would have only one chance to abscond, if he decided to do so, and he had to make it count.

As President Washington's second term came to a close, he prepared for permanent retirement at Mount Vernon. Hercules was growing more desirous for freedom and must have known that the window to escape was closing. He may have been buoyed by the successful flight of Martha Washington's longtime enslaved maid Oney Judge in April 1796 as well as of a couple of other of Washington's slaves. However, the fact that some slaves had successfully made their getaway meant that Hercules was being more closely watched. In fact, President Washington sought to minimize the risk of Hercules's escape by moving him back to Mount Vernon ahead of schedule. As Craig LaBan wrote,

> Oney Judge proved Philadelphia was a risk. But back at Mount Vernon, surely, Hercules would be secure. The once-trusted chef, also noted for the fine silk clothes of his evening promenades in Philadelphia, suddenly found himself that November in the coarse linens and woolens of a field slave. Hercules was relegated to hard labor alongside others, digging clay for 100,000 bricks, spreading dung, grubbing bushes, and smashing stones into sand to coat the houses on the property, according to farm reports and a November memo from Washington to his farm manager. "That will Keep them," he wrote, "out of idleness and mischief." When Hercules' son Richmond was then caught stealing money from an employee's saddlebags, Washington made his suspicions of a planned father-son escape clear in a letter: "This will make a watch, without its being suspected by, or intimated to them."[24]

Richmond's attempted theft confirmed President Washington's earlier suspicions of Hercules and put his former chef in a more precarious position. Washington thus took extra steps to make it more difficult for Hercules to escape. Yet, that doesn't mean we should count Hercules out.

In early 1797, Hercules dashed for freedom. The conventional wisdom held that he had escaped in Philadelphia *before* President Washington left the city and returned to private life at Mount Vernon. However, some recent historical detective work has caused researchers to reassess that timeline. Following up on recent discoveries by some Washington historians, LaBan wrote, "Before dawn on Feb. 22, 1797, he launched his quest for freedom. The recent discovery by Mount Vernon historian Mary V. Thompson of this key detail in the weekly farm report from Feb. 25, 1797 — '*Herculus* [*sic*] *absconded 4* [days ago]' — has finally solved two long-held mysteries: the place and timing of Hercules' flight."[25] In reality, Hercules made the gutsy move to leave on President Washington's birthday! Hercules must have shrewdly calculated that all of the activity surrounding the birthday festivities at Mount Vernon would distract others from noticing his absence.

The president's reaction to Hercules's escape played out for nearly a year's time, and Washington demonstrated a dogged refusal to accept that this master-slave relationship had ended. In January 1798, almost a year after Hercules took flight, the former president was still making inquiries and marshaling his resources to recapture Hercules. This is not so surprising, given the similar efforts Washington had made to recapture Oney Judge, Martha Washington's personal slave, who had successfully escaped to Portsmouth, New Hampshire, in May 1796. Several months later, the president had orchestrated an ultimately unsuccessful scheme to kidnap Judge and forcibly return her to Mount Vernon, Virginia. His key middleman was none other than Oliver Wolcott, his secretary of the treasury. In a 1 September 1796 letter to Wolcott, President Washington wrote, "I am sorry to give you, or any one else trouble on such a trifling occasion, but the ingratitude of the girl, who was brought up and treated more like a child than a Servant (and Mrs. Washington's desire to recover her) ought not to escape with impunity if it can be avoided."[26]

On 13 November 1797, nine months after Hercules had absconded, a still seething Washington fired off another letter to George Lewis. He wrote, "The running off of my Cook, has been a most inconvenient thing to this family; and what renders it more disagreeable, is, that I had resolved never to become the Master of another Slave by purchase; but this resolution I fear I must break. I have endeavored to hire, a black or white, but am not yet supplied."[27] Washington's temper is best described as "volcanic"—his eruptions were infrequent and intense. As presidential historian Thomas Fleming wrote, "Not many people made George Washington lose his temper. His self-control was legendary. But when he lost it, the explosion was something witnesses never forget."[28] This letter makes Hercules sounds indispensable to the Mount Vernon kitchen, but clearly the Washingtons had gone without his cooking before. Recall that Washington had Hercules working in the fields in the weeks prior to his flight. This suggests that the hard labor was temporary punishment to "teach Hercules a lesson" for thinking about escape while in Philadelphia. In addition, President Washington had numerous slaves that he could have forced to cook. Apparently, spite motivated the man whose presidency was a fading memory; running a slave-operated plantation was apparently now his primary occupation.

The former president sounded rather sad and depressed as he closed his 10 January 1798 letter to a Mr. Kitt: "We have never heard of Hercules our Cook since he left this [place]; but little doubt remains in my mind of his having gone to Philadelphia, and may yet be found there, if proper measures were employed to discover (unsuspectedly, so as not to alarm him) where his haunts are. If you could accomplish this for me, it would render me an acceptable service as I neither have, nor can get a good Cook to hire."[29] Martha Washington echoed this sentiment when she wrote to a friend on 20 August 1797. Brace yourself, for it reads like something right out of an episode of *The Real Housewives of Old Virginia*. Mrs. Washington complained, "[I] am obliged to be my one [*sic*] Housekeeper which takes up the greatest part of my time,—our cook Hercules went away so that I am as much at a loss for a cook as for a house keeper—altogether I am sadly plaiged [*sic*]."[30]

Once the reality of Hercules's successful escape sunk in, one must wonder: Where did he go? Given his awareness of the Fugitive Slave Act of 1793 and President Washington's efforts to kidnap Oney Judge, Hercules knew he had to get as far away as possible. If I were to indulge my imagination, I might wonder whether Hercules contemplated a foreign destination in the Americas—perhaps Canada, the Caribbean, Mexico, or Central or South America. They all would have been logical choices, and with the money he had made from selling leftovers, he certainly could have financed a lengthy sojourn.

Remarkably, a few clues might indicate that Hercules may have traveled even farther than expected by crossing the Atlantic. The trail leads to the Thyssen-Bornemisza Museum in Madrid, Spain, where a painting titled *A Cook for George Washington* is currently on display. The portrait is attributed to Gilbert Stuart, who also painted an iconic portrait of George Washington, but this attribution is disputed by some art historians. In assessing the clothing that Hercules wears in the portrait, Ellen Miles, the Smithsonian National Portrait Gallery's curator of painting and sculpture, said in a 2010 newspaper article interview that "the cut and fashion of the subject's white coat says late 18th century."[31] In the same article, Christine Crawford-Oppenheimer, a librarian at the Culinary Institute of America, added, "But his chef's hat is a tall toque that didn't become popular until the early 19th century."[32] Intriguing as they may be, these clothing cues get us no closer to the actual truth. The details of Hercules's escape itinerary remains a mystery.

One thing we know for certain is that Hercules never came back to Mount Vernon. While Hercules was away, Louis-Philippe, a French nobleman and future king of France, visited Mount Vernon a few months after the former chef's flight. Upon meeting Hercules's daughter Delia, he wrote in his travel diary, "The general's cook ran away, being now in Philadelphia, and left a little daughter of six at Mount Vernon. Beaudoin [Louis-Philippe's valet] ventured that the little girl must be deeply upset that she would never see her father again; she answered, *Oh! sir, I am very glad, because he is free now.*"[33] Hercules's heart must have ached from being separated from the four children he left behind — especially given that we know that his wife had died ten years earlier — but the risk of recapture was greater for an entire family than it was for one person.

Perhaps Hercules didn't go that far after all. In 1801, New York City's mayor, Colonel Richard Varick, who happened to be President Washington's former recording secretary, is on record as having spotted Hercules walking around town.[34] Perhaps Hercules, who had never worked for President Washington during his time in New York City, thought living there was much safer than hanging out in Philadelphia, where he would more likely be recognized. Varick immediately wrote to Martha Washington to apprise her of his discovery. The Fugitive Slave Act was still the law of the land, and Mrs. Washington could easily have forced Hercules's return. But she declined because, by this point, she had already freed her slaves. Hercules had likely gotten news of President Washington's death and, like the other Mount Vernon slaves, knew that Washington had desired to free them once he died.[35]

Varick's report is the last eyewitness account that exists of Hercules.

Yet his memory lived on in those who ate his food. In 1850, Margaret Conkling wrote in her memoirs of the Washington, D.C., dinners that she attended: "*Hercules*, the colored cook, was one of the most finished and renowned dandies of the age in which he flourished, as well as a highly accomplished adept in the mysteries of the important art he so long and so diligently practiced."[36] I like to imagine that Hercules vanished while at the top of his game to acquire something he desired more than fame—his freedom.

While Hercules made his mark preparing the very best in Virginia cuisine, African American cooks in elite circles became adept at making other cuisines besides southern food, and most often it was French food, the "official cuisine" of high society in America. Having a cook who could successfully execute French food was extremely important to maintaining social status as an excellent hostess. Jessie Benton Frémont was one of D.C.'s best-known socialites in the nineteenth century, and in her memoirs she gives us some valuable insight on how enslaved cooks were trained:

> There have always been admirable French cooks in Washington. The foreign ministers all brought them; when they returned—if not sooner—the cooks deserted and set up in business for themselves. These not only went out to prepare fine dinners, but took as pupils young slaves sent by families to be instructed. In that way a working knowledge of good cookery of the best French school became diffused among numbers of the colored people—and for cookery they have natural aptitude. [Well-known African American caterer James] Wormley, whose hotel in Washington was famous and who has lately died leaving over a million of property, owed his success to such training, as well as to his business capacity which turned it to profit.[37]

One can see the French influence in several soul food dishes like spoon bread, which is technically a cornbread soufflé. Most likely we owe such dishes to the French chefs who taught recipes and techniques to enslaved cooks.

With a few exceptions (namely the presidents named "Adams"), our early presidents were wealthy men who embraced the social customs of the elite households of their day. Some followed trends and others were trendsetters, and none exemplified the latter more than Thomas Jefferson and James Hemings, Jefferson's enslaved chef who was trained in classical

French cooking. Though his experience predated Jefferson's presidency, the culinary adventures and legacy of James Hemings reverberated for decades in terms of how White House food was prepared and perceived.

Hemings was the second-oldest brother of Sally Hemings, who is more well known today because of her now documented sexual relationship with Thomas Jefferson. Hemings was born in 1765, the son of an enslaved African woman named Elizabeth "Betty" Hemings and her enslaver, a white man named John Wayles. Wayles's daughter was Martha Wayles Jefferson, Thomas Jefferson's wife. That means that James Hemings was technically Martha Jefferson's half brother and Thomas Jefferson's brother-in-law. Hemings worked a number of jobs under Jefferson. From 1779 until 1783, while Jefferson was governor of Virginia, Hemings was a house servant and messenger and sometimes a carriage driver. Hemings's life may have been as mundane as the lives of the other Monticello slaves, but then his life took an unexpected turn.[38]

In 1784, the U.S. Congress appointed Jefferson to help Benjamin Franklin and John Adams negotiate treaties with European nations; Minister Jefferson thus had to go and live in France, and he took a nineteen-year-old Hemings with him. When they arrived in France, Jefferson quickly began Hemings's intensive, three-year study of European cuisine from 1784 to 1787. Hemings first apprenticed under a restaurant keeper named Combeaux and then learned pastry making in late 1786. Though Jefferson would poke fun at him, Hemings hired a French language tutor and was conversational in that language by 1787. Hemings then apprenticed under the cook for Prince de Condé [Louis V Joseph de Bourbon] in 1787, at great expense to Jefferson, on a country estate called Chantilly. He ultimately became chef de cuisine at Jefferson's Paris residence—the Hôtel de Langeac. While in this position, Jefferson paid Hemings a wage of twenty-four livres a week, which was comparable to or even higher than what free white servants who were his contemporaries made.[39]

Some historians theorize that Jefferson may have essentially been "paying Hemings off" because he faced a similar challenge to having slaves in Paris as President Washington had with keeping slaves in Philadelphia. Much like Pennsylvania, France provided the legal means for James and his younger sister Sally, who later joined him in France, to be emancipated. Unlike the situation that Hercules had to face in Pennsylvania, though, the Hemings siblings didn't have to wait. They were technically free as soon as they stepped on French soil under something called the "Freedom Principle." All that was needed was for a third party to sue for their freedom on their behalf. But this never happened, and it could possibly have been due to an arrangement that Jefferson made with both Hemingses, perhaps promising to keep their family intact back at Monticello. In the meantime, Chef Hemings kept preparing the superlative food that helped build Jefferson's reputation as an excellent host in Paris.[40]

Because of the combination of a new federal government being implemented at home and the rising social tumult in Paris, Jefferson, the Hemingses, and the rest of his staff left France in September 1789, a few months after the French Revolution began. Upon arriving in the United States, Jefferson found out that Washington had appointed him as the new government's first secretary of state.[41] Chef Hemings and now Secretary Jefferson took up residence in New York and then moved to Philadelphia when that city was designated as the nation's capital.[42] During President Washington's first term, White House steward Samuel Fraunces and Chef Hercules were in Philadelphia as well, and it is entirely possible that they were aware of each other given the friendship of their influential bosses. During his time in Philadelphia, Chef Hemings continued to see his share of historic moments.

One such moment was the "deal" that led to the District of Columbia. According to Chef Ashbell McElveen, founder of the James Hemings Foundation, Hemings

> was in the kitchen for the most historic dinner in early American history. On June 20, 1790, the meal—a delicious balm in his signature half-Virginian-half-French style—helped reconcile the bitter enemies Thomas Jefferson and Alexander Hamilton. Over lavish courses that included capon stuffed with Virginia ham, chestnut purée, artichoke bottoms and truffles, served with a Calvados sauce, and *boeuf à la mode* made with French-style *boeuf bouillon* instead of gravy, they forged an agreement to settle the young republic's biggest problem: how to finance the Revolutionary War debt. They also decided that the national capital would be situated along the Potomac.[43]

In 1793, Jefferson resigned from the secretary of state position and wanted to retire to Monticello. Coincidentally, Chef Hemings also wanted to retire—from being a slave. He asked Jefferson to free him, and Jefferson agreed under the condition that Hemings would teach others at Monticello how to cook, drawing on his accumulated knowledge and recipes that he had learned in France. This certainly would have saved

Inventory of kitchen utensils at Monticello, written by James Hemings, n.d.
Courtesy Library of Congress.

Jefferson the expense of training another slave, as well. Hemings accepted this condition and requested that Jefferson draw up a formal agreement on paper, perhaps showing that he didn't fully trust Jefferson. Thus, Hemings began a three-year culinary school for a select few cooking in the Monticello kitchen.[44] Only two of Chef Hemings's recipes exist to this day—though neither in his own hand—and they are both dessert recipes, one for chocolate cream and the other for "snow eggs." The one extant document in his handwriting is an "Inventory of Kitchen Utensils" in the Monticello kitchen, a list that he created in 1796.

Having fulfilled his obligations, James Hemings was freed in 1796 and immediately departed for Philadelphia. In 1797, Jefferson visited that city and spotted Hemings, later writing of their encounter, "James is returned to this place, and is not given up to drink as I had been informed. He tells me his next trip will be to Spain. I am afraid his journeys will end in the moon. I have endeavored to persuade him to stay where he is, and lay up money."[45] After some negotiation through a third party, Jefferson persuaded Hemings to return to the Monticello kitchen in 1801, but Hemings stayed only forty-five days. Had Hemings continued his professional relationship with Jefferson, he would very likely have been tapped to be Jefferson's White House chef. Tragically, that day would never come. William Evans informed Jefferson in a 5 November 1801 letter that Hemings had died in Baltimore: "The report respecting James Hemings having committed an act of suicide is true. I made every enquiry at the time this melancholy circumstance took place. The result which was, that he had been delirious for some days previous to his committing the act, and it was the general opinion that drinking too freely was the cause."[46] We have no inkling of the demons that drove James Hemings to drink. While his memory lived on in those who knew him, there is nowhere near as much written about him as there is about Hercules. Any descriptions of what he cooked for Jefferson in Paris, New York, Philadelphia, or Monticello wait to be discovered—or may be entirely lost to history. Thus, a most interesting life came to a tragic end, and we are left to wonder, "What if?"

When he became president, Jefferson needed someone to cook in the White House kitchen, but he was reluctant to have any African Americans on his culinary staff. As he wrote in 1804, "At Washington I prefer white servants, who when they misbehave can be exchanged."[47] Honoré Julien—a white Frenchman who coincidentally filled in as Washington's presidential chef when Hercules was removed from the position—was his first hire, and he was installed as chef de cuisine. Chef Julien would need additional help, so President Jefferson relented. As one Jefferson scholar wrote, "Despite having trusted enslaved domestics at Monticello, Jefferson brought only three slaves to the President's House, a succession of apprentice cooks." The first enslaved person to apprentice under Chef Julien was fourteen-year-old Ursula, who was named after her grandmother, a long-serving Monticello cook. Ursula had expertise in pastry making, but she lasted less than a year at the White House because she became pregnant. When she returned to Monticello, she rotated from kitchen work to fieldwork.[48] President Jefferson would have to select someone else from the Monticello kitchen, and he ultimately decided to pick two enslaved women—Edith "Edy" Hern Fossett and Frances "Fanny" Gillette Hern. Fossett came to work in the White House kitchen in the fall of 1802, when she was fifteen years old. Four years later, she was joined by her enslaved sister-in-law Hern, who was eighteen years old when she arrived.

Earlier I noted how Chef Walter Scheib believed that the White House was modeled after a plantation "big house." One big difference was in the kitchen. As plantation architecture scholar John Vlach notes,

> By the first decades of the eighteenth century, it was already customary for the owners of large plantations to confine various cooking tasks to separate buildings located some distance from their residences. This move is usually interpreted solely as a response to practical considerations: the heat, noise, odors, and general commotion associated with the preparation of meals could be avoided altogether by simply moving the kitchen out of the house. . . . There were, however, other important if less immediately evident reasons for planters to detach the kitchens from their residences. Moving such an essential homemaking function as cooking out of one's house established a clearer separation between those who served and those who were served.[49]

Fossett and Hern's primary task was to help Chef Honoré Julien maintain President Jefferson's sterling reputation for entertaining. President Jefferson was a culinary superstar in our early republic. He gets credit—probably too much—for introducing some popular European foods into American cuisine. Wealthy households were eager to mimic what the president served on his dinner table. A perfect example is macaroni and cheese—a dish that President Jefferson truly loved. By way of a backstory, Jefferson developed a macaroni mania while he served as the U.S. minister to France from 1784 to 1789. At the end of this diplomatic stint, Jefferson took great pains to have a macaroni-making machine sent from Naples to his Philadelphia residence. It is highly likely that Jefferson made sure that James Hemings learned how to make the dish during his "culinary school," and that culinary knowledge was passed on to the other Monticello cooks. The earliest recorded macaroni and cheese recipe appeared in *The Forme of Cury* cookbook printed circa 1390. This was the "go-to" cookbook for the royal courts of Richard II and Queen Elizabeth I, and the "macrows" recipe consisted of little more than pasta, (Parmesan) cheese, and butter.[50] Hemings's showed his French culinary influence by adding cream to the original macaroni and cheese recipe.

President Jefferson thought so highly of macaroni that he served it at a small dinner party he held at the White House on 6 February 1802. Reverend Manasseh Cutler, one of the dinner guests, started his recap of the evening in his diary with a note of disappointment before describing the whole meal: "Dinner not as elegant as when we dined before. Rice soup, round of beef, turkey, mutton, ham, loin of veal, cutlets of mutton or veal, fried eggs, fried beef, a pie of macaroni." Cutler then struggled to describe the new-fangled food, "which appeared to be a rich crust filled with trillions of onions, or shallots, which I took it to be." Then came the final verdict: "tasted very strong, and not agreeable." A Mr. Lewis, presumably Meriwether Lewis of Lewis and Clark expedition fame, explained to Cutler that he had just eaten an "Italian dish" and that the "onions" were in fact pasta. Cutler felt much better about the ice cream dish served for dessert, though. In terms of after-dinner entertainment, the party "drank tea and viewed again the great cheese," the latter being a two-ton piece of cheddar cheese that some Massachusetts dairy farmers sent to the White House as an inauguration gift for President Jefferson.[51]

We know from records of what he grew at Monticello that Jefferson incorporated many West African foods like benne (sesame seeds), black-eyed peas, and okra into his diet. As one historian notes, President Jefferson's White House menus "varied seasonally with foods often brought from Monticello. . . . Soups, whatever the season, were routinely served; a presidential favorite was savory tomato with chopped fresh herbs. One of Jefferson's prized desserts was a delicious crème anglaise–based queen of puddings filled with homemade damson [plum] preserves and covered with meringue." In addition, although he actually ate a prodigious amount of meat, President Jefferson espoused a primarily vegetarian diet while in the White House: " 'The English eat too much meat,' he once commented. 'I have lived temperately eating little animal food.' "[52]

Thanks to noted Jeffersonian expert Lucia Stanton, one gets a real sense of what a typical day was like in the White House kitchen.

On April 3, 1807, in the enormous room under the north Entrance Hall, the kitchen staff kept the fires burning in a fireplace, an iron range, and a stew-stove. Sandy the scullion filled a scuttle with charcoal for the latter, where pots of coffee and hot chocolate sat on grates above its cast-iron stewholes. After Fanny Hern scattered corn for the hens and ducks in the poultry yard and gathered up the new-laid eggs, she met the cart of Miller the dairyman and carried in the day's milk and cream. Edy Fossett was preparing the breakfast breads, while Julien and Lemaire put their heads together to settle on a menu for dinner. Mary Dougherty was on her way to the cupboards to get linens for the breakfast table. . . . While Jefferson, James Madison, Albert Gallatin, Henry Dearborn, and Robert Smith discussed impressments on the high seas, steam rose from copper stewpans of soup and beans in the kitchen and from a copper boiler in the wash house in the west dependencies wing, where Biddy Boyle wrestled with sheets and pillow cases. Julien directed Edy Fossett in putting together his specialty of the day, "partridge with sausages & cabbage a French way of cooking them." Revolving on the roasting jack before the hearth was a quarter of bear that Lemaire had purchased at market six days earlier. He was anxiously watching Fanny Hern stir an egg custard for the centerpiece of the dessert course.[53]

A similar scene played out several times during the Jefferson presidency, for Jefferson extensively used his dinner table to woo friend and foe alike.

Life outside of the White House kitchen—but still inside the White House basement—was another matter for Fossett and Hern. The White House basement was the live-in slaves' "world," an arrangement that wasn't unusual for urban slaves and servants in wealthy households. As an urban slavery historian noted,

These [slaves] generally lived where they worked, not so much because the wages were low, but mainly because of great difficulties in getting to work in the mornings; for colored neighborhoods were far away and the working days were long and hard. Sleeping quarters were generally spare places in the attics, basements and about the stables and barns, so that the men could feed the horses easily in all kinds of weather. House servants always lived in the house so that they could rise early and start the fires and have the old coal stoves hot by the time the white people came down to breakfast.[54]

Apparently, Fossett and Hern lived at the White House for almost the entire year, even though President Jefferson returned to Monticello during the summer months. At first, this seems odd since Monticello was not a great distance away, and transporting Fossett and Hern to their home shouldn't have been too burdensome. There are four factors in play here that may explain the president's behavior.

First, Fossett and Hern had the primary task of meeting the needs of White House staffers. As Monticello historian Leni Sorensen explains, "Edith and Frances didn't come home to Monticello when Thomas Jefferson did. He left them in D.C., probably because the White House was not completely abandoned when Jefferson left. There was always some staff that needed meals prepared for them."[55] Second, President Jefferson wasn't wholly dependent on Fossett and Hern's cooking because he had Peter Hemings and other enslaved cooks back at Monticello who could prepare top-notch meals. Third, as we learned earlier, slavery was legal and thrived in Washington, D.C. Thus, Jefferson didn't worry about emancipation laws like those that existed in France and Pennsylvania. What's unclear from the historical record is how closely Fossett and Hern's movements were monitored. In all likelihood, and unlike the other professional staff, these women remained at the White House. And the fourth and final factor is that President Jefferson could not have cared less about their wants and desires to be reunited with their entire families. They existed for only one purpose—to serve him or others as he directed. Nothing else about his enslaved cooks was of real consequence to him.

During his two terms, a number of familial events highlighted the human drama unfolding in the White House basement. Fossett and Hern surely ached from long work hours and fretted about the frequent illnesses of their young children. During the summer months, the White House basement regularly flooded after a good rainstorm, and the increased risk of contracting a disease took a serious toll. "The presence of young children (of the Doughertys and the enslaved cooks) meant the dreaded diseases of infancy stalked the cellars of the mansion," Lucia Stanton observes. "A boy died in Jefferson's absence in the summer of 1802, and whooping cough carried off Fanny Hern's child in November 1808. . . . Of at least five children born in the President's House to the

Monticello cooks, only two, James and Maria Fossett, survived to adulthood."[56]

If both of these enslaved women were omnipresent at the White House, how does one explain their pregnancies? It turns out that the long marital separations caused by their White House tenure were occasionally interrupted by visits from their husbands.

Fanny Hern was able to see her husband for a day or two, at intervals. David Hern, a wagoner, journeyed alone to the Federal City twice a year, transporting plants and supplies between Monticello and the President's House. Nevertheless, as former Monticello overseer Edmund Bacon recalled, they got into "a terrible quarrel," Jefferson was "very much displeased," and Bacon was summoned to the capital to take them to Alexandria for sale. When the overseer arrived, the Herns "wept, and begged, and made good promises, and made such an ado, that they begged the old gentleman out of it." Edy Fossett's husband, Joseph Fossett, made an unauthorized journey to Washington when he heard disturbing news from John Freeman or Jack Shorter, soon after their arrival with the president at Monticello in July 1806. The enslaved blacksmith left his forge and set out on foot on a road he had never before taken.[57]

As soon as President Jefferson found out about Fossett's unauthorized visit, he ordered a hot pursuit to bring Joseph back to Monticello. Although love drove these husbands to take tremendous risks to see their wives, President Jefferson was oblivious to how his enslaved workers showed their family values.

In March 1809, Jefferson's presidency ended, and Fossett and Hern returned to preside over the Monticello kitchen for years to come. According to Stanton, the former president and his guests were well pleased: "During the years of his retirement, Monticello visitors praised the 'half Virginian, half French style' of the meals they prepared."[58] Fossett and Hern cooked there until Jefferson's death in 1826. But after all of their years of service, Fossett and Hern did not ultimately get their just desserts. As Stanton writes, "Honoré Julien's enslaved pupils, after running Monticello's kitchen for more than 15 years, were both sold at the estate sale after Jefferson's death. Fanny Hern and her husband were purchased by University of Virginia professor Robley Dunglison. Edy Fossett and her youngest children were bought by her free relatives. Her husband,

Joseph, who had been freed in Jefferson's will, continued to work as a blacksmith to pay for the purchase of his wife and children."[59]

We know that the legacy of President Jefferson's table, both at the White House and at Monticello, lived on through his extended family and reached its fullest expression in the publication of Mary Randolph's book *The Virginia Housewife* in 1824. The progeny of the enslaved presidential cooks carried the torch as well. The most notable example is Peter Fossett, Edith Fossett's son, who was born at Monticello in 1816 and eventually became a successful caterer and Underground Railroad conductor in Cincinnati, Ohio. Peter Fossett made so much money through catering that he retired early from that business, became an ordained minister, and ultimately became known as the "Father of Ohio Baptists."[60] This was quite a feat for an African American man in nineteenth-century America. However, for most African Americans living in the nation's capital, racial progress turned into regress as the century advanced. Two events effectively describe D.C.'s deteriorating race relations from two distinct vantage points: a well-known race riot and a daring, unprecedented escape attempt.

The event that locals would later call the "Snow Riot" happened in August 1835. An eighteen-year-old enslaved African American named Arthur Bowen was arrested and jailed for the attempted murder of the white woman who owned him. A lynch mob formed at the jail to execute the accused, but the police intervened.[61] Author Jefferson Morley wrote a detailed account of the event:

> Prevented by the police from gaining access to Bowen and [a white abolitionist named] Crandall, they redirected their anger toward Mr. Beverly Snow's popular Epicurean Eating House, located nearby at the corner of Sixth Street and Pennsylvania Avenue NW. They ransacked the restaurant, destroying furniture and breaking liquor bottles, forcing Snow to flee the District. After looting Snow's restaurant, they continued their rampage by vandalizing other black-owned businesses and institutions, including Rev. John F. Cook, Sr.'s church and school at the corner of 14th and H streets, NW. Fearing that the mob would come after him, Rev. Cook fled to Pennsylvania. The impact of the Snow Riot lasted far beyond the few days of violence. As one of a number of clashes in the 1830s and 1840s, it was emblematic of the continued centrality of slavery in the nation's capital.[62]

Despite the deadly consequences if caught, enslaved people were ever vigilant for opportunities to escape to freedom. The most spectacular opportunity, and the second example showing D.C.'s poor race relations, came during the Franklin Pierce administration. At dawn on 16 April 1848, several wealthy Georgetown families awoke to a tremendous surprise: all of their slaves had disappeared sometime the night before. A range of thoughts must have raced through their minds and emotions through their hearts, for they now witnessed the impossible—a mass slave escape had occurred. Slavers were accustomed to individuals or small groups attempting to get away, but never before had such a large number of enslaved people pulled off a coordinated disappearing act. This episode came to be known as the "The Running of 1848," but I think this title is a misnomer. When those wealthy families faced the prospects of doing their own cooking and work—or at least of having to pay someone to do those tasks—the event is best described as "The Panic of 1848."

Sometime the night before, seventy-six fugitive slaves and three white crewmen slipped out of Washington, D.C.'s harbor, and they sailed down the Potomac River aboard the schooner *Pearl*.[63] The night was calm, and only the current propelled the ship downstream. After traveling about half a mile, the *Pearl* was stalled by the incoming tide and had to anchor. Near dawn, a fresh breeze arose from the north, and the ship and her passengers once again headed north, toward freedom. At the mouth of the Potomac River, the *Pearl* encountered strong northerly winds that prevented it from sailing up the Chesapeake Bay, and again it anchored, causing the passengers to lose even more of their head start.

A local African American man who was aware of the escape plan snitched on the others.[64] As a result, around noon on the following day, the steamboat *Salem*, with about three dozen armed white men on board, hurriedly left Washington in hot pursuit of the fugitive ship. Fourteen hours later, as the passengers and crew on board the *Pearl* slept, the *Salem* caught up. After all of the extensive planning and being so close to freedom, the enslaved passengers' hearts certainly sank as the *Salem*'s armed men boarded the *Pearl* and awakened its captain—a white abolitionist named Daniel Drayton. Since they were unarmed, Drayton advised the *Pearl*'s crew and passengers to exhibit restraint and not resist. Drayton, Edward Sayres (the *Pearl*'s owner), and Chester English (Drayton's helper) were taken aboard the *Salem* for questioning, and everyone else remained on the *Pearl* as the steamer towed it back to Washington.

The daring escape attempt made national headlines, and its fallout rippled far beyond Georgetown. Paul Jennings, a formerly enslaved body servant for President James Madison, and Daniel Webster, a sitting U.S. senator from Massachusetts, had secretly helped plan the getaway, but they were never charged with any crime for their involvement. The plight of two young sisters, Emily and Mary Donaldson, who were involved in the attempted flight inspired Harriet Beecher Stowe, in part, to write *Uncle Tom's Cabin*. Ultimately, the unsuccessful escapees were returned to work in the homes of their masters or sold into slavery elsewhere.[65]

Yearning for freedom was not limited to the streets of D.C. and Georgetown; it was also felt by those who worked within the walls of the White House kitchen. One of the most pernicious justifications for slavery was the supposed existence of the "happy slave." This falsehood asserted that African Americans preferred and enjoyed slavery in an alien, but civilized, Christian nation rather than being free in the savage, pagan country that they once called home. For our purposes, the relevant permutation of the happy slave stereotype was that an enslaved cook should feel "honored" to have the privilege to cook for the most powerful person in the country—regardless of the circumstances. Yet, the jarring, internal inconsistency of the term "happy slave" did not stir the presumption of privilege so established in the minds of many white people or cause them to reassess the status of African Americans in American society. Few accounts captured this juxtaposition more perfectly than this remarkable conversation transcribed in an article titled "A Modern Pharaoh," which appeared in the *Liberator*—a widely read, controversial antislavery newspaper founded by noted abolitionist William Lloyd Garrison:

> Mr. ——. to the Colored Man. Are you a free man?
> Colored Man. No, Sir, I am a slave!
> Mr. ——. Well, I suppose you do not care for that—you must be happy and contented in such a situation as this, and withal, a slave to the President; are you not?
> Colored Man. I do not know, Sir, why you should ask me such a question, or suppose any such thing.
> Mr. ——. Why, it is because we at the North often hear our southern men, and some northern men, too, who have travelled at the South, say "the slaves are very happy and contented," and much better off than free colored people.
> Colored Man. I don't know how that can be, Sir,—that a man as a

slave can be better off than a free-man, seems impossible. I guess
if they had to take my place, and be hired out by their master, as I
am here to PRESIDENT TYLER, for $30 a month, and receive only
$3 of it to support their families, as I do, they would not think
their condition was so mighty nice.

Mr. ——. How many slaves has President Tyler?!!

Colored Man. Only four, Sir, at the white house. Did not know how
many he had elsewhere.

Mr. ——. Have you a wife?

Colored Man. Yes, Sir, in Virginia; I have not seen her for months.

Mr. ——. Do the slaveholders ever separate husbands and wives,
then—and families?

Colored Man. Certainly, Sir, whenever they choose. Two of the slaves
of the President have not seen their wives since the President came
to Washington. And they often sell them forever apart!![66]

Such was life for the "happy slave." Fortunately, by the time President
Abraham Lincoln arrived at the White House, hope was building. As one
survey history noted, "Washington has been from the first a kind of show-
case city. Abolitionists, temperance advocates, zealots and reformers of
every stripe made their mark here. The District was the first place where
the domestic slave trade was abolished by federal legislation, the first
place where slaves were emancipated, the only place where slave owners
were recompensed by the government."[67]

President Zachary Taylor was the last known chief executive to bring
his own slaves to Washington, D.C., and have them take up residence
in the White House. Presidents Millard Fillmore, Franklin Pierce, and
James Buchanan didn't own slaves, but they may have used loaned slaves
to handle the domestic White House duties during their administrations.
Though President Lincoln ended the White House's dependence on slave
labor, his domestic staff did not fully escape slavery's legacy. As historian John E. Washington wrote, "When Lincoln came to Washington he
found that in the White House nearly every servant could trace his ances-
tors from slaves who had grown up as house servants."[68] One of President Lincoln's greatest accomplishments for race relations was subtle.
He simply treated the African Americans who worked for him with dig-
nity—something that had not happened in decades. Rosetta Wells, a
seamstress in the Lincoln White House, remembered "that [President
Lincoln] treated the servants like 'people' and would laugh and say kind

things to them, and that because he was President he wasn't 'stuck up,' and things had not gone to his head."[69]

One of those White House workers whom President Lincoln is on record as having treated well was Mary Dines. Dines cooked for the Lincolns when they would retreat to the Old Soldiers' Home in upper northwest Washington, D.C. Her birth date and year is currently unknown, but we do have some great details about her life. Dines was born in slavery on a farm in Prince George's County, Maryland. Dines's master was a wealthy bachelor who, reportedly, rarely beat his slaves. Upon his death, Dines was sold to a family in Charles County, Maryland, that was much harsher with punishment. Dines somehow ingratiated herself with the new master's white children, and they secretly taught her how to read. With that education, she plotted her eventual escape to Washington. She fled utilizing the help of friendly slaves, hiding in hay wagons and staying at "stations" along the Underground Railroad. She eventually made it to a contraband camp near present-day Howard University. In this camp, Dines quickly made a reputation with her singing ability, eventually becoming "the leading soprano of the camp" and, thanks to her secret education, "also the principal letter writer" for the illiterate elders in the camp.[70]

President Lincoln frequently passed this camp en route to the Old Soldiers' Home from the White House. Sometimes he would stop and talk with people there. During one of Lincoln's visits, Dines was tapped to be an impromptu choir director, and though incredibly nervous, she led the gathered throng in singing songs like "Nobody Knows What Trouble I See, but Jesus," "Every Time I Feel the Spirit," "I Thank God That I'm Free at Last," and "John Brown's Body." President Lincoln was moved to tears, for he "was very fond of the hymns of the slaves and loved to hear them and even knew most of them by heart." The next time President Lincoln visited the camp, he expressly asked for Dines to lead another extended singing session. It's not clear how Lincoln found out that she could cook, but she would eventually render such services at his summer retreat from the White House.[71]

As historian Matthew Pinkser explained, "Originally known as the Military Asylum, the Soldiers' Home was an institution created in the early 1850s for disabled army veterans who could not support themselves. . . . The cottages at the Soldiers' Home offered an attractive alternative to the White House, especially in hot weather, because they were well situ-

Old Soldiers' Home. Washington, D.C., 2015. Author's photograph.
. . .

ated on cool, shaded hills."[72] President Buchanan was the first president
to use this retreat and likely recommended it to President Lincoln. Dines
was cooking for the Lincolns in this location by 1862, and she was quickly
beloved by the Lincolns and the federal troops guarding the location.
Dines probably endeared herself to Lincoln by making his favorite dish
of cabbage and potatoes, and she curried favor with the troops by giving
them the leftovers from the president's table. During her cooking stint,
the troops presented her with a dress to show their gratitude.

Even under the unimaginable weight of waging a war and implement-
ing emancipation, President Lincoln still had to deal with domestic matters such as a grumbling staff. Days after firing the rebellious Union army
general George McClellan, President Lincoln wired First Lady Mary
Todd Lincoln to ask for advice: "Mrs. [Mary Ann] Cuthbert & Aunt
Mary [Dines] want to move to the White House because it has grown
so cold at the Soldiers' Home. Shall they?" Willard Cutter, one of the
guards, wrote in a letter contemporaneous to the president's telegraph
that Dines "had already told him that she would be gone in a matter of
days."[73] Dines's request was apparently granted, for she did cook at the
White House for a short period of time. But by the next summer, she was
no longer working for the Lincolns. Pinkser notes, "What happened that
summer to Mary Dines is not clear. . . . She might have run into trouble
with Mary Lincoln, perhaps over her habit of providing meals to the Sol-

diers who guarded the cottage. The first lady had always been notoriously hard on her domestic help. . . . Or perhaps the contraband singer, caught up in the spirit of post-emancipation Washington, might have tried something new in this year of freedom."[74] Eventually, Dines was reinstated as the retreat's cook in the fall of 1864, and in no time she relayed Mrs. Lincoln's concerns for her husband's safety to other members of the domestic staff.[75]

Lincoln's gradual dismantling of legalized slavery in Washington, D.C., and the rest of the nation endeared him not only to his staff but also to millions of African Americans and white abolitionists. Those executive actions to end slavery also ushered in an era where independent, free-labor culinary professionals ruled the White House kitchen. And as hope swelled in the hearts of millions, the White House kitchen itself became a symbol of hope. Haley G. Douglass, one of Frederick Douglass's grandsons, recorded the following anecdote:

> It was the custom of Lincoln to sit at the window while reading a book or paper and occasionally gaze out of it. One evening, Lincoln called his messenger and said, "William, who is that old colored man outside with an empty basket on his arm? I have noticed him for some days, as he comes regularly, and leaves with the empty basket. Go downstairs, get him and bring him up here to see me." The command of the President was instantly obeyed and in a few minutes the old man was hobbling into the presence of his Emancipator. Embarrassed and too full of emotion to speak a single word, he endeavored to say "Good evening," but just could not get it all out.
>
> Realizing the nervousness of the poor old man, as he was trying to get himself together, Lincoln said, "Well Uncle, I've seen you coming here for several days with your empty basket and then in a few minutes you go away. I've waited to see if you would come again and if you did I intended to send for you to learn your story. What can I do for you?" "Thank you, sir," he said. "You know Mr. Lincoln, I heard that you had the Constitution here and how it has *provisions* [another word for food] in it. Well, as we are hungry and have nothing to eat in my house, I just thought I'd come around and get mine." After a hearty laugh Lincoln told Slade to carry him downstairs to the kitchen and fill his basket. The grateful old fellow departed bowing low with gratitude and thanking God, and Lincoln too.[76]

The change in their legal status was an important pivot in the course of presidential foodways. Yet, the African American struggle to be fully integrated into American society had not ended with slavery's demise. It merely changed the context of servitude.

In antebellum America, enslaved cooks used numerous protest strategies: doing the job poorly, sabotaging the equipment they used, poisoning their master and his family, or running away. Given the high profile that comes when cooking for the First Family, few of these strategies were practical for African American presidential cooks. Except for Hercules, who successfully escaped, and James Hemings, who negotiated his way out of slavery, most enslaved presidential cooks felt a kinship with Edith Fossett and Frances Hern, who were literally trapped in the White House basement.

After emancipation, African American presidential cooks felt trapped in a different way. Though they now had more liberty than ever, African Americans were free to choose a profession only from a very limited set of options. Having success in any other field besides a service occupation exposed them to violent retribution from racist whites on their physical bodies and their personal property. In essence, they continued to live in a "professional career ghetto" and were expected to work in jobs that served white people.

One thing that differed in post–Civil War America was that African Americans now had leverage. Whites had become so dependent on black cooks that few white hostesses could cook themselves, and there weren't enough ethnic Asian or European immigrants to take the place of black cooks in the kitchen. As we'll see in the next chapter, black cooks used their leverage, not always successfully, to negotiate for pay equity and better treatment. The fact that black cooks had the gumption to demand fair treatment or even decline to work in the White House kitchen evidenced how much things had changed.

Second in importance was the growing political clout of the black vote. Since the 1870s, Democrats and Republicans have alternately courted African American voters, whose vote could make a difference in close elections. The White House didn't have its first African American presidential cabinet member until President Dwight D. Eisenhower appointed E. Frederic Murrow as "Administrative Officer for Special Projects."[77] Before the 1950s, the potential white backlash that presidents faced from having a black appointee on the White House staff far outweighed the possible benefits. Many presidents took a pass on making such appointments. It was perfectly fine, though, for a president to have a black cook on his staff, and these cooks became de facto cabinet members. Knowing what their black cooks meant to the larger black community, presidents had to change the ways in which they related to African American cooks. Emancipation ushered in an age where, over time, presidents increasingly relied on their black cooks for advice on race relations. This is the time that the president's kitchen cabinet began being built in earnest.

Recipes

HOECAKES

In his culinary biography of the Washingtons, Stephen McLeod writes: "Family members and visitors alike testified that hoecakes were among George Washington's favorite foods. He invariably ate them at breakfast, covered with butter and honey, along with hot tea — a 'temperate repast' enjoyed each morning."[78] Try these instead of pancakes for a delicious breakfast.

Makes eight 4-inch hoecakes

1/2 teaspoon active dry yeast
2 1/2 cups white cornmeal, divided
3–4 cups lukewarm water
1/2 teaspoon salt
1 large egg, lightly beaten
Melted butter for drizzling and serving
Honey or maple syrup for serving

1. Mix the yeast and 1 1/4 cups of the cornmeal in a large bowl. Add 1 cup of the lukewarm water, stirring to combine thoroughly. If needed, mix in 1/2 cup more of the water to give the mixture the consistency of pancake batter.
2. Cover the bowl with plastic wrap and refrigerate for at least 8 hours, or overnight.
3. When ready to prepare, preheat the oven to 200°F.
4. Add 1/2 cup of the remaining water to the batter.
5. Add the salt and egg and blend thoroughly.
6. Gradually add the remaining cornmeal, alternating with enough additional lukewarm water to make a mixture that is the consistency of waffle batter.

7. Cover the bowl with a towel and set aside at room temperature for 15–20 minutes.
8. Heat a griddle on medium-high heat, and lightly grease it with lard or vegetable shortening.
9. Preparing 1 hoecake at a time, drop a scant 1/4 cup of the batter onto the griddle and cook for about 5 minutes, or until the bottom is lightly browned.
10. With a spatula, turn the hoecake over and continue cooking another 4–5 minutes, or until the bottom is lightly browned.
11. Place the hoecake on a platter, and set it in the oven to keep warm while making the rest of the cakes.
12. Serve the hoecakes warm, drizzled with melted butter and honey or syrup.

SNOW EGGS

As Damon Lee Fowler notes in *Dining at Monticello*, "This is classic French *ouefs à la neige*, which the enslaved cook James Hemings almost certainly learned in France. The recipe appears three times in the Jefferson family manuscripts, twice attributed to Hemings."[79]

Makes 6 servings

5 large eggs
5–6 ounces (2/3–3/4 cup) sugar
2 tablespoons orange flower or rose water
2 cups whole milk
2 tablespoons sherry or sweet white wine

1. Separate the eggs, setting aside the yolks, and place the whites in a large metal or glass bowl.
2. Beat the whites with a whisk or an electric mixer fitted with the whisk until thick with froth.
3. Gradually add 4 tablespoons of the sugar and continue beating until the mixture forms firm, glossy peaks. Beat in 1 tablespoon of the orange flower or rose water. Set aside.
4. Stir together the milk, the remaining sugar, and the remaining flower water in a heavy-bottomed 2-quart saucepan.
5. Bring to a simmer over medium heat, stirring frequently to prevent scorching.
6. Reduce the heat to medium low.
7. Working in batches, drop heaping tablespoons of the meringue

(no more than four at a time) into the pan and poach, turning once with a skimmer or slotted spoon, until set, about 4 minutes. The meringues will puff considerably as they poach but deflate to half the volume as they cool.

8. Lift them out with a slotted spoon or frying skimmer and drain briefly in a wire mesh colander or on a clean kitchen towel.
9. Transfer to a large serving bowl or individual serving bowls (about three per bowl) and poach the remaining meringue.
10. Whisk the egg yolks in a medium bowl until smooth and gradually beat in 1 cup of the hot milk mixture.
11. Slowly stir this back into the simmering milk and cook, stirring constantly, until the custard thickly coats the back of a spoon.
12. Remove from the heat and stir until it has cooled slightly.
13. Stir in the sherry or wine and strain the custard into a bowl through a wire mesh colander. Stir the custard until cool.
14. Pour the custard over the meringues and serve at room temperature, or cover and chill before serving.

BAKED MACARONI WITH CHEESE

Macaroni and cheese is often a glorious, goopy mess, but this recipe is closer to the earliest iterations of the dish. Thomas Jefferson served something like this to Rev. Manasseh Cutler when he dined at the White House on 6 February 1802.

Makes 6 servings

4 cups whole milk
4 cups water
1 pound tube-shaped pasta, such as small penne
6 tablespoons unsalted butter, cut into small bits
8 ounces imported Parmesan cheese or extra-sharp Farmhouse
cheddar

1. Position a rack in the upper third of the oven and preheat the oven to 375°F.
2. Stir together the milk and water in a large pot and bring to a boil.
3. Add the pasta, stirring well, and return to a boil. Reduce the heat and simmer, stirring occasionally, until the pasta is tender, 8–12 minutes.
4. Lightly drain it in a colander (it should still be a little wet) and return it to the pot. Season with salt to taste and toss well.

5. Lightly butter a 2-quart casserole dish and cover the bottom with one-third of the pasta.
6. Dot with one-third of the butter and shave one-third of the cheese over it using a vegetable peeler or mandoline.
7. Repeat the layers twice more, finishing with a thick layer of cheese and bake until golden brown, 20–30 minutes.

4
Semisweet

PERSONAL AND PROFESSIONAL
PRESIDENTIAL COOKS AFTER
EMANCIPATION

Thou art the King of rail-splitters, O Abe!
Thou art the everlasting son of the late Mr. Lincoln.
When thou lookest upon thee to run for the Presidency and deliver the Union,
thou didst humble thyself to stand upon the "Chicago Platform."
When thou didst overcome the sharpness of election, thou didst open
the White House kitchen to all believers.
From the satirical poem "To Abraham Laudamus," 1862

Lincoln's presidency and the circumstances of the Civil War set several things in motion. First, in antebellum America, recently freed slaves, particularly those with professional skills, flocked to the nation's capital, which has earned several nicknames over time due to its allure for African Americans: the "Colored Man's Paradise," the "Negro Mecca," and "Chocolate City." In 1800, 783 free blacks could be found in D.C.; by 1830, 6,152; and by 1860, 11,131, and they far outnumbered the enslaved population.[1] Why were freed slaves drawn there? Many slaving states required freed slaves to leave either immediately or within a short period of time. Free blacks were dangerous to the South's racial caste system because they could be actively working on a slave rebellion, assisting runaway slaves, or simply inspiring other blacks to pursue freedom. In the states where free blacks were permitted to eke out an existence, there were often so many regulations on their economic activity or ability that it wasn't worth it to stay. After the Civil War began and the conflict raged on, thousands of enslaved blacks journeyed to the nation's capital from both north and south to live in the contraband camps near the city. Millions of African Americans were physically on the move during the war years.

Second, a significant number of D.C.'s African Americans were moving up the socioeconomic ladder, though the top rungs remained out of reach. From the earliest founding of the city, blacks established schools, built churches, and opened up businesses. The entrepreneurial spirit flourished in other ways. A wealthy white woman named Anna Maria Brodeau wrote in her diary she kept in 1800 that she "bought a wooden tray of a Negro Man, who has purchased his freedom by making them & bowls at his leisure time."[2]

Third, blacks were quickly asserting their political power, but it wasn't easy. In 1867, the Radical Republicans pushed through Congress a bill that gave D.C. blacks the right to vote. This measure was wildly unpopular with whites, and President Andrew Johnson vetoed the bill. But Congress overrode his veto, and the bill became law. That year, "thousands of blacks voted in District elections. In 1868 blacks were elected to local office for the first time. By 1869 there were seven black councilmen. By 1870 the City Council prohibited discrimination in hotels, bars, restaurants and places of amusement. For a short time, at least, segregation had officially ended."[3]

Alarmed by the rising political clout of D.C.'s African Americans, members of Congress took steps to make sure that power was muted. The key move was to prevent self-determination, and Congress actually removed the right to vote from all of Washington's citizens. John Tyler Morgan, the senator from Alabama, starkly explained the legislative action on the Senate floor in 1890: "It was necessary, he said, to 'burn down the barn to get rid of the rats . . . the rats being the negro population and the barn being the government of the District of Columbia."[4] Yet, Congress couldn't stop all black progress, as historians Harry S. Jaffe and Tom Sherwood point out:

> What Congress denied in the form of political power, the federal bureaucracy gave back in the form of jobs. A government job was a ticket to the American Dream, and Washington developed the largest and most stable black middle class in the nation. . . . The black middle class was sandwiched between a small class of black aristocrats and the poor blacks who couldn't make it out of the alleys. The result was a rigid caste system reflected by skin color. "It was a segregated city among blacks," says Calvin Rolark, Jr., who came to Washington from the South in 1952 and started a weekly newspaper. "The lighter-skinned blacks didn't associate with the darker blacks, and the Howard University black didn't associate with anyone."[5]

In terms of workplace status, African Americans were figuratively on the move as well. As free laborers, professional cooks could apply for the job, get courted for the job, bargain for a good wage, show their skill, and, if they so choose, stay on the job through changes in presidential administrations. To understand these dynamics, this chapter looks at the experiences of Cornelia Mitchell, Dollie Johnson, Lucy Latimer Fowler, Alice Howard, Sergeant John Moaney, and Zephyr Wright.

Cornelia Mitchell was the first presidential cook to run the White House kitchen in post-emancipation America. She was a carryover employee from James Buchanan's administration, and she lived in the White House servant quarters with her children. She was remembered fondly by a coworker for "her meals [that] were always well cooked and good enough to set before a king. . . . Cornelia was cultured and of a splendid old Southern family background. She was well educated for a colored girl of her day, and could prepare any dish from 'old corn pone and cabbage' so much liked by President Lincoln, to the finest dishes with lobster and terrapin. She was noted as one of the best cooks in the District."[6] Mitchell handled almost all of the cooking duties for private and public events, but extra cooks and kitchen help were hired for big events.[7] Mitchell also supplemented the presidential meals with fresh vegetables from a White House garden kept at that time.[8]

As the Civil War raged on, Mitchell's kitchen operations remained rather routine. Still, there were some unexpected interruptions. The most significant was moving the White House kitchen from the basement's Central Hall to its present location. As one Lincoln historian explains:

> The White House's lower-level kitchen was originally located in the center of the ground floor, which could be considered a partial basement. It had north-facing windows. Sometime in the middle of the nineteenth century, the kitchen was relocated to the northwest corner. This may have been one of Mary Lincoln's improvements to the living conditions of the White House. After the North Portico was constructed in 1830, the kitchen windows were blocked by this new entrance to the White House. Relocating the kitchen to a corner with windows made sense.[9]

Another interruption occurred in late August 1861, while President Lincoln was at the Old Soldiers' Home, some unexpected dinner guests arrived—the Norway Light Infantry of Maine. According to what we would now describe as an "embedded reporter" with the infantry, the "grub" was bad for a few days, and so our heroes strolled "down town" to see what could be done. They proceeded directly to the President's House. Without ceremony they wended their way quietly into the broad kitchen—"bowing to a tall man" on their passage—and, carefully selecting what they thought would "go round," made the following speech to the cook: "Look, here, we've sworn to support the Government; for three days we've done it on salt junk [salt pork]; now, if you *would* spare us a little of this, it would *put the thing along amazingly!*" It is needless to say that the boys had an abundance that day.[10]

The "tall man" in this anecdote may have been the butler Paul Brown; the unnamed cook was Cornelia Mitchell. Whatever the soldiers ate from the White House larder, I think that it's safe to say it was not salt pork.

Mitchell was just one person in a collection of culinary stars working in our nation's capital during the nineteenth century. Before her were free entrepreneurs of color like the aforementioned Beverly Snow, who ran D.C.'s finest, and possibly earliest, modern restaurant in the 1830s. Another notable figure was Augustus Jackson, who cooked in the White House as late as the Andrew Jackson administration before leaving to stake his claim as an ice cream empire maker. Many now credit him with inventing an eggless ice cream "made of sweetened-and-flavored cream and nothing else." This would eventually be called "Philadelphia-style" ice cream, as compared to the more familiar "New York–style" ice cream made with an egg-based custard.[11]

Yet Augustus Jackson did not always get the credit he deserved. Three different ice cream origin stories floated around in American popular culture during the 1800s. The first claimed that an unnamed African American cook for Abigail Adams accidentally invented an eggless strawberry ice cream in a hurried effort to please the Adamses' special guest: President George Washington. Another theory was that it was Elizabeth Schuyler Hamilton (Alexander Hamilton's wife) who invented this type of ice cream, also to cap off a dinner served to President Washington.

The most enduring origin story goes to Dolley Madison, the former First Lady. As the story goes, while Augustus Jackson worked for President Jackson, he simply followed the ice-cream-making directions he received from Dolley Madison, who handled White House entertainment for the widowed president. In time, Dolley Madison became synonymous with ice cream. By the 1930s, "Dolly" Madison ice cream stores started to

Domestic staff for President Hayes, March 1877.
Courtesy Rutherford B. Hayes Presidential Center.

. . .

proliferate around the country; many of these stores stayed in business for decades.[12] Whatever we make of the competing origins, Augustus Jackson did in fact know how to make an eggless ice cream, and he used the knowledge to run "a confectionary store in Washington, filled quart cans with custard and embedded them in tubs of ice. These he sold for $1 each. Others followed him, but he retained the reputation for making the best ice cream, and became rich as a result."[13] Jackson ultimately relocated his business to Philadelphia in the 1830s, perhaps because of the increasingly restrictive black codes enacted in D.C. The clear message was that D.C. whites were hostile to black success.

Another notable black entrepreneur in Washington was the caterer James Wormley, who operated a high-end hotel not far from the White House and catered some White House events. As one newspaper posthumously reported of the Wormley Hotel, "All the late presidents, Mr. Hayes excepted, enjoyed the hospitality of its well-known proprietor."[14] Another newspaper recounted, "When Tad Lincoln was sick the president sent for Wormley and he nursed the boy at the White House."[15] By some accounts, he was the only African American man in the room when

President Lincoln was on his deathbed and served as an honorary pall-bearer at Lincoln's funeral.[16] Wormley was also in the presidential lime-light for nourishing a mortally wounded President James Garfield with a beef tea made from the boiled-down essence of porterhouse steaks.[17]

Wormley was an immensely wealthy and socially connected man, and he used both resources to press for racial justice. He was friends with many of the Radical Republicans of the 1860s and 1870s, particularly Senator Charles Sumner of Massachusetts. One newspaper noted that, even though his hotel was for "whites only," "among the colored popula-tion [in D.C.] Wormley was held in the highest esteem. He had more in-fluence than Fred Douglass, for the reason that Douglass has always been suspected of trading his power with them for his personal advantage. Wormley, on the contrary, studiously avoided the whirlpool of politics, and devoted himself almost exclusively to his hotel business, in which he amassed a considerable fortune."[18] But the picture is complicated by another newspaper account, which reported that "Mr. Wormley did not enjoy any great popularity among the people of his own race. He was con-sidered by them as austere, remote, and desiring to live apart and to cul-tivate the society of whites."[19]

We know, however, that Wormley made several contributions to the local black community. He led the successful effort to convince Congress to create the first free school for African Americans, went on to fund a number of schools for African American youth, and supported local sta-tions in the Underground Railroad. Wormley also used his talents to en-hance social events for black elites. For example, on 10 October 1865, he catered a banquet for the First District of Columbia Colored Troops Regiment that was "talked about town" for some time.[20]

Wormley's legacy with respect to race relations in D.C. garnered a mixed assessment in the press. His last major involvement was indirect, dripped with irony, and sent shockwaves throughout the nation. The compromise of the 1876 presidential election—which delivered the presi-dency to Republican candidate Rutherford B. Hayes over Democratic candidate Samuel J. Tilden and effectively ended the Reconstruction ex-periment in the South—was finalized in his hotel.

Along with the reconstituting of southern political power, certain tra-ditions in southern culture waxed in influence as well, such as southern cooking: "Naturally when a Southern gentleman went to Washington to represent his state in the House or the Senate he took his cook along. Southern cooking predominated in the White House for a good many years. It was here that Mammy turned professional and went to cook for the famous restaurants, and Washington's culinary reputation was born."[21] The use of the term "Mammy" did not bode well for the prospect that black people would be accepted in the post-Reconstruction era.

Numerous black cooks made their living in D.C.'s private wealthy homes, but they also starred in high-end restaurants and hotels. John Chamberlin ran an eponymous restaurant that was also one of D.C.'s fanciest in the late 1800s. As one local newspaper observed, "It was long known as the highest priced restaurant at the capital; in fact, Chamberlin prided himself on the altitude of his rates, as well as the excellence of his cuisine. . . . Mr. Chamberlin had no French chefs and no foreign cookery. His cooks were negro women, but it was his taste that dominated everything. He bought the best to be had in the market, and by many, his restaurant was considered superior to anything in New York."[22] Emeline Jones was one of Chamberlin's cooks, and she, and her food, became indispensable to any dinner, public or private, hosted by a member of Congress during the 1880s. Her terrapin dish graced the White House table during the brief Garfield administration.[23]

Wealthy private homes and fancy restaurants proved to be excellent talent pools for cooks for the chief executive's kitchen. During his first term, Grover Cleveland, according to the *Boston Herald*, suffered first under an Irish cook and then under a French cook before seeking help. He entreated Chamberlin to "find a colored woman who understood the art of cooking in the Maryland style, and could do up oysters, clams, crabs, and terrapin in a superior manner."[24] The president called on the right man. A local newspaper gleefully reported that "Mr. Chamberlin had an old 'nanny' at his restaurant, and offered to loan her to the President for the Summer, while business was dull, and in the mean time would try and find a substitute. The offer was accepted, and now the presiding genius of the White House basement is an old colored woman, weighing about 300 pounds, black as coal, and wearing a yellow plaid turban."[25] Even as this black woman was being celebrated for her professional achievement, the writer still felt it necessary to end the newspaper article by reviving the mammy stereotype that would take several decades to die.

The most celebrated African American presidential cook of the latter nineteenth century was Laura "Dollie" Johnson.[26] She took an unusual path to the White House kitchen in that she neither was the personal cook of a presidential candidate nor was already living and working in the

Dollie Johnson in the White House kitchen, circa 1890.
Courtesy Library of Congress.

. . .

Washington, D.C., area when offered the job. Johnson, who was biracial, was born in Louisville, Kentucky, circa 1852.[27] Other than this fact, there are competing versions of Johnson's biography and path to the White House that play out in various newspapers. One version establishes Johnson as a successful caterer and chocks up a win for black chefs in their rivalry with French chefs. "[President Benjamin] Harrison complained that [White House chef] Madame Pelounard's sauces and pastries were too rich and 'laid him out,'" according to one newspaper report of the times.[28] The president asked for simpler fare, but she refused—so the president fired her. First Lady Caroline Harrison wrote to Mrs. H. M. Skillman of Lexington in search of a Kentucky cook. Skillman recommended Johnson, a well-known Lexington caterer, the *Lexington Leader* reported on 3 December 1889.[29] Another version is that Johnson had previously cooked for the Harrisons while they lived in Indiana, well before Harrison become president.[30] Of all the "how Dollie got the job" anecdotes, the following is my favorite.

At the time of her hire, Johnson was described as "about thirty-seven years of age, and is a mulatto. She has a dignified and refined appearance, and has a fairly good education. Some three months ago she left Col. [John Mason] Brown's service, and went to her old home in Lexington, having accumulated quite a sum of money, intending to take life easy for the remainder of her days."[31] As fate would have it, an up-and-coming politico named Theodore Roosevelt once dined with Brown and feasted on Johnson's cooking. Roosevelt would later describe it as "one of the best dinners he ever had" and highly recommended her to a friend in search of a cook. That friend happened to be President Benjamin Harrison.[32] Not knowing of Roosevelt's lobbying effort, Johnson received a random letter from President Harrison's White House steward, Hugo Zieman, which requested her services at the White House. She didn't respond immediately but sought the counsel of her friends and Colonel Brown. Only then, and several months after the Harrison presidency had begun, did she agree.

Regardless of how she got there, Johnson's hire made an immediate splash. Newspapers across the country boldly announced her hire and even included her full name without putting "Aunt" or "Auntie" before it. This was a rarity during a time when most media took every opportunity to belittle African Americans and indicates how much cultural cachet Johnson had. Even so, many articles in the news were disparaging, dwelling, along with Johnson's cooking prowess, on her physical appearance.

Johnson's second stint in the White House kitchen, under President Cleveland, stoked a simmering interstate cooking rivalry. One newspaper editorialized, "Mr. Cleveland, in selecting those to fill important posts in his household, official and domestic, has, we think, discriminated in favor of Kentucky. Two important positions so near to the President, are too many for any State — South Carolina could certainly have furnished most superior material for at least one of these offices."[33]

However, Johnson did have some detractors. Political patronage had become such a problem that the U.S. Civil Service Commission was formed so that government jobs would be filled based on merit rather than due to cronyism. Her hire seemed like just the kind of backroom deal that a politically astute Roosevelt and President Harrison would have known to avoid. Under such scrutiny, a scratch cook like Johnson who lacked any formal culinary training seemed unqualified for such a prestigious job when compared to a typical French chef — that is, until one tasted her food and all doubt about her qualifications were banished. President Harrison and White House steward William Sinclair brushed aside the criticism, and Dollie Johnson got the job. This appointment thrilled the president's African American constituents. One newspaper announced, "There was a great deal of joy among the colored people of

Washington over the announcement that a negro cook had been selected for the White House."[34] Such news was a relief to President Harrison, whose nascent administration was dogged by rumors that his First Lady, Caroline Harrison, did not want any black employees at the Executive Residence. Had that been the case, it would have been a real political problem for a Republican president for whom African Americans were a core constituency.

Johnson's biggest critic was Madame Pelounard, mentioned earlier as the French cook who already had the White House's head cook job.[35] In a newspaper interview soon after the hiring, White House steward Zieman said Pelounard

> had been cooking for the English Legation, and I gave her the same place in the White House and told her husband [Marcel] that I might make him butler. He went away to Europe. While he was gone Mrs. Harrison became disgusted with the woman's cooking. The President's wife wanted plain food and the cook insisted on serving rich pastry and sauces. Mrs. Harrison never was used to that sort of thing. Plain meat, potatoes and white bread suited her better. The President is troubled with indigestion sometimes and the new cook's dishes laid him out. So I discharged her.[36]

This very French cook had some very American reactions to the entire situation. She filed a lawsuit against President Harrison seeking monetary damages for unlawful discharge (a presidential first), and then she went to the press.

Pelounard attempted to spin the press coverage back into her favor by dishing on the bad food habits of the First Family. She disparaged their diet by describing how stingy they were and how gauche their diet was because they ate ham and eggs all the time and even had pie for breakfast. The *St. Louis Post-Dispatch* editorialized, "Large allowances must be made for the tongue-lashing propensity of a French woman scorned as a professional cook, but a bad lot of civil service appointments has long satisfied the public that there was something wrong in the White House bill of fare. A constant diet of fried ham and eggs is a very plausible explanation of the trouble, and the liberality of Indianapolis packers may in the next four years inflict untold misery upon the country at large."[37] The fact that diet may affect political appointments brought new meaning to the term "food policy." Pelounard's case was ultimately resolved out of court and never made it to trial.

With the controversy behind her, Johnson could finally focus on cooking, and things went well. A contemporary newspaper reporter noted,

> The busiest place in the whole executive mansion is the two rooms in the basement over which Dolly Johnson, the colored cook, presides. . . . Mary Robinson, a dark-complexioned African American from Virginia, makes the pies, bakes the bread and fries the crullers, and is the assistant of Mistress Dolly Johnson, who confines [Mary's] ambitions to browning soups and basting meats. The two of them can get up a dinner that would put Phillipini, Nicollini, and all the other $10,000 *chefs* to the test. Delmonico has no more juicy meats than Dolly draws from her oven, and Vanderbilt's own chef cannot put up a better pastry than the "Vaginny girl."[38]

The article went on to describe their cooking wardrobe: "They both wear tidy dresses of Dutch blue calico, and big white aprons that cover them from head to foot. Dolly wears a bandanna crossed on her capacious bosom in a picturesque fashion, but neither of them wear caps, as the least suggestion of livery is unallowable at the White House."[39] Once again, the mammy imagery rears its ugly head.

Johnson and Robinson plied their trade under trying conditions. It wasn't that the president, the First Lady, the White House steward, or any other humans made their life difficult—it was all of the critters that frequently visited the White House kitchen. Thanks to accounts from Hugo Zieman and First Lady Caroline Harrison, a shocked public learned that the White House kitchen (and other rooms as well) were overrun with red ants, cockroaches, and rats. Zieman accentuated the point by admitting, "I never saw anything to equal the way that old house is overrun with vermin." Zieman also claimed that the hungry rats ate a painting of Abraham Lincoln hanging in the Cabinet Room.[40] The Harrisons tried to use such revelations to their advantage, hoping that their plight would allow them to both relocate and build a new White House or drastically renovate the current location. Neither Congress nor the American public had an appetite for either, so the Harrisons had to keep calm, persevere, and exterminate extensively.

Dollie Johnson's White House tenure was not long. In less than a year, she returned to Kentucky to tend to her sick daughter. However, at least one of her White House meals was memorialized. Here's the menu, formatted as the *Chicago Tribune* reported it:

The Christmas dinner for the President and his Cabinet will be like yours. They will have their turkey and their plum pudding, and at the White House the menu which has been written out for you by the President's cook will be as follows:

PRESIDENT HARRISON'S CHRISTMAS DINNER
MENU
Blue Point Oysters, Half Shell
Soup.
Consommé Royal.
Entrée.
Bouches à la Reine.
Roast.
Turkey, Cranberry Jelly.
Potatoes Duchesse. Stewed Celery.
Terrapin à la Maryland.
Lettuce Salad. Plain Dressing.
Sweets.
Mince Pie. American Plum Pudding.
Desserts.
Ice Cream. Tutti Fruitti.
Lady Fingers. Macaroons. Carlsbad Wafers.
Fruits.
Apples. Florida Oranges.
Bananas. Grapes. Pears.
Black Coffee.[41]

When Grover Cleveland succeeded President Harrison, he had White House steward William Sinclair, an African American man, try to woo her back. At the time, she was cooking for Mrs. Rosa Vertner Jeffrey, a well-known poetess in Lexington.[42] In President Cleveland's second administration, Johnson returned to work as the White House's head cook.[43] Jerry Smith, an African American man who performed a variety of odd jobs around the White House, salivated for Johnson's return. After heavily criticizing French cooking, Smith said, "The introduction of a colored woman from the South into the White House to preside over its kitchen would be one of the greatest acts of the present Administration, and added years to the lives of the members of the Executive Family."[44]

In the last chapter of her life, Johnson returned to Lexington, where

DOLLY,

The famous White House Cook, has opened a

Dining Room

at 152 S. Limestone St.

she married Ed Dandridge on New Year's Day 1894, took her new husband's surname, earned a living hosting special engagements at high-end venues for about a decade, and began opening a succession of restaurants in that city. In 1905, Dandridge opened her first restaurant at 152 S. Limestone Street. Dandridge's notoriety drew all kinds of customers, ranging from U.S. senators to curious schoolgirls.[45] Dandridge closed that restaurant within the next five years, and by 1910 she was on to a new venture:

> The [*Lexington Leader*] reported on November 30, 1910 that Dolly (often spelled Dollie) Dandridge would soon be opening a restaurant, the White House Café, at 215 E. Main St. "She will serve regular meals and also special orders, and will make this the headquarters of her general catering for entertainments," the newspaper reported.
>
> But by March, the Leader reported, she had closed the café because she was hired to reopen the dining room at the Central Hotel at the corner of Short and Upper streets. Over the next few years, Dandridge moved her business to several other downtown locations. "Dollie Dandridge, the White House cook, has closed her dining room at 203 South Upper Street for the summer, owing to the heat and the torn-up condition of the nearby streets," the *Leader* reported on July 11, 1912. "She will devote her entire attention to catering for weddings and parties."[46]

The next year, Johnson performed her last known presidentially related culinary act when she sent President Theodore Roosevelt's daughter Alice a pecan cake to celebrate her nuptials with an upstart politico named Nicholas Longworth. Despite her fame, Dandridge's life came to an obscure end. As Tom Eblen of the *Kentucky Herald Leader* wrote in a tribute piece, "Dandridge died Feb. 1, 1918, at a niece's home, a small shotgun house behind Hampton Court, and was buried in African Cemetery No. 2 on East Seventh Street. The *Leader*'s funeral notice—the third small item in the 'Colored Notes' column on page 11—made no mention of her fame."[47]

Johnson's life illustrates an African American presidential cook at the height of her profession and loaded with bargaining power. Being unfettered to a particular president gave her the freedom to control the duration of her White House stint. A cook who worked for someone before he became president felt more pressure to stay during an entire presidency and return to private life with the retiring president. During the Reconstruction era and beyond, more chefs made it their career to be a presidential cook on staff through several administrations. Though most of these staff cooks were anonymous to the general public and toiled in relative obscurity, a few were profiled in the media. One exception to the enduring anonymity was Lucy Latimer Fowler.

According to a newspaper article, Fowler was born in an elite household in Georgetown, Maryland, and "belonged to the Mackall family, one of the most aristocratic and influential of Maryland's famous gentry. The Mackalls are connected with the Bowles, Keyes, and other prominent families of Prince George['s] county."[48] The same article condescendingly added, "It was an admitted fact that Lucy's mother was related by blood to one of the fine old families of Maryland, which no doubt accounts for the unusual intelligence and refinement of this little colored woman and her exceptional characteristics."[49] Though she was born in slavery, her white slavers taught her how to knit and sew and, unusual for those times, how to read and write.

Upon her master's death in 1857, she was freed as a fourteen-year-old and went to live in southwest Georgia. As an adult, she returned to Washington, D.C., and ended up working for Horace Porter, a former Union army officer who then served as private secretary to President Ulysses S. Grant. When the Grants dined with the Porters, they were repeatedly impressed by Fowler's hot rolls and Washington cream pies. The Grants were also floored by a meal that she once prepared for their train ride from Long Branch, New Jersey, to Washington, D.C., in the days before railway dining cars. With those successful "auditions," President Grant hired Fowler to be his White House cook.[50] Fowler worked for three more presidents after Grant, but it wasn't always smooth sailing.

One incident involved President Rutherford B. Hayes. On a morning in late November 1876, President Hayes's day started off with a bang—or more precisely, with a loud crash he heard coming from the White House basement. He dispatched his security detail to investigate the noise, and they discovered that Fowler was fighting with one of the butlers. One newspaper reported, "Lucy Fowler, a colored cook, struck John D. Whitton, a colored waiter employed there, a vigorous blow over the head with a rolling pin, inflicting a severe wound. John rallied and struck Lucy in the neck with a large plate. The President heard the commotion in the kitchen and sent one of the police officers detailed in the White House down to the kitchen to make a reconnaissance. The officer arrived just in time to prevent a renewal of hostilities and quelled the disorder by arresting both belligerents."[51] Fowler was described as "a small mulatto woman, scarcely over five feet tall."[52] Given her height, I do wonder how she was able to hit someone upside the head, but it happened. No reason is given for the skirmish, so we are left to speculate that perhaps it was due to mounting pressure to cook an excellent Thanksgiving meal later that week. However, Fowler did not come up short in terms of publicity. One newspaper decided to have some fun with the incident and printed a hyperbolic headline that read, "War has begun in the White House, and Sherman has now the opportunity to take the field."[53] The Fowler incident made the Washington, D.C., *Evening Star*'s crime section, where it was reported that she got "bonds to keep the peace."[54] Remarkably, Fowler and Whitton returned to work, side by side, in the executive kitchen without further incident.[55]

Only one other person had the guts to cross Fowler, who was now known as someone who took no mess. That brave soul was White House steward William T. Crump. Crump fired Fowler for stealing, and she responded by filing a $10,000 wrongful termination suit against Crump.[56] Fowler's lawsuit was ultimately resolved, and once again, she got her old job back. Her tenure ended when President Chester Arthur decided to hire a French chef. Fortunately, her former employer Ulysses Grant retained fond memories of Fowler's gingerbread. Upon hearing that Fowler was now available, the former president immediately hired her to be his and Mrs. Grant's private cook—a position she held until Grant's death in 1884.[57]

Alice Howard was another notable White House assistant cook who

Samuel Fraunces, presidential steward, n.d.
Courtesy Fraunces Tavern Museum, New York, N.Y.

Gilbert Stuart, A Cook for George Washington, *a portrait of Hercules, circa 1795–97.* © *2016 Museo Thyssen-Bornemisza/Scala, Florence.*

Eserline Dewberry (third from right) *and Raymond Jackson* (far left)
with the Kennedy administration White House kitchen staff, circa 1961.
Courtesy John F. Kennedy Presidential Library and Museum.

Charles Ficklin, White House maître d'hôtel, circa 1959.
Courtesy National Geographic.

Eisenhower era head chef Pedro Udo (left) *and an unidentified White House kitchen staffer, circa 1959. Courtesy National Geographic.*

Franklin Blair, White House kitchen staffer, circa 1967.
Courtesy National Archives.

White House kitchen staff preparing for a Ford-era state dinner, circa 1974. Courtesy National Archives.

President Reagan shakes hands with a White House Mess chef, 1986. Courtesy Ronald Reagan Presidential Library and Museum.

John Ficklin, White House maître d'hôtel, n.d.
Courtesy Ronald Reagan Presidential Library and Museum.

State dinner place cards for John Ficklin and his wife, 1984.
Courtesy Ronald Reagan Presidential Library and Museum.

Senior Master Sergeant Wanda Joell, Air Force One *flight attendant, 2010. Courtesy Wanda Joell.*

White House Mess executive chef Charlie Redden with President Clinton. Courtesy Charlie Redden.

worked for several presidents. There isn't much biographical information available on Howard, but there are many accolades to her culinary
skill. A 1914 newspaper article described her as "colored, widow, fifteen
years assistant cook in the White House kitchen, whose well prepared
dishes did more to put weight on William H. Taft than anybody else's,
and whose remaining at the White House has been responsible for the
ex-president's having thirty-five pairs of trousers cut down at the waist
line."[58] Reportedly, Presidents Theodore Roosevelt and Woodrow Wilson loved the way she made chicken, hoe cakes (a lightly leavened or
unleavened cornbread), griddle cakes, and waffles.[59] But as much as the
press wrote about the presidents showing appreciation and love for her
food, it was her own love life that gave her notoriety.

One day in January 1914, without any advance warning to anyone at the
White House, Alice Howard eloped with a African American stonemason
named William Clements. Howard's white colleagues seemed rather
ambivalent about her nuptials except for how it would impact her colleagues' White House lives. One of the lingering questions in the media
was where the newlyweds would live. One newspaper sought answers
from Howard's White House kitchen colleagues and got some limited and
unsatisfactory responses:

> "Where's she going to live now?" "Too much for me. She's always
> had her quarters here. Hardly think that she could bring her hus-
> band here." Even in the kitchen information as to Alice was mighty
> scarce. The cook and the other assistants are white girls who claim
> that matrimonial affairs have no interest to them, and all they knew
> was that the assistant cook was absent on leave. . . . There was unani-
> mous agreement on one point among the White House help — Alice
> is a crackerjack cook, and if William Clements is able to supply the
> raw materials, he will have mighty good eating around where the
> two make their home.[60]

Alice Howard eventually left the White House to cook in the home of
Admiral Cary T. Grayson, President Woodrow Wilson's physician.

During the presidential culinary adventures of Johnson, Fowler, and
Howard, D.C. was a place of increasing contradiction. A number of
blacks were flocking to the city for a chance at the good life, and many
got to live it, as evidenced by a growing black upper-middle class. The
local newspapers printed several accounts of "The Colored Aristocracy"
and members' colorful social customs. Yet, in sharp contrast to increas-

ing black success within D.C., the slight economic, political, and social gains that African Americans made after emancipation were being erased in all segments of society. Though slavery was now illegal, a new racial caste system reconstituted itself with the 1896 U.S. Supreme Court decision of *Plessy v. Ferguson*. That court case marked the official birth date of "Jim Crow," a nickname for legalized racial segregation. Oddly, and counterintuitively, elite attitudes about black servitude were changing as well during this time period. More and more press reports surfaced about the "servant problem" that whites had with blacks. Newspaper editorials increasingly called for ethnic emigrants from Europe, not necessarily considered "white," to be hired instead.

Segregationist thinking and the growing preference for non-black servants infected life in the White House. Though blacks like Alice Howard were on staff as assistant cooks, every president from Theodore Roosevelt to Herbert Hoover had either an Irish or a Swedish woman installed as the head cook of the White House kitchen. President Taft's housekeeper, Elizabeth Jaffray, segregated the residence staff's dining area, and Woodrow Wilson hosted a private screening of the incredibly racist film *The Birth of a Nation*. Whites (mainly in the South, but also in the North) lost their collective mind when Theodore Roosevelt had lunch with Booker T. Washington and when Mrs. Herbert Hoover hosted Jessie DePriest (wife of Congressman Oscar DePriest) for a traditional, annual congressional wives' tea. President Roosevelt tried to explain away his controversial meal with the prominent African American by saying it was just an impromptu meal at his work desk, not a formal dining scene. It didn't work, and the racists raged on for several weeks in newspaper pages and in the chambers of Congress.[61]

During this time, members of the Executive Residence staff ate their meals in the White House out of convenience and necessity. In 1907, an anonymous essay titled "What It Means to Be Colored in the Capital of the United States" appeared in *Independent* magazine. Though not written by a White House employee, the author makes some poignant observations on what Jim Crow life was like in the "Colored Man's Paradise": "As a colored woman, I may walk from the Capitol to the White House, ravenously hungry and abundantly supplied with money with which to purchase a meal, without finding a single restaurant in which I would be permitted to take a morsel of food, if it was patronized by white people, unless I were willing to sit behind a screen."[62] Jim Crow's wings were slightly clipped within the White House when Eleanor Roosevelt became the First Lady. One of her first acts to end segregation among the residence staff was to fire all of the white people save for the supervisor. Thus, technically, there could not be any segregation since every servant was of the same race. I'll let you decide if that's "racial progress."[63]

One of the most interesting White House kitchen teams ever assembled was the staff that cooked during the Franklin D. Roosevelt administration. The head cook was an African American woman named Ida Allen. Allen was described by her immediate supervisor, White House housekeeper Henrietta Nesbitt, as "temperamental," "a born leader," and "someone who could meet any culinary challenge."[64] Allen's main assistant cook, known as the "second cook," was Elizabeth Moore, another African American woman and transplant from the Roosevelt home in Hyde Park, New York, who had a "wonderful disposition."[65] Akin to Edith Fossett from the Jefferson administration, Moore had a child during her White House stint (delivered at a local hospital rather than in the basement, as Fossett had), and her baby was known as the "firstborn to the White House household."[66] An all–African American kitchen thus nourished one of the most consequential presidencies in our nation's history. However, there was just one problem: the food served in FDR's White House had a horrible reputation, to the point where invited guests thought twice about accepting the invitation or decided to eat before they headed to the White House for an event. What led to such a problem with good food in the FDR White House? The answer lies in the old adage "It's good to have friends in high places."

Henrietta Nesbitt was the only white staffer exempted from Eleanor Roosevelt's turnover of the Executive Residence staff. Nesbitt survived because she had a special place in the First Lady's heart. Nesbitt had become friends with Mrs. Roosevelt back when Franklin Roosevelt was governor of New York. Eleanor Roosevelt, who was active with the League of Women Voters while her husband had campaigned for the governorship, asked Mrs. Nesbitt, who ran a successful bakery in Albany, if she could supply the campaign with baked goods. Later, Mrs. Nesbitt went on to supply the Governor's Mansion with her locally renowned bread and pies. Eleanor admired Nesbitt's pluck as the main wage earner in her household, as her husband was often down on his luck. When it came time to hire a White House housekeeper, Eleanor remembered her friend Henrietta and tapped her for the position.[67]

But Mrs. Roosevelt, unfortunately, was not sufficiently concerned about Nesbitt's qualifications for the job. In his memoirs, White House chief usher J. B. West shared the president's blunt assessment: "Mrs. Roosevelt didn't pay much attention to White House food . . . but the President did. He couldn't stand it. 'I wish we could do something about Mrs. Nesbitt,' he said to [White House usher] Mr. Crim, in mock surrender, 'but Mrs. Roosevelt won't hear of it.' Henrietta Nesbitt prided herself on her friendship with the First Lady, and blithely instructed cook Elizabeth Moore to carry out her menus, no matter what the President requested. 'The food around here would do justice to the Automat,' the President said."[68] White House maid Lillian Rogers Parks remembers Nesbitt standing behind White House cooks Ida Allen and Elizabeth Moore as they worked and ordering them to adjust food preparation from what they would normally do.[69] All of this spelled culinary disaster in the White House kitchen. Normally, one would expect Nesbitt to be fired for such results, but FDR had ceded all control of the domestic operations to his wife, and he wouldn't intervene.

Yet, no matter what obstacles are thrown his way, a president is going to get the food he wants to eat. Rather than sit idly by in perpetual indigestion, FDR resorted to a strategy of confrontation and subterfuge. He ordered that a small kitchen be built on the White House's third floor and relocated Mary Campbell, a white cook from the Hyde Park residence, to the White House to cook in this new kitchen. He then bypassed the main kitchen and had Campbell prepare a number of his meals. Eleanor Roosevelt and Nesbitt protested, but there was nothing they could do.

Another type of presidential servant is a valet. Many of our military veteran presidents had African American valets who served them both in the military and in private life (such as John Amos for President Theodore Roosevelt), but hardly any relationship was closer than that of Sergeant John Moaney and President Dwight D. Eisenhower. Traditionally, a valet is not a cook but rather more like a personal servant who does everything else—much of it unglamorous. But Moaney did help with some food preparation. For example, Moaney usually began his White House workday by waking President Eisenhower up at 6 A.M. and assisting in dressing him by holding out the presidential undershorts—which the president would step into![70] Moaney then typically prepared the following for President Eisenhower's breakfast: "orange juice, a little fried egg, a piece of bacon and toast and pineapple jam."[71] According to Moaney, this simple breakfast was indicative of the president's tastes. "All the other meals, he never liked them real fancy—always liked just plain cooking," Moaney once said.[72]

John Moaney Jr. ("Moaney") grew up in Easton, Maryland, and was drafted into the U.S. Army in 1942.[73] In September of that year, he became General Eisenhower's personal valet and served in the European theater and Africa during World War II. After the war, when Eisenhower went into private life, Moaney and his wife, Delores, whom he married in 1946, became the primary personal servants for the Eisenhowers, with John continuing as Dwight's valet and John's wife becoming Mamie's maid in 1948. One of Sgt. Moaney's first assignments when he was back in the U.S. at Fort Meyer, Virginia, was to feed General George Marshall's chickens.[74] The Moaneys worked for the Eisenhowers during their days at Columbia University; at their winter home in Palm Desert, California; at the White House; and finally in their retirement at their farmhouse in Gettysburg, Pennsylvania. Though initially hired for other tasks, the Moaneys soon became a culinary duo with Delores as the family's private cook at Gettysburg and John serving as the presidential sous chef.[75]

During his military service, Moaney earned a reputation for making meals that "tasted like home."[76] Moaney shadowed General Eisenhower during the war and, along with another African American man named John Hunt, cooked most of the general's meals—even during the D-Day invasion of 6 June 1944.[77] Though they sometimes used local ingredients in Europe, they mostly cooked out of American rations.[78] Cooking for Eisenhower was easier than cooking for a number of other presidents, because Ike himself loved to cook and even installed a state-of-the-art grill on the White House rooftop. When the president grilled steaks, the rising smoke alarmed passersby on Pennsylvania Avenue.[79]

President Eisenhower and Moaney teamed up to make a variety of dishes: chili, fried fish, pancakes. Yet Ike's most iconic dish, and one of his favorite things to make, was a beef-laden vegetable stew. Lillian Rogers Parks remembered,

> President Eisenhower left the complete running of the house to his wife, except for his personal bouts in the kitchen with his cooking. He used to let the beef for his soup simmer in the kitchen next to my workroom for hours and hours until we would all be drooling. It had a most delicious odor. Every once in a while he would pop into the kitchen to check on it, and I would supervise the preparation of the vegetables until they were just so. He loved to don an apron and do his own mixing at the pot. Once, when he went to Palm Springs, California, for a rest, he took his whole container of soup with him

*John Moaney grilling with President Eisenhower, n.d. Courtesy Dwight D.
Eisenhower Presidential Library, Museum and Boyhood Home.*

. . .

because he hadn't had time to eat it at the White House. We love this
human touch in the dignified General-President.[80]

As a nod to his cooking abilities, Rogers also knitted him an apron as a
gift, which he proudly wore when he cooked.[81]

When it came to the famous dish, Moaney played a special role. Chief
usher West recalled, "'Ike's stew,' a recipe passed reverently around offi-

cial Washington, was known unofficially at the White House as 'Moaney's stew.' The good-natured sergeant chopped up the meat and onions in the diet kitchen on the third floor, assembled all the ingredients, and stood patiently beside the pot like a surgical nurse, handing the President parsley, paprika, garlic, as Mr. Eisenhower asked for each."[82] Moaney also recalled in an interview that in addition to the famous vegetable soup, President Eisenhower magnanimously taught him how to make other things like potato salad.[83]

The Eisenhower presidency witnessed several seminal events in the accelerating civil rights movement: the 1954 *Brown v. Board of Education* decision by the U.S. Supreme Court, the Montgomery bus boycott of 1955, and the use of federal troops to help desegregate Little Rock High School by nine African American students in 1957. Public perception of President Eisenhower's civil rights record was divided. Some believed that he took courageous, measured steps to advance the cause of black progress in the South and in Washington, D.C., by dismantling Jim Crow practices in federal government, appointing African Americans to key positions in his administration, and melting social taboos by entertaining African Americans at the White House.[84] Others felt that he never did enough.

As African Americans closely associated with President Eisenhower, the Moaneys felt a constant pressure to defend the president's civil rights record to other African Americans. Susan Eisenhower wrote in her biography of her mother, Mamie Eisenhower,

> Delores has always been perplexed and upset by the notion, conveyed by some, that Ike and Mamie were racist. . . . She remembers the Eisenhowers would decline invitations if Delores and Moaney were not given proper accommodations or treated equitably with their white counterparts. And neither of them would tolerate the expression of racism in their presence. Once, at the White House, a guest used a pejorative word for Negro, and Ike jumped from his seat with an angry retort: "You will not talk that way in my house again!"[85]

Yet the Eisenhowers seemed to pick their battles on advocating for racial equality. Traphes Bryant, the White House pet keeper who wrote a tell-all book, claims that Mrs. John Doud, the president's mother-in-law, used a racial slur within earshot of the president, but he didn't do anything about it.[86]

Still, Moaney and Eisenhower went together like beans and rice (and garlic and onions). When General Eisenhower decided to run for president and tried to relieve Moaney of his valet duties and say good-bye, Moaney reportedly replied, "Me and you can always make it. Don't worry about a thing." That remark cemented an enduring friendship. One newspaper reported, "Eisenhower was so heartened that he agreed to take Moaney with him. The veteran black sergeant became the closest man to Eisenhower. 'He woke him up and put him to bed,' said an associate, 'and nobody could get away with what Moaney did. Moaney was the only man to tell Ike what to do. He'd snap at Ike and tell him what suits to wear and so forth. And in Ike's presence, not a person uttered an unkind remark about Moaney.'"[87]

Moaney served Eisenhower until the former president died in 1969, and then he served Mamie Eisenhower at the Gettysburg farm where his wife, Delores, was securely installed as the cook. For his dedicated service to the president, Moaney was ultimately awarded the Legion of Merit for meritorious service.[88] There is probably no better benediction for this friendship than what the former president wrote a couple of years before his death: "Of Sergeant John Moaney, I have only this to say: He and I have been inseparable for almost a quarter of a century; in my daily life, he is just about the irreplaceable man."[89] John Moaney died on 19 February 1978, and Delores Moaney resided in the Washington, D.C., area until she died in 2014 at the age of ninety-eight.

Not all presidential personal cooks have been as "irreplaceable" as Sergeant Moaney, and that was certainly true of Pearl Nelson. Nelson was a private cook who worked for the Kennedys while they lived in Georgetown and came with them to the White House. She fully expected to make meals in the newly constructed second-floor kitchen. Even though JFK loved the way that Nelson cooked his favorite New England seafood dishes like clam chowder, First Lady Jacqueline Kennedy set her heart and mind on having a French chef handle all of the presidential cooking. She got her wish when she hired René Verdon to run the White House kitchen under the newly created title "White House Executive Chef." The First Lady tried to fire Nelson several times, but Nelson had a knack for talking her out of it every time the subject was broached, thus saving her job. Exasperated, the First Lady asked chief usher J. B. West to fire Nelson for her. The first time West tried to do so, Nelson put up a good fight, just as she had with the First Lady. West then resorted to bribery. He offered Nelson a free two-week stay in the White House as a guest, where she would get the VIP treatment from the residence staff—chef-made meals, her bed made up every morning, and chauffeured rides in presidential cars. Thus Nelson's mercurial White House stint came to an end. As West elaborated, "Mrs. Kennedy ran into me in the center hall during Pearl's first week in residence. 'I just saw Pearl!' she exclaimed, eyes wide. 'Did you give up, too?' 'Not at all,' I said, and explained my delicate maneuver. Mrs. Kennedy was delighted. 'That's splendid,' she said. 'Just splendid!' She grinned impishly."[90] Jacqueline was certainly color-blind in executing her plans. Seeing how skillfully West handled Nelson, she asked him to handle getting rid of a white staffer in the main kitchen.[91]

Lyndon Baines Johnson was the last president to bring a longtime African American personal cook to serve on the White House kitchen staff, and that person was a remarkable woman named Zephyr Black Wright. Zephyr Wright was born near Marshall, Texas, in 1915. She spent the first eleven years of her life on a farm being raised by her maternal grandparents. She later graduated from high school and then from nearby Wiley College, where she majored in home economics. As was common at the time, she planned to be the domestic servant or cook for some private family in her hometown. Little did she know that she was being prepared for something better. Two Wiley College professors, Dr. Melvin B. Tolson and Dr. Matthew Winfred Dogan, took an interest in Wright and mentored her on her critical thinking skills and public speaking. When Claudia Alta "Lady Bird" Johnson came to town seeking a family cook, the Wiley professors happily recommended Wright.[92]

Though they didn't know each other personally, Wright and Johnson had much in common: both were born in rural Texas, in towns not far from Marshall; both graduated from Marshall High School; and Wright's aunt had worked for Lady Bird Johnson's father. Wright remembered when she finally met Mrs. Johnson in person:

When I went to Wiley that September I talked with Dr. Dogan about working, and it was just a coincidence that Mrs. Johnson also went to Wiley and talked to Dr. Dogan about someone to work for her. He had told me that he thought I could help him in many ways, with even cooking and probably something in the office, or just work around there in order for me to go to school. Then after Mrs. Johnson had talked to him, he asked me how I would like to go to Washington. I was quite elated when he spoke of going to Washington, because I knew I'd never have an opportunity to go anywhere. You know, I just thought in terms of always being in Marshall.[93]

The chance to work in Washington greatly expanded her universe and possibilities beyond anything that Wright could have previously conceived.

Wright joined the Johnsons in D.C. soon after LBJ won his first congressional race in 1942. They quickly took to Wright's homey southern cooking, particularly her brownies, fried chicken, hash, popovers, peach ice cream, roasts, spoon bread, and Pedernales River Chili.[94] During Johnson's political career in the House and Senate, the broader Washington community became familiar with Wright's cooking through the many meals hosted by the Johnsons. Longtime and legendary Speaker of the House Sam Rayburn (D-Tex.) called Wright "the best southern cook this side of Heaven." Another said that Zephyr's dishes are "as light as her name."[95]

The Johnsons introduced Wright to the nation when they gave her a VIP seat at President Johnson's 1964 inauguration. As the *New York Times* reported, "Mrs. Zephyr Wright, the Johnson family cook for 21 years, occupied the Presidential box in the House gallery with Mrs. Johnson, members of the family and a few honored guests." Anticipating that a certain current White House executive chef might be reading, the *Times* also clarified that "Mrs. Wright is expected to cook for the family or for small private gatherings. She is not expected to take over the job now held by René Verdon, the French chef who has been in charge of state dinners and other social gatherings at the White House during part of the Kennedy Administration."[96]

Despite the initial excitement, life in the White House was not a rose garden for Wright. Her first challenge was forging a decent working relationship with Chef Verdon. As the Johnsons became increasingly dissatisfied with Verdon's French dishes, they asked him to prepare more familiar southern and Tex-Mex dishes. How did Verdon feel about cooking such fare? Well, he once derided the melted cheese dip called *chile con queso* as "chili concrete." Whenever Verdon messed up cooking a "homey dish," President Johnson would instruct Verdon to have Zephyr show him how it was done. I imagine that this irked Verdon a great deal. In time, Zephyr was doing all of the cooking, with Verdon handling the state dinners and family cooking on her days off. The last straw for him was when the Johnsons hired Mary Kaltman in 1965 to help control food costs and menus.

One can feel for Verdon as he endured such a sharp contrast from his elegant days in Camelot. He eventually resigned. The entire episode gave Wright a chance to leverage her importance into several raises that put her salary on a par with what prestigious French chefs could command ($9,000 a year). After the Jacqueline Kennedy and Pearl Nelson matter had ended a decades-long winning streak in the ongoing rivalry, an African American cook bested a French chef.[97] Following Verdon's departure, a classically trained Swiss-born chef named Henri Haller filled the vacant executive chef position and stayed there until he retired in 1987. When Wright found out about Haller's starting salary, she blew another gasket and successfully lobbied the First Family to be paid a better salary, since she had more seniority than the new chef.[98]

After kitchen relations went from boiling back to a simmer, Wright had the Herculean task of managing LBJ himself. President Johnson was notorious for coming back to the White House late in the evening to eat his meals, bringing more guests over for meals than were expected, and demanding perfection, regardless of how difficult he made the circumstances. The scheduling unpredictability—and the predictability of LBJ's temper—put a tremendous strain on Wright and the rest of the kitchen staff. However, decades of familiarity equipped Wright with the ability to roll with the punches and give back to LBJ as good as she got it. She dealt with unexpected invitees by coordinating with the butlers to liquor up the guests to keep them distracted and happy while staggering how the courses were served so that she could prepare additional items on the fly.[99] Ultimately, the job pressures took their toll. Wright, echoing the sentiments of previous presidents, called the White House "a prison." She gained eighty pounds in the five years she worked there, and she was very unhappy.[100]

Though her own health suffered, Wright was charged with keeping the president healthy. She was the primary enforcer of the low-fat diet Johnson had been on since he had experienced a heart attack in 1955.[101] That health event began an elaborate and repeated dance where Lady Bird Johnson planned and Wright cooked the president's low-fat diet—which the president broke whenever he could. This tragicomedy came into sharp relief when Johnson had a showdown with U.S. senator William Fulbright of Arkansas over the Vietnam War. Fulbright served as chair of the Senate Foreign Relations Committee during this turbulent time and was a strong critic of Johnson. Fulbright once said that under LBJ's leadership, the nation was "gradually but unmistakably . . . succumbing to the arrogance of power."[102]

President Johnson got wind of what Fulbright said and barred the senator from White House social functions but eventually relented and invited Fulbright to a diplomatic reception held in the White House's Blue Room in May 1966. When Johnson finally spoke with Fulbright, he said,

> "A man can hardly have an arrogance of power when he gets a note from his cook talking up to him like this." LBJ then took from his pocket a note that Wright had slipped under his dinner plate and read it to Fulbright: "Mr. President, you have been my boss for a number of years and you always tell me you want to lose weight, and yet you never do very much to help yourself. Now I am going to be your boss for a change. Eat what I put in front of you, and don't ask for any more and don't complain." With a smirk, Johnson re-inforced the point that "If and when I feel arrogance of power," he reassured the doubting Senator, "Zephyr will take it out of me."[103]

Aside from the Vietnam War, the civil rights movement was the burning social issue of the day, and unwittingly, Wright's personal experiences with Jim Crow became a powerful rhetorical tool. From the Civil Rights Acts of 1956 and 1964 to the Voting Rights Act of 1965, Congressman and then President Johnson made civil rights a cornerstone of his congressional and presidential legacy. He often consulted with Wright to check the African American pulse on what he was doing. As Wright said in an oral history interview, "He seemed very disappointed that I hadn't noticed what he had done for this civil rights bill [of 1964]."[104] Most of the time, Wright was abreast of the latest happenings and discussed things with the president. She firmly believed that her major contribution was to give LBJ a unique perspective on African American life. As civil rights leaders had approached Lizzie McDuffie (with FDR) and the Moaneys (with Eisenhower), they bent her ear several times in the hopes that she could bend the president's ear on some pressing issue. Whether she did or didn't often depended upon her mood. Above all, she felt that the president was doing a lot for African Americans, and she was mystified that others didn't agree.[105]

Before introducing legislation to Congress for the landmark Civil Rights Act of 1964, President Johnson began "working" members of Congress, the media elite, and the social set in Georgetown to support the bill. Though he made a number of arguments, his most well worn stories milked the Jim Crow experiences of Zephyr Wright. The essential facts were that the Johnsons and their staff would drive back and forth between their home in Stonewall, Texas, and Washington, D.C. As this trip ran through the Jim Crow South, any African Americans traveling with the Johnsons were denied hotel accommodation—even when Lady Bird Johnson argued with hoteliers to give them shelter. The indignities piled up so high that Wright finally had enough, and she stayed in Washington year-round rather than travel between the capital and Texas. The Johnsons thus had to find others to cook for them while they stayed at the LBJ Ranch. The president's stories got more action-packed and emotionally wrought with each telling, but ultimately he persuaded enough members of Congress to pass the Civil Rights Act of 1964. At the signing ceremony, hundreds of people attended, and he used several pens to sign the bill. When he finished, he gave Wright one of the pens and said, "You deserve this more than anyone else."[106]

That same year, the White House was embroiled in the "Great Chili Controversy of 1964," which electrified the voting public. The White House runs a great risk when it releases recipes, but it does so occasionally. Liz Carpenter, Lady Bird Johnson's press secretary, was always nervous when a Zephyr Wright recipe was released because she suspected that some key ingredients were purposefully left out. This is what is known as a "less-er-pe (less of a recipe)," and it's a much-utilized tactic by secretive cooks. Still, in her memoir, Carpenter could not help but laud Wright's strategy: "Zephyr remains one of the great cooks of the world by *not* divulging her recipes entirely."[107] On this occasion, Wright seemingly left one ingredient out of her recipe for Pedernales River Chili (named after the river that runs along the LBJ Ranch): beans. However, this was not an act of subterfuge on Wright's part but a bold adherence to a culinary tradition.

Ask any Texan, and they will tell you that a true chili is beanless. After all, "chili" is a contraction of the Spanish term *chile con carne* (chile peppers with meat), not *chile con frijoles* (chile peppers with beans). Yet people who live outside of Texas are accustomed to eating a bastardized chili loaded with beans. When the White House published the chili recipe, it "spilled the beans" that President Johnson ate a beanless chili. People who lived outside of Texas went nuts. The White House mailbox and switchboard were flooded with letters and calls from the public wondering if their president liked the "correct" version of chili. Better yet, they wanted to know if their president even liked beans. The public, though, failed to understand just how much chili meant to the Johnsons.

President Johnson once said, "Chili concocted outside of Texas is usually a weak, apologetic imitation of the real thing. One of the first things I do when I get home to Texas is to have a bowl of red. There is simply nothing better."[108]

With such expressed passion, one would have expected those in the Johnson White House to put up a fight. Instead, the fervor put them into spin control. Who could they call upon? Zephyr Wright, their own resident expert on chili and beans, answered the call. On 18 March 1964, President Johnson's private secretary Juanita Roberts phoned Wright to get the lowdown on the president's bean preferences. The fascinating conversation sounds like two experienced scratch cooks comparing notes rather than two White House colleagues doing some troubleshooting. For the first time for public consumption, here is the entire conversation transcribed from a tape in the Johnson Presidential Library Audiovisual Collection:

> Roberts: We have correspondence asking us if the president and the First Family, like beans. Well, I know enough to say "Yes" [*laughs*] but I wanted to check with you. What would you say if you were asked that question by a responsible person?
>
> Wright: Oh, I would say yes!
>
> Roberts: And . . .
>
> Wright: They didn't ask what kind, did they?
>
> Roberts: No, but I know that he, particularly likes, pork and beans.
>
> Wright: He like pork and beans, he like pinto beans, he like, lima beans, green beans . . .
>
> Roberts: And that's green limas or dried?
>
> Wright: Green limas.
>
> Roberts: Green?
>
> Wright: Mmm, hmm.
>
> Roberts: And the green, fresh green beans?
>
> Wright: And he like the Blue Lake canned green beans, you know, marinated and use it in a salad . . . marinated in French dressing. And he like—well that's not a bean though, it's a pea, I started to say green peas, but he just like beans.
>
> Roberts: Now the green limas—
>
> Wright: The baby limas—
>
> Roberts: The green baby limas . . . how do you prepare those for him?
>
> Wright: Just in salty water, cook 'em and add a little oleo-margarine

and pepper and cook them for a good long while until the juice in them is kinda thick.

Roberts: Yes. You used to use the Velveeta, but you don't do that anymore?

Wright: Well, I do that for parties. We use the Velveeta, also mushrooms. You know, you call it lima beans with cheese and mushroom sauce.

Roberts: And the pinto beans I guess you cook like I do, with salt pork or hambone?

Wright: That's right.

Roberts: The pork and beans, do you doctor them up?

Wright: Not for him, he like them just plain. He doctors them himself with some kind of pepper sauce or something like that.

Roberts: All right. Zephyr, do you know where any of the chili cards are, the chili recipe cards?

Wright: Hmm, hmm. I sure don't. I may have one or two here.

Roberts: Well, somebody's got one and I'll find it because I need that one also. Okay, nice talking to you.

Wright: Okeydoke.

Roberts: Thank you a lot. Bye.[109]

Ah, those recipe cards. The White House successfully doused the publicity brush fire, and the recipe cards, according to Lady Bird Johnson, were "almost as popular as the government pamphlet on the care and feeding of children."[110] Though the Pedernales River Chili recipe cards are long out of print, I've included the recipe at the end of this chapter.

In late November 1968, Wright announced that she would retire from private cooking once the Johnson administration ended. In a newspaper interview, she shared, "I'm going to be lost," and explained that she was "retiring because of her health." Wright added that "she enjoyed her job more when the Johnsons were a private family because in the White House 'it's a little hectic around here.'"[111] She also had dream projects for her "retirement": "One of the things that I really would like to do is this cookbook [. . .] showing how a menu or a recipe can be made into a diet recipe. Because this is what I had to do, use skim milk and Sucaryl [a sugar substitute] and stuff like that to make it where he [Johnson] could eat it and everybody else could eat it, too, and it would taste good."[112] It would have been a fascinating, groundbreaking read for its time, but it wasn't meant to be. Wright was so burned out after her White House

Paula Patton-Moutsos, White House assistant chef, 2003.
Courtesy George W. Bush Presidential Center.

. . .

experience that she didn't even return to Texas with the Johnson family after working for them for nearly three decades. She did, however, stay connected with the family. After a brief retirement, former First Daughter Lynda Bird Johnson Robb hired Wright to privately cook for her family. Wright lived out the rest of her days in Washington, D.C., and died there in 1987.

Zephyr Wright's tenure marked the zenith of African American influence in the White House kitchen. When Jacqueline Kennedy created the position of White House executive chef (before that, this person was just called cook, chief cook, or head cook) and hired Frenchman René Verdon to fill that position, she set—revived, really—the standard from the era of Thomas Jefferson: the White House kitchen should be run by classically trained (read European) chefs preparing European food. Since then, African Americans have served only as assistant chefs in the White House kitchen, with an occasional guest spot by an African American chef. But although African Americans lost some status in the main kitchen, they still presided over many other aspects of presidential food service. In the next chapter, we will see how centrally positioned African American staff was when it came to feeding our presidents when they traveled outside of Washington, D.C.

Recipes

PEDERNALES RIVER CHILI

Here's the chili that got the Johnson administration in a lot of hot water. You may vary the heat level or taste by changing the amount or type of chile powder used. I personally like to use 1 tablespoon of cayenne chile powder and 1 tablespoon of ancho chile powder. Please note that absolutely no beans were harmed in the creation of this chili con carne!

Makes 12 servings

4 pounds chili meat (coarsely ground round steak or well-trimmed chuck)
1 large onion, chopped
2 garlic cloves
1 teaspoon dried oregano
1 teaspoon cumin
2 tablespoons chili powder, or more to taste
1 1/2 cups canned whole tomatoes
2–6 generous dashes liquid hot sauce
1 teaspoon salt, or to taste
2 cups hot water

1. Place the meat, onions, and garlic in large, heavy pan or Dutch oven and cook over medium heat until light in color.
2. Add the oregano, cumin, chili powder, tomatoes, hot pepper sauce, salt, and hot water and bring to a boil.
3. Lower the heat and simmer for about 1 hour, skimming off the fat as it cooks.

PRESIDENT EISENHOWER'S OLD-FASHIONED BEEF STEW

Few presidents who lived in the White House enjoyed cooking as much as Eisenhower. Not only did the aroma of this stew linger around the Executive Mansion, but it also permeated homes around the country, since during the run-up to the 1956 election, the Eisenhower campaign widely circulated the recipe to supportive housewives who could host stew suppers in their homes and persuade their friends to vote for Ike.

Makes 8 servings

For the bouquet garni
  2 peppercorns
  1 bay leaf
  3 whole cloves
  1/2 teaspoon thyme
  Pinch of cayenne pepper
  1 garlic clove, halved
For the stew
  2 pounds beef stew meat
  3 cans beef bouillon
  1 pound small white potatoes
  1 bunch carrots, sliced
  8–10 small onions
  2 tomatoes, chopped
  3 tablespoons all-purpose flour
  3 tablespoons water

1. To create the bouquet garni, combine the spices, wrap them in cheesecloth, and tie with kitchen twine.
2. Place the bouquet garni, meat, bouillon, potatoes, carrots, onions, and tomatoes in a large stockpot and simmer on low heat for 40 minutes, or until the vegetables are tender.
3. Remove the bouquet garni.
4. In a small bowl, combine the flour and water and 3 tablespoons of stew stock until well-blended.
5. Add the flour mixture to the stew, stirring well.
6. Simmer until slightly thickened.

CAROLINE HARRISON'S DEVILED ALMONDS

No known recipes attributable to Dollie Johnson currently exist. Caroline Harrison, however, left some recipes behind, and it is not unlikely that Dollie Johnson had prepared these addictive snacks during her brief tenure in the White House kitchen. I've served these as an amuse-bouche at my presentations on African American presidential chefs, and I can testify that they are addictive.

Makes 4 servings

1/2 pound almonds, blanched
4 tablespoons butter
Cayenne pepper to taste
Salt to taste

1. Heat a large skillet over medium heat.
2. Add the almonds and butter and sauté the almonds until they are light brown.
3. Drain on paper towels.
4. Place the almonds in a cake pan and lightly season with cayenne and salt.
5. Serve hot.

5
Eating on the Run
PRESIDENTIAL FOODWAYS IN MOTION

After all is said and done the man who is chiefly responsible
for the comfort, and in a large degree for the welfare, of the presidential
party, rides in the last car of the train. He is a colored man, and he is in charge
of the culinary department of the presidential train. Before he is selected the whole
force of the road is carefully scrutinized. He is chosen as one among a hundred,
and as a rule feels not only the responsibility but the honor of his appointment.
It is told of the chief cook on a previous presidential journey that after an
especially fine breakfast the president expressed a desire to see and
congratulate the chef on his triumph. Word was taken to the magnate
in his special car and he sent back word that if the president
desired to see him he could be found in the kitchen.
"On the Presidential Train," *Coalville Times,* 17 May 1901

It is when the president departs the White House and goes on a trip that the presidential food story becomes most complex. George Washington found this out early in his presidency whenever he contemplated travel anywhere other than back home to Mount Vernon. As presidential historian Richard J. Ellis observes, "Americans in the early republic did not want the president parading like a monarch, but nor did they want him campaigning like a mere politician. . . . Americans wanted reassurance that their president traveled as one of them, unburdened by monarchical pretensions."[1] Most of a president's daily life is hidden from public view unless the White House grants access to outsiders. When the chief executive boards a train, plane, or yacht, these vehicles, infused with the presidential aura, become, for the press and the public, brighter, shinier objects than even the White House. Consequently, when a president travels, concerns about cost, diet regimens, food safety, presidential comfort, press interest, and public perception are heightened. Throughout American history, African American cooks have been on the move with the presidents to help manage the immense juggling act involved—and to attempt to assuage all fears.

Presidential travel cooks faced different challenges than their contemporaries who cooked in the (by comparison) comfortable White House kitchen did. They had less space to cook in and less downtime because they had to do shopping, preparation, and cleanup with fewer personnel. Also, those involved in mobile presidential food service have often had to perform multiple duties in addition to cooking. The reward was that the confined space of a boat, plane, or train often afforded the cooks more familiarity with the president. In this chapter, we learn about the railroad dining car cooks, yacht mess attendants, and flight attendants who nourished our presidents through the experiences of Joe Brown, John Smeades, William Letcher, Delefasse Green, Lizzie McDuffie, Daisy Bonner, Sam Mitchell, Ronald Jackson, Charlie Redden, Lee Simmons, and Wanda Joell.

With his restrictive views on presidential travel, President Washington set a precedent for later presidents from which they were reluctant to stray. Washington chose to travel in as low key a manner as he possibly could—he took few trips, and when he did he traveled by stagecoach with a small retinue of servants, he stayed at private homes as much as possible, and he often refused to be greeted with huge public fanfare. The biggest prohibition felt by presidents in these early years was traveling abroad. Why? Americans had such an aversion to monarchy that they didn't want their own president to be seen as if cavorting with monarchs—an inevitable occurrence when a president was received by a foreign head of state. A few presidents, including Benjamin Harrison and William McKinley, were so slavish to this early travel taboo that they hilariously tested it by going right up to the Mexican border but not crossing over.[2] Theodore Roosevelt finally broke the unofficial proscription in 1906 when he traveled to inspect construction of the Panama Canal. Since then, "modern presidents have typically spent between one-third and one-half of their time away from the White House."[3]

Presidents freely and exuberantly, however, explored every inch of domestic territory that they could. Before the 1820s such travel was by horse or stagecoach. When the journey lasted longer than a day, the president dined at a designated inn, at a restaurant, or in someone's home. By the mid-nineteenth century, the "iron horse," as railroads were nicknamed, greatly expanded a president's ability to conduct business and politick away from Washington, D.C. Yet, this mode of travel was never baggage-free, as Von Hardesty, a curator at the Smithsonian National Air and Space Museum, records:

The frequent use of trains by presidents in the nineteenth century and into the early decades of the twentieth century gave birth to renewed concern over the perceived monarchical aspects of the American presidency. Typically, presidents traveled in private cars, which often were richly appointed. By necessity, these train cars were borrowed from railway moguls and rich Americans, because no funds had ever been appropriated by Congress for the construction of special railway cars for the exclusive use of the chief executive. One private car, dubbed the "Maryland," served several presidents in grand style, including Rutherford B. Hayes, Grover Cleveland, Benjamin Harrison, and William McKinley. More a palace on rails, it was fifty-one feet long with four separate compartments. The parlor was lavish, with sofa, marble-top table, chairs, and decorative mirrors. Such luxury renewed the old debate on what is appropriate for presidential travel in a democracy.[4]

At first, presidents traveled merely as honored guests of the railroad companies—and sat among the regular, commercial passengers. Later, railroad moguls, as a matter of pride and also to curry favor, loaned their own private luxury railcars to the president to use. On 9 August 1849, President Zachary Taylor became the first president to travel in such luxury when he took a trip from Washington, D.C., to Baltimore. Ellis relates, "Affixed to the rear of the waiting train was a 'large, new and elegant car' that had been provided by the Baltimore and Ohio Railroad company 'for the exclusive use' of the president. Taylor, however, 'respectfully declined' to use the special car, preferring instead, the *Baltimore Sun* reported, to take 'his seat in common with other passengers.'"[5] Even then, President Taylor realized that the "optics" (to use today's political language) of having a tricked-out train were bad. Several presidents followed suit, and rail travel was discouraged unless deemed absolutely necessary.

After the Civil War, presidents felt less apprehensive about traveling in specially outfitted railcars, but the practice invited criticism. The postbellum decades saw a great increase in the power and wealth of railroad companies. Along with such growth came a deepening feeling among the public that railroad company owners and executives had politicians in their back pockets and influenced them to enact laws and policies that enriched the owners at the expense of the working class. Having presidents travel in luxurious railway cars only enhanced that sentiment, and it often seemed that what would most draw public ire was the absolute splendor of the railway dining cars. Yet, the public eventually, if begrudgingly, accepted that presidents were special people who deserved some comforts—including a loaned cook from the railroad, usually the railroad president's private cook. The ultimate in railroad comfort were the Pullman dining cars, so named after George Mortimer Pullman, who founded the "Pullman Palace Company" in the 1860s. The first Pullman dining car was constructed in 1868 and was appropriately titled the "President." According to the Pullman Company Historic Site website, the President was Pullman's "first hotel on wheels . . . a sleeper with an attached kitchen and dining room. The food rivaled the best restaurants of the day and the service was impeccable."[6] These dining cars were overwhelmingly staffed by African Americans—because that fit the social order of the nineteenth century:

> With the advent of the dining car, it was no longer possible to simply have the conductor and porters do double duty; a dining car required a trained staff. On the Delmonico, two cooks and four waiters prepared and served up to 250 meals a day. Later, depending on the train and the sophistication of the meals, a staff could consist of more than a dozen men: a steward, a chef, three or more cooks, and up to ten waiters. Pullman resolved the staffing issue by hiring recently freed house slaves. They were experienced and skilled at service, and he believed they would be polite and deferential to his passengers. Moreover, since they needed jobs, they would work for less money than whites. As discriminatory as his policy was, it did have some positive results. The Pullman Company became the largest employer of blacks in the country. Within the black community, working for Pullman meant steady employment, travel, and respect. One could take pride in wearing the Pullman uniform. Nevertheless, the men were underpaid and overworked even by the standards of the time.[7]

As the nineteenth century progressed, the railroads relied less on the labor of freed slaves but still drew heavily on a black labor force. While overworked and underpaid, Pullman workers, recent histories have shown, came to play a significant role in the development of workers' rights that benefited African Americans in particular and all American workers in general.

By the twentieth century, a racial division of kitchen labor developed on the railroads so that "generally chief stewards and chefs were white and assistant cooks and waiters were black. But blacks did become chefs and were able to add dishes they knew and loved to the menu."[8] One such example is Chef Joe Brown of the Baltimore & Ohio Railroad. Chef Brown was born on 22 January 1859 in Charles County, Maryland, near the village of Pomonkey. When he was of working age, he landed a waiter job at the Relay House, a famous dining spot along the B&O. Brown was eventually made a cook, and among his famous customers were President and Mrs. Rutherford B. Hayes. The Hayeses were so taken with Chef Brown's food that they arranged for him to be their personal railroad chef when they traveled to Deer Park, a summer resort in Maryland owned by the B&O.[9] Brown's encounter with a second president was much more tragic, given what he witnessed on 2 July 1882:

> There was burly, vigorous President Garfield, who would eat nearly anything the chef set before him. The memory of that incident in Sixth Street Station, Washington, is as clear in Joe's mind as on the day it happened. He had stocked his pantry with solid food and was waiting besides the special when the Presidential party came along. Mr. Garfield had greeted the chef and gone when Joe saw the assassin, Guiteau, leap forward. "I didn't know what was happening," he says. "There was the crack of the gun and the President fell into the vestibule. We were too dazed to stop Guiteau, and he ran from the station and Mr. Garfield was carried into the station."[10]

After Garfield was placed in the convalescent care of White House steward William T. Crump and caterer James Wormley, Chef Brown went on to serve thirteen administrations—from President Garfield to President Franklin Delano Roosevelt. During his amazing career as a railroad cook, fortunately, most of his experiences were less traumatic. The *Baltimore Sun* reported, "One of the secrets of Chef Brown's long, successful service is that he always tried to remember what his 'regulars' liked. He knew the appetites of the presidents and catered to them. Most of them . . . liked plain food well prepared. A notable exception was President Franklin D. Roosevelt, whose tastes ran to richer foods, and especially to game."[11] Brown's story would make a fascinating book—just think of all the historical, social, and technological change that he witnessed during his career of fifty-plus years.

While we have few descriptions of the interior of presidential railcars, the *Kansas City Times* reported that in March 1893, President-elect Grover Cleveland rode from New York to the B&O railroad station in

Washington, D.C., in an electrified railcar with "an observation room at the rear, a dining room, two bedrooms, a kitchen and a wine cellar."[12] Railcars took a more luxurious turn in the early 1890s, based on this description of the dining car used by President Benjamin Harrison:

"Coronado" is the name of the dining car. The furnishings of the dining car proper are supremely aesthetic. Seats and seat backs are of pearl gray straw, harmonizing thoroughly with the silver lamps and silvery metal work and contrasting artistically with oak woodwork and green plush curtains. The kitchen is presided by an experienced Afro-American cook, which fact is noted cheerfully by the people of his race as a slap at the French "chef." The steward's pantries and refrigerators are laden to their utmost capacity with bottled goods.[13]

Even railway dining cars could not seem to escape the ongoing rivalry between African American and French cooks.

Dining cars like the Coronado set the standard for presidential rail travel for years to come. And don't think that just because the president dined in a railcar that there was a steep decline in the quality of his meals. When President Ulysses S. Grant traveled by rail on the Chicago, Alton & St. Louis Railroad circa 1869, the St. James dining car had the following bill of fare for an eight-course meal:

Soup — St. James soup; Fish — Baked white fish with tomato sauce; Boiled — Leg mutton with caper sauce, ham with champagne sauce, pressed corned beef and tongue; Roast — Lamb with mint sauce, loin beef, chicken with giblet sauce; Entrees — Prairie chicken with Huntsman sauce, Mallard duck with currant jelly, Queen fritters with cream sauce, Maccaroni a l'Italienne, chicken sauté with rice; Vegetables — Green corn, hot slaw, lima beans, stewed tomatoes, squash, new beets; Pastry — Peach pie, jelly tarts, apple pie, sponge pudding in brandy sauce, and finally for the Dessert course, wine jelly, brandy jelly, ice cream, watermelon, apples, tea, chocolate and coffee.[14]

Railroad chef John Smeades, who first cooked for President Theodore Roosevelt, got national attention for his cooking exploits on the dining car Ideal during President William Howard Taft's cross-country railroad trip in September 1911. As discussed in chapter 1, perhaps no other president used his train to play hooky from his diet more than Taft, and he must have considered Chef Smeades his accomplice-in-chief. The First Lady and White House physician couldn't have been pleased with press reports of the president's prodigious railcar eating like this one printed in the *St. Louis Post-Dispatch*:

> John Smeades is a big man and a black one. He has to be big for he cooks for another big man, and that is a big job. And it is likely that his color helps him withstand the heat that is part of his job. John cooks for the President; rather to be accurate, he has cooked for the President during the long journey across the continent and back that began on September 15. Cooking for William Howard Taft is no child's play. It is Big Business with capital Bs. The President eats heartily, and eats often, so John Smeades rarely has any spare time.[15]

Smeades went on at great length about the various foods favored by Taft: a big, thick, juicy steak with the blood oozing out and a side of bacon; "plenty of green vegetables, a delicious salad of romaine and quartered tomatoes, with plenty of French dressing thickened with Roquefort cheese"; fried cauliflower, "a couple of chops and two or three lightly boiled eggs makes a breakfast menu"; fruit before and after every meal, including "grapes, peaches, oranges, oranges, melons, pears, apples, plums"; and chicken, shellfish, boiled salmon, and game (canvasback duck, elk, and deer). Chef Smeades also clarified, "But [President Taft] is not a greedy eater. He eats just what he feels he needs, and will never suffer from overeating."[16]

President Woodrow Wilson, a tall and thin man, set a sharp contrast to Taft in many ways, but he loved food just as much and had a knack for getting the best cooks the railroads had to offer, including Chef William "Letch" Letcher. Decades in the making, the extraordinary reputation Letcher achieved as a chef could not escape presidential attention: "'Letch' is the Pullman company's official chef to President Wilson en route, just as he has been commander of the kitchen aboard presidential cars for a number of years. And when it comes to cooking—well, 'Letch' gets all the medals. He can cook a steak with a touch of real art. He makes a jelly omelet that is worthy of poetry. And his rolls, his fried chicken, his coffee, and other dishes are beyond description even by a connoiseur [*sic*] in the good things in life."[17]

Another chef in President Wilson's railroad kitchen was Delefasse Green, who was described in a newspaper as a "king of cooks." Green started as a butler after finishing high school and before becoming a railway cook. He first cooked for President Taft when he traveled by train and later became one of President Wilson's favorites. When a local newspaper interviewed him, Green gave readers a rare peek into the work life of a high-end presidential railroad cook. The newspaper even described how he handled grocery shopping:

> Whenever the private train drew up for a stop in any city, there would presently emerge a stoutish neat, bustling colored man, who would hail a taxicab and hurry away to the best available market. Here he would shop around as might any busy housewife, and no market-man would be aware of the fact that he was selling food for the table of the President. Receipts for the purchases would be made to Green and payment made in cash. So fresh food was always available. No product out of a can was ever used.[18]

Sounding a bit like an early spokesperson for the Paleo diet, Green continued, " 'Food should be cooked and served plainly. There should be few mixtures and few sauces. The manner of cooking followed by the early huntsman was the right method. Such food retains its flavor and is good for the stomach.' "[19] Keenly aware of the public scrutiny our presidents received during the Prohibition era, Green took the extra step of reinforcing their collective virtue, stating that "one peculiar thing about his ten years of service as cook for presidents is that he never saw a man in that office smoke a cigar or cigarette or take a drink of intoxicating liquor. He wonders if there is something in the Constitution which forbids these indiscretions."[20]

President Franklin Delano Roosevelt loved traveling by train, particularly to Warm Springs, Georgia. On these trips, Elizabeth "Lizzie" McDuffie and Daisy Bonner teamed up to provide presidential food service. Fortunately, their culinary adventures were documented, thus allowing history a unique window on how a president eats when on vacation. The first half of his dynamic duo in Warm Springs was Lizzie McDuffie. She mostly served the president's food when he traveled but would help with cooking when asked. McDuffie was an interesting personality and has an amazing backstory wholly apart from what she did in the kitchen.

McDuffie, a native of Newton County, Georgia, was the Roosevelts' most trusted maid, and she pitched in with cooking duties when the president traveled. She entered the Roosevelts' orbit because her husband, O. J. McDuffie, had been FDR's valet since 1927. Lizzie had a big personality, and her high school classmates predicted that she was des-

Kitchen staffer during the Kennedy administration, circa 1961.
Courtesy John F. Kennedy Presidential Library and Museum.

. . .

tined for a stage career. Fellow maid Lillian Parks Rogers remembered, "FDR counted on Lizzie for her sense of humor, her sense of the outrageous. Even when we have guests — the old intimate friends, that is — FDR might send for Lizzie to liven things up a bit. Lizzie had show biz in her veins so she loved it. She had two Early-Muppet-style dolls and she would put on a show using various voices. One of the dolls was named Suicide and the other, Jezebel. FDR loved their fights and misadventures and roared with laughter."[21] McDuffie almost had a real chance at show business when a movie executive, who was dining in the White House, took one look at Lizzie and wanted to cast her for the role of "Mammy" in the blockbuster film *Gone with the Wind*. But despite FDR's bragging,

Eleanor Roosevelt's personally lobbying the movie studio, and several newspaper reports, McDuffie was never seriously considered for the part that ultimately went to Denver, Colorado, native Hattie McDaniel.[22]

McDuffie had a political operative side as well. She half-jokingly called herself the "Secretary of Colored Peoples' Affairs," but there was much truth to it. When African American leaders couldn't get the ear of the president, they would contact her with the hopes that she could draw his attention to a particular issue. McDuffie carried such weight because her political clout went well beyond the White House walls. In the 1936 presidential election, which wasn't a guaranteed win for FDR, McDuffie was strongly motivated to get the president reelected, and she stumped for FDR in several cities that had an appreciable African American vote. The *Baltimore Afro-American* reported on her activities:

> "No man is a hero to his valet." For over 350 years since the Prince de Conde made the above statement, the world has debated on both sides of it. Last week, Mrs. Elizabeth H. McDuffie, White House cook and wife of President Roosevelt's valet, taking the stump before an audience of 700 in St. Louis, classed Roosevelt with Lincoln "whose love of his fellow men has been something akin to the divine." Here is a valet's wife to whom her husband's employer is a hero. That is news. But bigger news is the spectacle of the White House cook doing a swell job as a campaign speaker. Mrs. McDuffie was cheered in St. Louis, Chicago, and Gary. She went out to make one speech, did make three and could have made twenty-four more before returning to Washington in order to cook the President's meals.[23]

This is arguably the first time an African American White House employee openly courted the black vote. Newspapers reported that McDuffie campaigned "gowned in black lace over a pink slip [with] her bobbed hair . . . combed straight back, and long pearl earrings dangled from her ears."[24] Her White House colleagues worried that McDuffie's stumping blatantly violated the Hatch Act that passed earlier that year and prohibited federal employees from campaigning while on the government payroll. Remarkably, McDuffie was never charged, or chastised, for violating the new law. Newspapers described her as a "Special Assistant to the President" (much to the envy of White House housekeeper Mrs. Henrietta Nesbitt), and FDR summoned her to the Oval Office the day after the election to personally thank her for her efforts.[25]

FDR often brought McDuffie with him to Warm Springs, where he sought relief for his polio. He built a complex there that would eventually be called the "Little White House." FDR loved his time there, and as Lillian Rogers Parks noted, "To understand the true FDR, you would have to see him at Warm Springs, Georgia."[26] His primary cook there was Daisy McAfee Bonner, an African American woman loaned to the president by a local wealthy family. Bonner was born in Ft. Valley, Georgia, and followed in her brother's footsteps by going to Warm Springs to work at the Meriweather Inn. She learned to cook at the inn and then went into service in private homes.[27] FDR started visiting Warm Springs in the 1920s while he was governor of New York. When he arrived, Bonner would be on campus ready to cook. During the entire gubernatorial and later presidential sojourns, Bonner stayed on campus and lived in a small servant cottage about twenty-five yards from the main building.

Bonner took every opportunity to get FDR hooked on southern delicacies like fried chicken, pigs' feet (broiled, not the sweet-and-sour version that he liked), turnip greens, hush puppies, and cornbread. President Roosevelt really loved a dish called "Country Captain," a chicken curry dish popular in Georgia. As to the dish's origins, legend has it that in the 1700s, a wayward captain sailing from India to the West Indies accidentally landed in Savannah with a boatload of curry and other spices as well as the recipe for this particular dish. As for Bonner's version, a frequent guest at presidential dinners at Warm Springs noted that FDR "told everybody, falsely, that her recipe was a secret, with 45 ingredients, which was a joke between Roosevelt and Daisy."[28]

Whenever Roosevelt's wife, physician, or meddlesome relatives were in Warm Springs, the dieting games began. In essence, according to presidential historian Jim Bishop, it was FDR, his stomach, Bonner, and McDuffie against the world:

> Lizzie McDuffie could see the President by squeezing her face diagonally against the window screen. Daisy Bonner said, "You think the President looks feeble?" Lizzie nodded, "Yes, but he looks better than when he came here." Like most women who were close to Roosevelt, Mrs. McDuffie and Miss Bonner loved the President. Daisy was possessed of the magical nostrums of cooks; if you feed a "peek-ed" man right, he will recover. "I know what I'm going to do," she said. "I'm going to give him the things he likes to eat." . . . She would feed him these things. . . . Daisy cooked; Lizzie served.

Daisy Bonner at Warm Springs,
Georgia, n.d.
Courtesy Franklin D. Roosevelt
Presidential Library and Museum.
. . .

When relatives maneuvered the menu, Miss Bonner obeyed, but she whispered a word to Mrs. McDuffie to take the platters to the table and whisper to the President "Don't eat any of that." Mr. Roosevelt never disobeyed the admonition of the cook. Sometimes, guests like Miss Suckley and Miss Delano would say, "Franklin, aren't you going to eat what Daisy made?" Mr. Roosevelt would say, "I will eat some of that tomorrow."[29]

Their teamwork was one of the reasons that Warm Springs was so beloved by FDR, and Bonner took great pride in cooking for him. "Daisy always said she longed to 'reach the top of my talent . . . so someday I might be president of cooking.'"[30]

Thursday, 12 April 1945, at the Little White House started as any other morning. That day, according to Bonner, "the President was 'up' and had breakfast in his room at 9:30. 'He was always up at 9:30,' [she said]. That day he had his usual breakfast, orange juice, oatmeal, melba toast and a glass of milk."[31] A few hours later, Bonner went about preparing FDR's lunch, with a cheese soufflé as the starring attraction, which he was to eat while he read newspapers and sat for an artist's sketching. The sequence of what happened next varies depending on who is telling the story, but the essential facts are the same. The *New York Times* offered a Bonner-centric version:

> At 1:15, Mrs. Bonner had the cheese soufflé ready and she told the valet, Arthur Prettyman, "Get the President to the table. The soufflé's ready." The President always said, "Never put the soufflé into the oven until I come out of my room," Mrs. Bonner explained. He was reading the *Atlanta Constitution* when the soufflé was ready. The papers had come late because of the bad weather and "Mr. Roosevelt had been worried about the mail. He'd asked the third time for the papers. So he'd gone right to reading when he came out." The artist was sketching him—"He'd never sit for her—she had to catch him when she could"—the cook says. . . . Then, just as he went in, the President said what a terrific headache he had, and he slumped over in his chair. He never ate that soufflé, but it never fell until the minute he died.[32]

FDR died two hours later, so anyone who has made a soufflé knows that it would be miraculous for it to "stand" for a couple of hours. Bonner alerted the White House switchboard operator of the tragic occurrence, and, grief-stricken, she penciled on the kitchen wall her last tribute to the great man: "Daisy Bonner cooked the first meal and the last one in this cottage for . . . President Roosevelt." It remains on that wall, preserved under a glass panel, to this day.[33]

A year later, Bonner shared her wonderful FDR memories in a newspaper interview. She considered opening up a business to honor the late president, in the way steward William Crump had done to memorialize President Garfield: "Soon though, she plans to sit in a little café museum, rock and tell the story of the President as she knew him. On Sundays she will supervise the making of 'Country Captain,' an involved chicken dish. It will be the only café in the world where 'Country Captain' can be had fit for a President. It was."[34] Bonner's museum dream never came true, and she died on 22 April 1958 in Warm Springs, Georgia.[35]

Samuel Clayton "Mitch" Mitchell was the last great presidential railroad cook to serve during the glory days of rail travel. According to a 1952 newspaper profile of him, Chef Mitchell, a South Carolina native, worked for Presidents Herbert Hoover and Franklin D. Roosevelt, but his big promotion came when he was put in charge of President Truman's dining car.[36] "Mitch, former Pullman porter, is major-domo on U.S. Car No. 1. He readies the car, plans the menus, and gets the food aboard. If he needs extra help, he requisitions it from the presidential yacht Williamsburg."[37] Chef Mitchell nourished Truman on his famous whistle-stop tours around the country, including his famous "comeback" train ride at the end of the 1948 presidential election. On that trip, the iconic photo of the president smiling and holding up the *Chicago Tribune* with the headline "Dewey Defeats Truman" was taken. Many have concluded that he was smiling because of the huge reporting error, but I like to think that he was recalling a savory meal recently prepared by Mitchell. Presidential rail travel became obsolete with the dawn of the jet age, but Samuel Mitchell was able to keep up with the times, eventually becoming the majordomo of the reception room in the Kennedy White House.[38]

While presidents took to the rails for work and play, certain types of boats—notably yachts—were exclusively for presidential leisure. According to presidential yacht historian Walter Jaffee, "Abraham Lincoln was the first president to use a yacht. In May of 1862 he steamed down the Potomac River in the revenue cutter *Miami* to review his troops. Three years later the sidewheel paddle steamer *River Queen* was chartered for him, becoming the first vessel dedicated and maintained for a president's use."[39] A succession of different boats used for play followed: the *Despatch* (Rutherford B. Hayes in 1880); the *Dolphin*, an unarmed cruiser (Benjamin Harrison to Harding); the more elegant *Sylph* (Theodore Roosevelt); the *Mayflower* (Roosevelt to Hoover); the *Potomac* and the *Sequoia* (Franklin D. Roosevelt); the *Williamsburg* (Truman); the *Barbara Anne* and *Susan E.* (Eisenhower); the *Honey Fitz* (Kennedy); and the *Sequoia* (Johnson to Carter).[40]

Presidential boat travel was typically controversial because it involved yachts, and few words scream snobbery more than "yacht," as Captain Giles M. Kelly, who has written about the presidential yacht *Sequoia*, observes:

Presidential yacht USS Mayflower, *circa 1912. Courtesy Library of Congress.*

. . .

The term "yacht" has been a problem for *Sequoia* because some political figures, Presidents Jimmy Carter and Dwight D. Eisenhower among them, believed that close association with anything called a yacht while in office would tarnish their image because it might seem ostentatious. For that reason even today some congressional and administration leaders are reluctant to support her, let alone use her, though she is indeed a very modest yacht for the government of a superpower. At her inception, her designer referred to her not as a yacht, but as a "houseboat."[41]

The prestige factor of the presidential yacht did cut both ways. Kelly related, "Years later, during his retirement, Gerald Ford was asked how he viewed *Sequoia*. '[She] was a superb yacht for special entertaining of presidential White House guests. The *Sequoia* was more informal than the White House itself, but significant as recognition of the prestige of the special guest. . . . I strongly believe [*Sequoia*] was a White House asset that could be used for constructive presidential entertainment.'"[42]

Aside from class perception, one of the biggest yacht-inspired headaches had a racial undertone, but this was not a black-white racial dynamic. While the railroad revived the French-versus-American cooking rivalry, a new, and artificial, ethnic culinary rivalry roiled the seas — African Americans versus Filipinos. A sad aspect of our military history

Eating on the Run

was the continued denial of African Americans' right to serve in combat positions, particularly in racially integrated military units. The powers that be knew that demonstrated heroism and patriotism would confer instant humanity upon the heretofore second-class citizen—and the real loser would be Jim Crow. Despite African Americans' long years of dedicated service as cooks and servants to the U.S. Army's elite officers, the U.S. Navy, puzzlingly, curbed even those opportunities as early as 1917. A newspaper article printed that year described the advancement difficulties that black sailors faced:

> Quartermaster Boyd, of the local navy recruiting station, has just received word from Washington that a limited number of negroes may be enlisted in the navy as mess attendants. Only desirable applicants who have had previous experience in hotels, clubs, restaurants or private families will be accepted in this rating, and then only upon presenting recommendations from previous employers. . . . The duties of a mess attendant consists in waiting on officers' messes and taking care of officers' room and clothing.[43]

Because of all the extra hoops to jump through, few African Americans became "mess boys." And when it came to presidential cooks, it was often through the ranks of the U.S. Navy that such cooks were promoted.

Strikingly, the next year the U.S. Navy ramped up its efforts to recruit Filipinos as servants and cooks:

> Gunga Din, the humble servitor, immortalized himself by carrying water to the fighting heroes of another day. These cousins of his, Phillippine Americans, face the same chance at immortality by carrying soup and coffee to the U.S. Jacktar, on patrol or in battle. They have been permitted to join the navy as messboys, replacing those of other alien races in Uncle Sam's flotilla. The first group of 152, soon to be supplemented by others, arrived at San Francisco from Manilla [sic] recently and were assigned to various naval units. Their training has run the gamut from soup serving to submarine spotting. And their mild faces camouflage fighting hearts.[44]

According to the history of the White House Mess that is printed on the back of its menu, it was aboard the USS *Despatch* that the U.S. Navy began its long affiliation with presidential cooking: "Since that time, the Navy has assigned their best Stewardsman to the White House to prepare the finest foods and provide outstanding food service for the president around the world."[45]

By the time of Calvin Coolidge's administration, only whites and Asians (a Chinese national named Lee Ping Quan and several Filipino mess attendants) served on the presidential yacht. The advancement prospects for African American mess boys improved, but civil rights leaders were eyeing the desegregation of the officers' ranks. As the opening paragraph of a 1947 memorandum to the President's Committee on Civil Rights stated, "The armed forces are one of our major status symbols; the fact that members of minority groups bear arms in defense of the country, alongside other citizens, serves as a major basis for their claim to equality elsewhere. For the minority groups themselves, discrimination in the armed forces seems more immoral and painful than elsewhere."[46]

The legendary A. Philip Randolph, who successfully organized black labor in the 1930s and 1940s, pressed the issue on the White House. The discussion that Randolph had with President Franklin D. Roosevelt and Secretary of the Navy Frank Knox went like this, according to a book by William Doyle based on actual White House tape recordings:

> FDR: I think the proportion is going up, and one very good reason is that in the old days, ah, up to a few years ago, up to the time of the Philippine independence, practically, oh, I'd say 75 or 80 percent of the mess people on board ship, ah, were Filipinos. And, of course, we've taken in no Filipinos now for the last, what is it, four years ago, two years ago, taken in no Filipinos whatsoever. And what we're doing, we're replacing them with colored boys—mess captain, so forth and so on. And in that field, they can get up to the highest rating of a chief petty officer. The head mess attendant on a cruiser or a battleship is a chief petty officer.
>
> Randolph: Is there at this time a single Negro in the navy of officer status?
>
> Knox: There are 4,007 Negroes out of a total force at the beginning of 1940 of 139,000. They are all messmen's rank. (*chatter*)
>
> FDR: I think, another thing Frank [Knox], that I forgot to mention, I thought of it about a month ago, and that is this. We are training a certain number of musicians on board ship. The ship's *band*. There's no reason why we shouldn't have a colored band on some of these ships, because they're *darn good at it*. That's something

we should look into. You know, if it'll increase the *opportunity*, that's what we're after. They may develop a *leader* of the band.[47]

FDR's reluctance to seriously grapple with the issue was discouraging, but the civil rights leaders pressed on in that particular conversation and beyond the White House. Thanks to dogged efforts of civil rights advocates, the officers' ranks were progressively opened up to blacks in the 1940s and 1950s.

Yet, the presidential yacht's culinary team remained made up of all Filipinos. Though African Americans rarely worked on the yacht, it is instructive to see what life was like for the Filipino crew. Fortunately we have a detailed account from Jack Lynch, a white crewman who served in the 1930s, of how they ate on the presidential yacht:

> Since nearly everybody stood some kind of watch, there was a lot eating by shifts; one group would get up and another would be seated, etc. There was also a lot of informal eating—"snacking"— on board. There was always coffee and fresh milk in the pantry, and pies, cakes and breakfast pastry were delivered every day in port and left available in the pantry too. There was always a pot of soup on in the galley and sandwich materials were there, too. All hands had free run of the galley and the cooks really didn't have too much work to do except underway.[48]

Fellow crewman Paul Harless added, "We could tell the cook what we wanted for meals or go into the galley at any time and fix our own. We called it 'open galley.'"[49] According to Jack Lynch, the crew ate typical fare on holidays—and made something unique out of the leftovers:

> Thanksgiving, we had, of course, the traditional Navy holiday meal—turkey and so forth. The cooks took all the leftovers and concocted a great turkey soup, which was kept simmering on the rear of the galley range for days. That happened to be an early and especially cold winter [1941] and there was a steady procession of guys coming off watch, or taking a respite from work, into the galley for a bowl of soup. As the supply dwindled, the cooks kept adding new ingredients from whatever was handy, ham, vegetables, even oysters, until its original makeup, even its color, changed several times. At Christmas, when turkey parts again became available, it resumed

its initial character. The cooks called it "perpetual soup" and it was still bubbling away on the last day of January when I left the ship.[50]

Creole food aficionados may find this "perpetual soup" akin to a bottomless pot-au-feu.

Speaking of "perpetual," FDR fished nearly every weekend from May until November where the Potomac River emptied into the Chesapeake Bay. The crew joined him, and the cooks would prepare the day's catch on the spot. When they caught eels, "the Filipino cabin boys loved them."[51] Even when away from 1600 Pennsylvania Avenue, the president often saw some of his White House favorites show up on the yacht's menu. Lynch noted, "I recall that a favorite supper of President Roosevelt's when we'd be returning on a Sunday night was scrambled eggs and little link sausages. When he had that, our cooks would prepare the same thing for the crew. We liked it, too."[52] The Roosevelt presidency was certainly high tide for presidential yacht use.

During the Truman administration, the growing idleness of the yacht's crew yielded a benefit in that it helped to solve an emerging labor shortage at the White House. President Truman's relationship with Congress was acrimonious, to say the least. But how much cooperation could the president really expect after he famously nicknamed the Eightieth Congress (January 1947 to January 1949) the "Do Nothing Congress"? After that, members of Congress acted as if they had nothing to do except exact revenge on President Truman during the budgeting process, especially regarding budget appropriations for the White House Executive Office.

The extensive White House renovations of the 1950s had created a need for more residence staff. The installation of air conditioning units had had a huge impact on work habits — as White House usher J. B. West recalled, "With air conditioning, Washington became a year-round city, the White House a year-round house."[53] But both West and the Trumans knew that getting more staff, especially for the refurbished kitchen, was a nonstarter with Congress. President Truman, who mused aloud about where to get White House kitchen help within earshot of White House chief usher Howard Crim, posited that the only option was military personnel. When West succeeded Crim as chief usher, Mrs. Truman, who had obviously been thinking about the same challenge, said, "Mr. West, I have an idea. We aren't planning to use the *Williamsburg* as much as we have been now that it's so pleasant up here [presumably due to air conditioning]. Could [we] bring some of the Filipino stewards in to be house-

Eating on the Run

White House Mess during the Reagan administration, 1986.
Courtesy Ronald Reagan Presidential Library and Museum.

. . .

men and kitchen helpers? Do you think the Navy would approve?" That set the bureaucratic wheels in motion. West reports that "the Navy quietly acquiesced, assigning three seaman to the White House pantry and as housemen to help with heavy cleaning, vacuuming, waxing floors, and washing walls upstairs. Beginning with Mrs. Truman, the seamen became a White House fixture. Some even stayed on as White House employees after retiring from the Navy. Until that time, though, the Navy paid their salaries."[54] Some of the Filipino mess attendants were employed as butlers, but most went to staff a newly created dining space in the White House's West Wing called the White House Mess.

President Truman's naval aide, Rear Admiral Robert L. Dennison, first recommended the idea of a mess, and it became official by executive order on 11 June 1951.[55] This navy-run, semi-exclusive dining space was immediately criticized as elitist. Critics also pointed out that, though staffers paid for their meals, the food often went for below market price. During the Nixon administration, diners were known to "get everything from soup to dessert—including a selection of meat or fish entrees—for two dollars. Those who really want to live it up can treat themselves to a steak or a double loin lamb chop, with the works, for $2.75. And, we note, no tipping is allowed."[56] By the time I worked in the White House, the prices had definitely increased. Those who had privileges but didn't eat in the mess either brought their own lunch, ate in the Dwight D. Eisenhower Executive Office Building, or went outside of the White House compound.

Bradley H. Patterson Jr. of the Brookings Institution gave a nice description of this clubby, private dining room in his seminal work on White House operations:

> Managed by the Navy, the White House Staff Mess consists of three adjacent dining rooms in the lower level of the West Wing that seat forty-five, twenty-eight, and eighteen, respectively, in paneled decorum, for each of the two noonday shifts. Some two hundred staffers and the cabinet are eligible [to dine there]. Dinners are now served as well—a reflection of the lengthening White House workday. Private luncheons in their own offices are available for West Wing senior staff, and carryout trays are provided for harried aides on the run. At the entrance to the mess, hanging noiselessly under glass, is a hallowed symbol: the 1790 dinner bell from the USS *Constitution*.[57]

I myself—when serving as a special assistant to President Bill Clinton—was promoted to the senior staff level at the White House, thus becoming one of those "harried aides." And I had the privilege of eating in the very same White House Mess. I dined in the room only once (I can't remember what I ate), but I often ordered carryout if I was working late, and I can personally attest that the mess's cheeseburger at that time was absolutely glorious.

Significantly, while the White House Mess is located within the White House, it "is entirely separate from the first family's kitchen and dining facilities in the Residence. The mess and the valets—a staff of fifty—are supervised by the presidential food service coordinator. Those who eat in the mess pay for their food, but the salaries of the Navy service personnel are borne by the Navy. When the president travels, mess attendants prepare some of the first family's meals, and when the chief executive hosts a dinner during a state visit abroad, mess personnel oversee the food preparation."[58] And, also significantly, once the "presidential food service coordinator" position was created, African Americans were finally in the White House Mess mix.

Ronald L. Jackson served a long time as the presidential food service coordinator, starting in the Lyndon Johnson administration and working at least until the Reagan administration. Jackson, who achieved the rank of navy commander, did much to make sure that the mess upheld high dining standards. He once told the *New York Times* that the mess's "soups and pies are all homemade" and explained how the skill of improvising, learned so beautifully while aboard a ship, affected everything the mess staff did, from carving realistic-looking flowers from vegetable peelings for the salad bar to making "puffy, crisp and buttery soufflé crackers that melt in the mouth."[59] Jackson wasn't afraid to seek outside opinions to improve food service. When famous gourmet Gene Lang once ate at the White House Mess, Jackson asked for some recipes from the Four Seasons hotel to put on the mess menu.[60]

During Jackson's tenure, the two worlds of the mess and the First Family directly interacted, typically, only on the Thanksgiving holiday, when the First Family would eat at Camp David, and on international trips. The Thanksgiving meals were supervised by Jackson and prepared by the White House Mess staff, and the dishes planned and served were fairly standard. For example, on the 1972 Thanksgiving holiday, Jackson supervised a meal of "roast turkey, bread dressing and giblet gravy with whipped potatoes, green peas and onions, and hot dinner rolls. Salad will be fresh cranberries with minted pears and dessert will be pumpkin pie with whipped cream."[61] However, selecting a traditional menu was not always a safe route for all presidents. When Jackson wrote a memorandum to the Carters proposing a similar menu for their 1977 Thanksgiving dinner meal, someone (presumably First Lady Rosalynn Carter) crossed out a certain side dish and wrote in the margins, "Jimmy doesn't especially like green peas."[62]

Jackson had plenty of additional opportunities to address presidential food quirks, and he was almost always a cool customer. Note, for example, something that Jackson experienced during the Nixon administration:

At Key Biscayne [a vacation spot favored by President Nixon], an automatic ice maker was purchased without authorization from the Secret Service. GSA [General Service Administration] officials said it was solely for the use of Secret Service and military personnel stationed there. But a GSA memo revealed that Cmdr. Ronald Jackson, the White House mess chief, had visited Key Biscayne on May 24, 1975, and noting the lack of an ice machine, said, "The President does not like ice cubes with holes in them." The $421 machine was installed five days later. More recently, a Secret Service agent conceded the ice maker was for Nixon's use and said it was "to ensure the President was not using poisoned ice."[63]

Though President Nixon spent a good chunk of his second term in political crisis, he managed to shine in some emergencies during an election year. One time, he did so, interestingly enough, with White House food. In the wake of Tropical Storm Agnes, a devastating flood hit Wilkes-Barre, Pennsylvania, in late June 1972. A couple of months after the floodwaters receded, President Nixon visited the ravaged area to see how relief efforts were progressing. A Tennessee newspaper reported, "During the tour, he presented a $4 million disaster relief check to a local college to help its reconstruction. Told there was not enough food for a volunteer-organized Sunday picnic, the President later arranged to send Navy Cmdr. Ronald Jackson, chief of the White House mess, and six stewards to Wilkes-Barre Sunday with enough hamburgers, hot dogs, potato chips and soft drinks to feed more than 1,000 people."[64] I never before envisioned *Air Force One* being used as a food delivery vehicle, but this was a politically shrewd gesture on President Nixon's part. He used the ultimate presidential perquisite to show that he cared. If "the train symbolized the president's accessibility to the people," historian Richard Ellis writes, then, "in contrast, *Air Force One* projects the power and majesty of the presidency."[65] Nixon illustrated that and more in one fell swoop.

Back aboard the presidential yacht, the mess crew moved back and forth between it and the White House Mess. Sometimes, other navy personnel were used to staff the yacht whenever the president wanted to sail. President John F. Kennedy probably went yachting the most frequently of all the presidents, doing so for relaxation. President Lyndon Baines Johnson used it extensively to lobby members of Congress. But the use of the presidential yacht came to an end when President Jimmy Carter implemented an austerity plan that eliminated many perks. President Carter never used the presidential yacht *Sequoia*, and it was on the top of his permanent hit list. The boat was thus auctioned off for a reported $286,000 in May 1977.[66] Members of Congress were outraged that President Carter would sell a piece of his presidency to the highest bidder, and some tried to persuade wealthy friends to purchase it and donate it back to the Executive Office. Believe it or not, a private group did eventually purchase the *Sequoia* for more than $1 million. It was presented to President Ronald Reagan, but he refused to use it. That ended the illustrious history of presidential yachting at taxpayer expense. Now, our presidents may sail with wealthy donors at their expense or on their own time.[67]

Plenty of job opportunities aside from the White House kitchen exist in the presidential food system, but to obtain such jobs one typically must be in the military, which has been tasked to handle different aspects of said service. The U.S. Navy, as already mentioned, operates the White House Mess and food operations at Camp David, and the U.S. Air Force handles food on *Air Force One*. A recent example of an individual taking advantage of this military option is Chef Charlie Redden.[68] Redden grew up in inner-city Wilmington, Delaware, while being the sous chef for a couple of "country girls"—his grandmother and mother—who liked to cook. Years ahead of Michelle Obama's effort to change school lunches, Redden grew tired of the lunch offerings at Howard Williams High School. One day, while he was walking the hall, he peeked in on a commercial food preparation class and saw that students were eating much better food than what he was getting. He immediately made a plan to get in that class.

After apprenticing at a high-end hotel, Redden joined the U.S. Navy. While doing menial tasks aboard a ship, he noticed that the food service guys ate better than the rest of the crew. (Are you noticing a theme here?) He thus became a culinary specialist in the navy. Given his previous restaurant experience, Redden was quickly promoted and soon cooking for the highest-ranking officers wherever he served. In 1995, while he was stationed in Jacksonville, a spot opened up in the White House Mess, and—at an admiral's suggestion—Redden applied. During the interview, he was asked why he should get the job out of the three hundred competitors. Without missing a beat, Redden promised to cook the current chefs there "under the table." That got a hearty laugh from the interviewers, and Redden won the job. At the White House complex, he supervised the mess's catering department, and in his spare time he earned an executive chef certificate from the American Culinary Federation. He thus became the first executive chef to work in the White House Mess.

During his stint with the Clinton administration, Chef Redden "traveled extensively with the Clinton retinue, checking out hotels and restaurants in advance of the First Family's arrival, and preparing soups, pizzas, and spaghetti meals for their personal use." But despite his high achievement, he still had to deal with issues of race at work. When he did advance work for presidential trips, the person on the other end of the phone would often assume that he was white, given his position. This happened most frequently when he planned the food operations for the president's foreign trips. He would often walk into the kitchens of high-end hotels unannounced, only to have security called on him. Once he showed his credentials, the kitchen personnel would be astonished that an African American had such responsibilities. Even presidential chefs can experience "Cooking While Black." Redden stayed on through President George W. Bush's first term and left because he could no longer advance in rank, given his current job. His last event with President Bush was a trip to his hometown of Wilmington, where the president spoke at a predominantly black Boys and Girls Club. Today, Chef Redden does private catering in Maryland.

Though the American public grew weary and wary of presidential yachts, it has been in awe of presidential planes. Franklin Roosevelt was the first president to take to flight, though infrequently, on the presidential plane named the *Sacred Cow*. President Truman often flew on the *Spirit of Independence*, and President Eisenhower flew even more often on the *Columbine*. President Kennedy was the first president to utilize an airplane with the call sign *Air Force One*, which is technically any plane with the president aboard. First Lady Jacqueline Kennedy consulted with a well-known artist to create the plane's signature colors and design, which last to this day.

The plane evokes elegance, grace, and style—but can the same be said of the food? Since *Air Force One* took to the skies, the flight attendants not only serve the food but cook it as well. They work out of two galleys. The galley in the front section handles meals for the president, VIP guests, and senior staff. The remaining passengers have their meals cooked in the rear galley. Though the flight attendants can make a wide range of foods, fried food is a nonstarter because, for safety reasons, no fryer is on board. French fries have been served, but they are reportedly "always soggy."[69] All told, "the crew can store enough food and beverages on *Air Force One* to serve everyone three meals a day for two weeks."[70] Presidential grocery shoppers wear civilian clothes while looking for the freshest, highest quality ingredients, sometimes getting "enough victuals for up to two thousand meals. Working in an area that occupies two full-size galleys, the steward crew can prepare up to one hundred meals at a sitting."[71]

As it was on the presidential train, the comfort and safety of the president are always primary considerations. Former *Air Force One* steward

Howie Franklin shed light on the established protocol in an interview with presidential historian Richard Norton Smith:

> The flight attendants are responsible for making sure that nothing on *Air Force One* will cause a problem, even an upset stomach, for the commander in chief. "We make sure that anything that could be consumed in any way, shape, or fashion has not been tampered with," says former chief steward Howie Franklin. The flight crew receives an itinerary from the White House and determines how many meals or snacks are needed for each day of a trip. Then the flight attendants propose a menu and submit it to the White House Mess, partly to avoid redundancy. "We wouldn't want to serve salmon when the president had salmon the night before," Franklin told me.[72]

After safety first, it's comfort second. According to Kenneth T. Walsh, in his history of *Air Force One*, "The White House provides a list to the *Air Force One* crew of every new president's likes and dislikes. The list also includes a rundown of the commander in chief's health problems, allergies, and anything else the crew might find helpful in serving him."[73] The *Air Force One* culinary team consists of two teams of three people — a team for each of the two galleys. One person serves as the cook and is responsible for finishing the partially cooked food in the plane's on-board microwave or small ovens. Another flight attendant helps with the prep work, and the remaining flight attendant is the bartender.[74]

As we learned with President Reagan's unsuccessful attempts to get Bavarian cream apple pie, the potential excesses of this airborne cornucopia of food might be controlled only by the First Lady or by the White House physician. Walsh writes, "Particularly during the Bush and Clinton eras, the presidents and First Ladies have insisted on more low-fat meals and have preferred bottled water or diet soda rather than sugary soft drinks or alcohol, all for health reasons. Under Ford and Carter, breakfast would often be scrambled eggs with cream cheese, hefty sausages, fried hash brown potatoes, a biscuit or danish, and a small fruit cup. Today, breakfast on board tends toward bran muffins, cereal, fresh fruit, and yogurt."[75] Walsh further wrote, "During the Clinton years, it was First Lady Hillary Rodham Clinton, not the president, who set the tone for everything on board, including the food. 'If Mrs. Clinton was with us, the menu leaned heavily to chicken Caesar salads with low-cal dressing,' [CBS news correspondent Mark] Knoeller said."[76] Still, just as in President Taft's heyday, a president could indulge in eating any food if he really wanted to do so. "If the president was traveling alone, you could usually get a good old-fashioned cheeseburger," Knoeller added.[77]

Not everyone was a fan of the aircraft's bill of fare. Former Clinton White House press secretary Mike McCurry didn't mince words when he said, "Not to offend the Air Force, but it's basically military chow."[78] The most famous example of a disgruntled diner may have been when a famous broadcast journalist disapproved of the offerings: "The food service was a source of constant complaint. When Gerald Ford went to China in 1975, TV personality Barbara Walters flew on *Air Force One* and was not pleased when the stewards served her the dinner of the day — stuffed pork chops, which she spurned as too heavy. A flight attendant returned a few minutes later with a deli sandwich, and she was so displeased that she complained about the food on television."[79] Kenneth T. Walsh elaborated on the perspective of the *Air Force One* crew when he wrote, "Passengers are expected to eat what they are served. And the stewards are not pleased if a guest rejects a regular meal. That means more work for the galley. When a passenger asks for a substitute, such as a chicken-salad sandwich or similar light fare, the stewards try to handle the requests diplomatically but aren't happy with the disruption of their routine."[80]

The Obama *Air Force One* menu had a chef-driven vibe to its makeover of presidential plane food. The *New York Times* listed the meals offered on a 2012 flight: "a blue-cheese burger with lettuce, tomato and garlic aioli, accompanied by Parmesan-sprinkled fries. Chocolate fudge cake. Pasta shells stuffed with four cheeses, topped with meat sauce and shredded mozzarella, and served with a garlic breadstick. Cake infused with limoncello. Buffalo wings with celery, carrots and homemade ranch dip."[81] Nodding to one of President Obama's most notorious campaign stumbles, a former staffer helpfully added some perspective to the common perception that President Obama's plane food is always of the healthier variety: "It's American fare, in that it's not going all arugula on people," said Arun Chaudhary, who was President Obama's videographer from 2009 to 2011. "It's not aggressively nutritious."[82]

All in all, complaints about *Air Force One* provisions have been heard only now and then. A happy stomach often led to camaraderie among the crew. This would happen especially when a president took interest in specific crew members who assisted with presidential food service. Lee Simmons, who became an *Air Force One* flight attendant and presidential steward, shared his experiences in an oral history collected for the Gerald R. Ford Presidential Library. Simmons was more involved in presidential food service as a steward, not as a cook, and he developed a remarkable friendship with President Ford.

Simmons was born in Akron, Ohio, and grew up in "the sticks of Alabama" but returned to Akron to work in a rubber factory before enlisting in the air force. During the Kennedy administration, Simmons recalled, "I was the first African American to be assigned as a crew member [as part of the presidential flying squadron that included *Air Force One* and a couple of backup planes. At first, Simmons flew on the backup planes.]. There were other African Americans flying on the airplanes in other capacities — White House staff or whatever. Or even maintenance people — some African Americans were in the maintenance squadron, and security. But as a crew member, which are [called] wings, I was the first one."[83]

Being the only African American steward left Simmons in some awkward off-duty social situations:

> I felt very welcome. I felt very comfortable. Of course, there were times when I knew that I should not be going to dinner with these guys in certain parts of the country — we'd go down in Texas. When they went to these hillbilly joints at night — I don't want to say hillbilly, I'm sorry. Or go to the country and western restaurant to eat, I figured, ah, maybe I ought to skip that and stay at the hotel. But mostly the crews treated me nice. I was, for about ten years, the only African American on the crews whenever we flew overseas or stateside.[84]

Simmons also encountered professional difficulties because of his race. The higher-ups in the command chain wouldn't assign him to serve on *Air Force One* or give him jobs that would put him in the pipeline to serve on *Air Force One*. Consequently, Simmons frequently flew on the backup planes and built up enough miles to create a "friends and family plan" with First Lady Pat Nixon. That opened the door of opportunity that he sought.

> As a matter of fact, I flew with Mrs. Nixon — that's where they made the mistake — they let me fly with Mrs. Nixon and the girls, so we got to be friends. And then occasionally I would get to fly on the main airplane, on *Air Force One* itself, instead of the backup — occasionally. Well, anyway, Mrs. Nixon saw me one day, she said,

"Oh, there's my friend, Lee." From then on, later on, I was assigned as his personal steward on *Air Force One*—President Nixon. And he would tell me whenever there was a trip that Mrs. Nixon didn't go with him, when she would represent the United States to inaugurations and to other functions for the government, he would tell me personally, he would say, "Lee, I want you to go with Mrs. Nixon. She's going to Africa." And I went to Africa with her.[85]

Mrs. Nixon took such a liking to Simmons that she even invited him and his wife, Jeannette, to attend a state dinner.[86]

Simmons had interesting encounters with President Nixon as well. On a return flight from Moscow, the president requested some eggs. Simmons dutifully went to the galley to fulfill the order, but the cook informed him that, being on the back end of a ten-day trip, the eggs had been deemed old and thrown away. Simmons informed President Nixon, who, with his chief of staff, Bob Haldeman, standing there, asked, "Well, do you have any chickens?" Simmons said he would check when Haldeman interjected, "No, the President was making a joke about chickens producing eggs." Simmons added, "That's what I remember about President Nixon's humor."[87]

Like so many other people involved with presidential food service, Simmons was an eyewitness to history and featured in this account of Nixon's last flight on *Air Force One*: "Shortly after takeoff, Nixon asked Master Sergeant Lee Simmons, first personal steward, for a martini, which was unusual. He was a light drinker on *Air Force One* and rarely had alcohol at all in the morning. But on this day, he was, understandably, deviating from his routine. . . . He and Press Secretary Ron Ziegler sipped martinis in the president's cabin, and ate a lunch of shrimp cocktail, prime rib, baked potato, green beans, salad, rolls, and cheesecake."[88] As Nixon's presidency ended, Simmons enduring friendship with President Gerald Ford began.

Simmons first met Ford in 1972 on the way to Miami, where Ford would serve as chairman of the GOP convention.[89] Simmons and then congressman Ford hit it off. After Ford became president, he picked Simmons be his personal steward while aboard *Air Force One*. Over time, they frequently dined together, particularly when Ford didn't have guests:

He would say, "Lee, you got anything to do today or for dinner tonight?" And I would say, "No, sir." I never had anything to do if the president wanted me to have dinner with him or lunch. I'm always available. "If you're not doing anything, why don't we just eat together." Sometimes he would say, "Why don't you find a restaurant — ask the Secret Service to find a restaurant close by someplace and let's just go out and have dinner." It would just be he and I. Of course, I ate that up. I thought that was great. Here I am sitting in the corner with President Ford having dinner and I'm sure the public is looking there and seeing this African American guy over here saying, ummm, wonder who that is? Must be the ambassador from Africa or somewhere — some diplomat.[90]

As part of his official duties, Simmons did what he could to satisfy President Ford's craving for butter pecan ice cream — while playing "cat and mouse" with the White House physician. "*Air Force One* always had that ice cream aboard when President Ford flew," Simmons said. "One day [White House physician] Dr. [William] Lukash put Mr. Ford on a diet and sent us a list of proper foods, and butter pecan ice cream was not on it. By mistake a lunch tray was handed the President with butter pecan ice cream on it. President Ford ate it up before touching anything else on the tray and told us not to tell Dr. Lukash.'"[91] After all, that's what friends are for.

Years after he had stopped flying on *Air Force One*, Simmons repeatedly spoke of President Ford's enduring kindness: "He always was very thoughtful. I'd have dinner with him, [and] if we were at some function that he was going to make a speech, regardless of where it was at, he would always introduce me. He would tell people, 'This is Lee Simmons, who has been on my staff for *x* number of years,' and that kind of thing."[92] President Ford showed Simmons several more acts of kindness — he gave Simmons a job as his personal assistant after his presidency and flew Simmons to California as a guest on *Air Force One* to start the new job, giving him one last opportunity to sip "the famous *Air Force One* lemonade" while he was waited on by his former colleagues.[93] After twenty years of service on the presidential plane, Simmons spent ten more years with Ford as personal assistant and valet.[94] Their relationship proved that "flying the friendly skies" went both ways for them.

The skies are not always friendly. On 11 September 2001, our nation's skies were filled with fear and terror. Senior Master Sergeant Wanda Joell, the first African American woman to serve on *Air Force One*, worked that day. Her military training and life experience kept a truly terrifying situa-

Reagan-era Air Force One, *rear galley, 2015. Author's photograph.*
. . .

tion from becoming overwhelmingly chaotic. Joell, a native of Bermuda, wanted to be a flight attendant ever since her family flew on a plane to immigrate to the United States when she was six years old. "I don't remember the exact airline—it had blue and white colors—possibly Eastern or Pan-Am, but I remember the flight attendant," Joell related. "She was so nice to me, and made me feel comfortable. If I talked to someone who can draw, I could describe her exactly. That's how much of an impression that she made on me. From that day on, I knew that I wanted to be a flight attendant."[95]

Joell held on to that dream all through high school, and after graduation she immediately applied with several commercial airlines to be a flight attendant. The airline industry was going through a series of booms and busts at that time, so her application languished. She then decided to enlist in the military and get flight attendant experience there and apply later. She first spent some time at a military base in Texas acquiring some culinary training (though not as extensive as one would get with a commercial airline) before being assigned to a traffic management office position at the Royal Air Force base in Suffolk, England, jointly operated by the U.S. Air Force and the Royal Air Force. It was during that three-year stint (1982–85) when Joell learned that U.S. active duty personnel were serving as flight attendants on military flights. When she transferred to Grissom Air Force Base, Indiana, in December 1985, she immediately applied to become a flight attendant. She was interviewed on a Gulf Stream military plane that stopped at the base, and her paperwork was sent to Andrews Air Force Base in December 1986. In no time, she was officially a military flight attendant.

No one starts off working on *Air Force One*, so Joell first worked on planes that carried members of Congress. Joell noted that supervisors scrutinized "your customer service skills, appearance, timing, how you prepare a meal, etc. These things determine your prospects for promotion. Flight attendants are also rotated through different positions to see how you do." Joell was promoted to the vice president's plane (George H. W. Bush held the position at that time), also known by the call sign *Air Force Two*, and soon was splitting time between *Air Force One* and *Air Force Two*. In 1990, Joell became a full-time flight attendant on *Air Force One*.

On the culinary side, gearing up for a presidential trip on *Air Force One* involves extensive teamwork. According to Joell, "Before planning a meal, we got a list of the president's dietary needs, likes, and dislikes from the White House. We then came up with a menu and sent it back to White House for approval. In addition to the approved menu, we made two or three extra meals, just in case." Once the menu was approved, Joell and the other flight attendants shopped for the groceries. At this point in the process, the ground crew at Andrews Air Force Base pre-cooked most of the meal's component parts, which were then frozen until reheated and further cooked by the flight attendants once the plane was in the air. Joell admitted that her team became known for some of their dishes, especially a French toast dish they developed on *Air Force Two* where they used Hawaiian bread. "We got a lot of compliments on that one," Joell proudly said.

Joell has a lot of fond memories from working for four presidents, from

President George H. W. Bush ("Bush 41") until she had to mandatorily retire in 2010 for length of service while flying with President Obama. She had served the military for twenty-eight years and flown on presidential planes for twenty-four years. Yet, 9/11 was the most memorable day. On the tenth anniversary of that tragic day, Joell reminisced to a Suwanee, Georgia, television station, "We had to remain calm for our passengers as flight attendants, but at the same time, you're still worried about the country," she said. "I felt safe. I felt *Air Force One* was safe, but you're still worried in general about what's going on back home."[96] Still, Joell and her team were able to keep it together: "Everyone was doing their thing. It wasn't chaotic. Everyone had a plan. We knew what we were supposed to do."[97] Joell has no problem focusing on the positive aspects of her service on the presidential plane: "I've got special memories that I can keep forever," Joell said. "It's still a special place in my heart."[98]

Presidential travel cooks had a full range of experiences using limited equipment for a limited period of time. Their main concern was to take care of nourishing the chief executive—whether traveling by train, boat, or plane—until the desired destination was reached. As these travel cooks learned, presidents needed food, and food often served as comfort for the presidents.

Recipes

DAISY BONNER'S CHEESE SOUFFLÉ

Here's the recipe for the miraculous soufflé that Daisy Bonner prepared the day that her beloved president, Franklin D. Roosevelt, died. Bonner always served this dish with stuffed baked tomatoes, peas, plain lettuce salad with French dressing, Melba toast, and coffee.

Makes 5 servings

1 tablespoon butter
2 heaping tablespoons flour
Pinch of salt
1/2 teaspoon prepared mustard
1/2 cup whole milk
3/4 cup grated sharp cheddar cheese
5 eggs, separated
1 teaspoon baking powder

1. Preheat the oven to 375°F.
2. Melt the butter in a saucepan and blend in the flour, salt, and mustard. Gradually add the milk, whisking constantly, to make a thin sauce.
3. Beat the egg yolks slightly and add them and the cheese to the sauce. Stir to combine.
4. Set aside to cool until ready to bake.
5. When ready to bake, beat the egg whites stiff with the baking powder.
6. Fold the egg whites into the cheese mixture.
7. Transfer the mixture to an 8 × 8-inch baking dish and bake for 30 minutes.
8. When the soufflé is done it should be very high and brown but soft in the middle.
9. Serve immediately.

HAWAIIAN FRENCH TOAST

Given the small galley on *Air Force One*, Wanda Joell had little latitude to create a lot of dishes, but this was one of her creations. She came up with this dish on one presidential trip because the crew wanted to do something new. This was one that President Clinton really enjoyed, and I think you will, too.

Makes 4 servings

1 cup eggnog
1 teaspoon vanilla extract
1 teaspoon cinnamon, plus more for serving
1 teaspoon ground nutmeg
8 slices King's Hawaiian bread
Sifted powdered sugar to taste

1. Heat a frying pan over medium heat and coat with butter or nonstick cooking spray.
2. Thoroughly combine the eggnog, vanilla, cinnamon, and nutmeg.
3. Dip the bread in mix on both sides.
4. Fry until golden brown on each side.
5. Remove from the pan and dust with powdered sugar and extra cinnamon.
6. Serve with butter, fresh fruit, maple syrup, and a choice of meat.

Chef Charlie Redden takes great pride in this dish because it was the very first thing that he cooked for President Clinton. The White House Mess had a pita pizza on its regular menu, and Redden adds jerk chicken, a standby in Jamaican cuisine, to give it a unique spin. This was another one of President Clinton's favorites.

Makes 4 servings

4 pita breads
12 tablespoons pizza sauce
1/2 teaspoon dried oregano (optional)
1/2 teaspoon dried basil (optional)
Sliced chicken breast strips
2 tablespoons jerk seasoning (I recommend Island Jerk Seasoning by Tropical Pepper Co.)
1 cup low-fat shredded mozzarella cheese
4 tablespoons Parmesan cheese
1/2 cup thinly sliced red onion (optional)
1/2 cup thinly sliced green bell peppers (optional)
Red pepper flakes, to taste

1. Place the pita breads on a cookie sheet.
2. Spread 3 tablespoons of the pizza sauce onto each pita.
3. Sprinkle 1/8 tablespoon each of oregano and basil, if using, onto each pita.
4. Toss the chicken strips with the jerk seasoning and arrange them on the pizza.
5. Top each pita with 1/4 cup of mozzarella cheese and 1 tablespoon of Parmesan cheese.
6. Top each pita with 1/8 cup each of the onions and bell peppers, if using. Season to taste with red pepper flakes.
7. Place the pizzas in the oven and broil for about 4–5 minutes at 425°F (recommended).

6

Seeing through a Glass Darkly

AFRICAN AMERICANS AND PRESIDENTIAL DRINKWAYS

❦

In that fierce light that beats upon Kings, potentates, and Presidents,
no detail of personal conduct is too trivial to escape public observation and
comment. The habits of all our Presidents in respect to the use of spirituous liquors
have been subjected to the keenest scrutiny, and the tide of gossip about the use
and non-use of wine at the White House or by its occupant has often risen so high
that all questions as to the policy of official conduct of the President seemed
to be quite submerged.
"The President and the Wine Cup,"
New York Times, 26 November 1899

Presidents have long recognized the value of feeding the voting public some occasional tidbits about the food they eat. Not only do their food habits humanize and personalize them, but they also give presidents the opportunity to show that they share things in common with average Americans. Presidents could achieve the exact same goals with beverages, but they are far more tight-lipped about their drinking habits. Why? Americans have historically had a very complicated relationship with one drink category—alcoholic beverages—and they want assurance that their president is not a drunk. In fact, one finds that for many Americans, alcohol should never pass a president's lips. Besides the belief that the president should serve as an exemplar for moral behavior, there are practical concerns that one of the most powerful people on Earth—one with access to nuclear weapons and a powerful military—should not be an alcoholic.

Thus, the American public highly values sobriety from and sober judgment in its president, so much so that even presidents who only moderately drank alcohol couldn't escape harsh judgment in the court of public opinion. Such intense public scrutiny has caused presidents to play a cat-and-mouse game with the press corps that is trying to inform the public. And time and time again, African Americans butlers, cooks, and stewards have also had to play this game because they are immersed in presidential drink culture, just as they are with food. African Americans once fit the expected social order by doing the work to produce alcoholic beverages, laboring in jobs where they served such beverages to whites and also drinking alcohol themselves, under certain controlled situations. The fear in the past was that inebriated blacks, particularly in interracial social settings, were primed to commit acts of moral depravity and racially motivated violence. In this chapter, we'll sidle up to the presidential bar with William T. Crump, Howard Williams, Arthur Brooks, John Ficklin, Alonzo Fields, Henry Pinckney, Tom Bullock, and President Barack Obama to sip sequentially from five different presidential drinking glasses: wine, punch, eggnog, cocktails, and beer. But first, one needs to understand how social attitudes in the United States toward alcohol have changed over time.

Liquor lubricated social life during the federal period, and its elevated status was due in part to necessity and not solely to entertainment purposes. European colonists had problems with the indigenous American water supply from day one. To them, the water was just plain nasty. As an alternative, white colonists, young and old, consumed a number of wines and "small beers" (the latter had a lower alcohol content than what we typically consume today). In time, though everyone was drinking alcoholic beverages of some type, class differences emerged in consumption patterns. American elite whites drank gin, Madeira, rum, and wines, while working-class and poorer whites consumed harder stuff, namely alcohol made from grains, like whiskey and corn liquor. Few important decisions were made or social occasions happened without alcohol. Even Alexander Hamilton and Thomas Jefferson decided where to locate the nation's capital while drinking wine.[1]

People of West African heritage living in the United States came from a drinking culture that featured low-alcohol beverages. For millennia, West Africans brewed mild alcoholic drinks from native grains and palm tree sap. In the Americas, slave owners purposefully hooked enslaved West Africans on drinks with a higher alcoholic content mainly as a matter of incentive and control. President Thomas Jefferson added alcoholic drinks to the food rations he issued to his White House slaves and free laborers to create the illusion that he was doing something really special for them. As a result, the enslaved would be pacified, and free workers would be more reluctant to ask for a raise.[2] This was consistent with the southern plantation practice of rewarding the enslaved with jugs of cheap liquor (mainly corn liquor) for large projects involving lots of hard work. Though African American drinking habits were the most ridiculed in the press and popular culture, there was growing concern in America's burgeoning faith community about the fact that everyone, not just blacks, drank to excess.

Contemporaneous to the rise in drinking culture, or perhaps because of it, young America experienced a religious and cultural phenomenon called the "Great Awakening." The increased religiosity sparked in the 1730s, and the momentum kept growing with each passing decade. By the late 1800s, these religious change agents had grown a movement large enough that they could flex their political muscle and push for temperance—the prohibition of alcohol. The ascent of the temperance movement had consequences for political candidates, especially those running for president. It took time, but by the 1850s, serious presidential candidates felt obligated to declare their stand on temperance. If they favored temperance, they were described as "dry"; if they were against temperance, they were described as "wet." The temperance movement set its sights on the president because participants believed that he should set the moral example. Temperance advocates were alarmed by the example William Henry Harrison set in 1840 with what historians call the "first national presidential election campaign." President Martin Van Buren was portrayed by his political enemies as an elitist who sipped champagne. Harrison sharply contrasted himself for voters by projecting the humble image of himself living in a log cabin and drinking hard cider.[3] Harrison cruised to victory that Election Day.

Lest you think that the question of a "wet" or "dry" White House went the way of the dodo once Prohibition ended, think again. There was much press about what the White House drinking policy would be after teetotaler and unabashed Southern Baptist Jimmy Carter was elected. A *Washington Post* writer described it this way: "Still unclear is the answer to the question of whether the White House of Jimmy Carter will be wet or dry, or somewhere in between with the low proof compromise of wine only. It has floated to the top of the current sea of speculation about the Carter style, like slices of fruit in a punch bowl, because of Mrs. Carter's indication that she may serve only wine, as she did in the Georgia Statehouse."[4]

When temperance advocates failed in getting "dry" candidates elected, they readjusted their strategy. If they couldn't change a president's private drinking habits, perhaps it was possible to keep presidents from serving alcohol when they entertained guests. Yet many temperance advocates begrudgingly eased their criticism of serving wine, since there are numerous biblical references that permit its use. The next target involved

White House renovations, so to speak—getting rid of the White House wine cellar.

President Jefferson, a noted oenophile, created the White House wine cellar by purchasing "some bottled wine by the case, but more often it arrived in barrels. They were stored under lock and key, first in the White House basement and later in a wine cellar which Jefferson dug on the grounds. The first Presidential wine cellar also served as an icehouse and was usually referred to by that more democratic name. A contemporary report described it as round, about 16 feet deep, lined with bricks and topped with a wooden shed."[5] The first location for the wine cellar was under what is presently the West Wing, and it was stocked with Madeira and Spanish dessert wines, including Pacaret.[6] After Jefferson vacated the White House, the wine cellar was on the move. In a modern article on wine in the White House, the *New York Times* reported, "By then [1834], the wine cellar had been brought into the White House. It was just beneath the State Dining Room. According to one report, racks for bottles and barrels were built along the walls behind heavy wooden doors and there was room for not only wine but hard liquor and beer."[7] Though there are periodic accounts of wine being served, we don't really hear much about the wine cellar until the time of Rutherford B. Hayes, who was an alleged teetotaler.

The high point for temperance advocates, and the low point for D.C. drunkards, came during the Hayes administration. At some point during his presidency, President Hayes entertained Wagon manufacturing magnate Clem Studebaker. Studebaker requested something to drink, and President Hayes directed White House steward William T. Crump to take Studebaker down to the White House cellar. Along the way, Studebaker daydreamed about what he might drink, his mind ultimately settling on presidential brandy. When they reached the wine cellar, Crump yelled out to an African American cook nearby, "'Miranda? Miranda! Where's that jug of buttermilk?' 'It broke me all up' said the wagon-maker. 'I fancy that I can taste that executive brandy yet.'"[8] President Calvin Coolidge was the only other president to make a show of having no alcohol in the wine cellar, and he stocked it with "his cigars, fruit, raisins, candy, nuts, etc., which were sent to him from time to time by admirers. When he had among his guests at the White House personal friends of long standing, he had the habit of solemnly escorting them to the wine cellar, allowing the ponderous outer door to be opened by the colored porter, then with his own private key, opened the wine chamber, where he would select some little treat and hand it to his guests."[9]

Despite the earlier anecdote, President Hayes was dodgy about his true commitment to temperance, and the advocates kept the pressure on him. As one newspaper editorial inquired, "But what is to be Mr. Hayes's policy on the liquor question, now that his Southern policy may be considered settled? We think we have the key to it in that White House dinner and the Presidential apologies that have followed it. It will be one of attempted compromise, adopted in the expectation of winning the favor of both temperance and anti-temperance people. We do not think Mr. Hayes is capable of pursuing any other policy on any question."[10] The press did report several instances where President Hayes was known to either request or actually drink alcohol. By the end of his term, one newspaper even speculated that Hayes banned liquor in the White House only because he didn't want to pay for it and enjoyed drinking at others' expense.[11]

First Lady Lucy Hayes was not squishy at all on the temperance topic, and the first clue is that her nickname was "Lemonade Lucy." Accordingly, the "within-the-White-House-temperance-movement" started off swimmingly. President Hayes banned all intoxicating beverages from official White House functions and declined to host any state dinners in order to "avoid the wine question."[12] Hayes diluted his stance because his secretary of state, William Evarts, persuaded him that foreign dignitaries were used to having wine with their meals. To deny them this pleasure would prove too difficult a hardship and make a poor impression internationally.[13] In the end, President Hayes proved a lost cause to the temperance folks, and Mrs. Hayes could never do enough to please them. She eventually had her name stripped from a temperance society named in her honor merely because she and the president were passengers on a steamboat that served claret.[14] As we'll see later, the conflicting versions of the infamous state dinner where White House steward William Crump either served or did not serve alcohol certainly didn't help the Hayeses' case.

President Chester Arthur, however, was an unabashed wine enthusiast who took office and restored the wine cellar to its Jeffersonian glory. The *Wheeling Register* of Ohio reported:

This place has been enlarged and cleaned out, only to be filled up again however. Before the cellar was too damp to keep wine in long.

It would be apt to become spoiled. This may account for the frequent calls General Arthur made upon it, probably not wishing to see any of the wine destroyed. The cellar has been refilled and in its present shape I am told by people who profess to be well posted about such things, that wine will keep there for years and the longer it is kept the better is will become. "There is one thing Arthur does understand," said a Congressman this morning, "if he is faulty in statesmanship, and that is wine. You can't fool him."[15]

With the first wine aficionado living in the White House since Jefferson, President Arthur called upon Howard Williams, his African American steward, to choose the very best wines.

Williams took a familiar nineteenth-century path to the White House. He was born in Baltimore in 1837 and moved to the D.C. area shortly before the Civil War began.[16] Williams would later be described as "a colored man of very fine personal appearance, well educated . . . [who] has made a triumph of his stewardship."[17] For his first professional job, he cooked for U.S. representative Samuel Hooper (R-Mass.).[18] Williams supervised dinners that one newspaper reported "had never been equaled."[19] After Hooper died in 1875, Williams became the personal chef for U.S. senator Roscoe Conkling (R-N.Y.) and then filled the White House steward position after Crump resigned in May 1882.[20] When hired as steward, Williams teamed up with a French chef named Alexander Fortin to make President Arthur's meals world-famous—especially the state dinners. In a rare newspaper interview, Williams gave details on how he and Fortin dazzled guests with "architectural gastronomy" ("One of the rules is that no dish be served flat. It must be raised up in some way"), elaborate table decorations, and an endless variety of food ("Not a dish is brought to the table that appeared at the previous dinner").[21] Yet, as was often the case for presidential cooks, Williams's excellence could not overcome a change in presidents. In May 1885, shortly after his election, President Cleveland relieved Williams and Chef Fortin of their duties.[22]

Though the Arthur administration represented a high tide for wine during the Gilded Age, the temperance movement crested to the point where a White House wine cellar seemed obsolete. One newspaper reported, "All presidents of the United States have at times set wine before their guests. Until Theodore Roosevelt became president the White House had a wine cellar and a dark room in the attic set aside as a storeroom for liquors. He did away with both of them. The cellar is now used

Arthur Brooks, White House wine cellar custodian. Trenton Evening Times, *3 October 1919.*

. . .

for machinery and the dark room is a part of the quarters for the servants."[23] Despite this description of the White House wine cellar at its darkest hour, the African American influence on the White House wine scene began to wax. The key personalities involved were Arthur Brooks, John Ficklin, and Alonzo Fields.

The wine cellar's last hurrah before Prohibition was enacted happened under the watchful eye of a highly regarded servant, "Major" Arthur Brooks. Brooks "guarded" the wine, may have been an informal sommelier, and certainly served wine in the White House. Brooks was born in Port Royal, Virginia, on 25 November 1861. While he was a boy, his family moved to Washington, D.C. Brooks made his mark as a national guardsman in what would eventually be called the First Separate Battalion of the District of Columbia National Guard and achieved the rank of major; he retired with the rank of lieutenant colonel. Why he was nicknamed with a lesser rank is unknown. Brooks might have seen a military career as a means for black progress; according to an African American newspaper obituary, Brooks organized and instructed a "High School Cadet Organization, and is due much credit for the interest of our people in military affairs."[24]

Brooks entered the orbit of elite men when he took a job as a messenger to Secretary of War George W. McCrary in the Hayes administration.

He continued to serve in that position with succeeding secretaries of war until he got a custodian position in the Taft administration.[25] Here, as one newspaper of the time observed, the term "custodian" was not meant in the janitorial sense but meant that he was the "bonded custodian of all furnishings and personal effects."[26] In addition, Brooks "directed the care of the President's personal wardrobe and advised more than one President, it is said, in matters of personal attire."[27] Clearly, Brooks found multiple ways to become a valued member of the White House staff.

Brooks prided himself on his ability to keep secrets and earned a sterling reputation for trustworthiness and military acumen. For the latter, President Woodrow Wilson even brought Brooks with him to Paris to advise him as he negotiated the Treaty of Versailles in June 1919. President Calvin Coolidge described Brooks posthumously as "'one of the finest men in Washington,' not as one of the finest Negroes," and also as "a cherished friend."[28] It's no surprise that Coolidge gave Brooks the keys to the White House cellar. White House housekeeper Elizabeth Jaffray remembers, "Brooks it was who always looked after the White House wines. When President Taft came in he had sent from Europe a cellar of fine wines. There were two keys for the wine cabinets — one that I kept and one that I gave Brooks. Before any big dinner I would give Brooks a list of the wines wanted and instructions as to just how they were to be served."[29] It is unclear how much discretion Brooks had in choosing wines, but he was integral to its service. On 9 January 1917, under the direction of Jaffray, Brooks served "18 quarts of Champagne, 2 quarts of Claret, 5 quarts of Hock, 2 quarts of Sherry, 2 quarts of Scotch, and a quart of Brandy."[30]

Around 1924, Brooks developed heart trouble, and the problem persisted. In 1926, the Coolidges were so concerned for Brooks's health that they made an extraordinarily heartfelt gesture, given the racial climate of the time. According to the *Chicago Defender*, "When President and Mrs. Coolidge left Washington for their summer White House at Paul Smiths, N.Y., Major Brooks was their house guest." Coolidge hoped "the mountain air and complete rest would help him to regain his health."[31] But the attempted remedy didn't work, and Brooks returned to Washington for constant care by his wife until his death in 1926. Ever mindful of his duties, when Brooks felt death was near, he summoned someone from the White House to his home so he could reveal the combinations for the locks to the silver vaults.[32] To punctuate the friendship between the president and the trusted servant, Coolidge was described as "deeply aggrieved" upon hearing of Brooks's death.[33]

The wine cellar was mothballed during the Prohibition years, though presidents kept a private stash or drank once they got outside of the White House grounds. It wasn't until the Eisenhower administration that the White House wine cellar was again fully stocked, and that was due to outside contributions. "The wine industry helped set up an American wine cellar for Dwight D. Eisenhower. The Kennedys served American wines proudly, as well as their excellent French labels. At present the White House has no wine cellar. Like many American homes, when a party is in the offing a quick order is simply put in at a nearby liquor store in downtown Washington," the *New York Times* noted.[34] Now that drinking wine was less of a concern, the public focused on what kind of wine was served, where it came from, and how much it cost.

By the time of the Kennedy administration, the American wine industry had recovered from the lost years caused by Prohibition and was producing fine wines on a regular basis. If the nineteenth century was fueled by a rivalry of French cooks versus American cooks, the twentieth century was about American wines versus French wines. The Kennedys' Camelot image definitely spoke with a foreign accent, which translated into White House dining menus written in French and French cooking served at meals accompanied by French wines. Though the American public devoured the Camelot image, they soured on all of the Frenchness, asking, "Can't American culture be classy and celebrated as well?" As the criticism mounted, the Kennedys went on the offensive, especially with the press, which did a lot to propagate the Camelot image. Ben Bradlee, a Kennedy family friend who would go on to edit the *Washington Post*, remembered getting personal calls from Jacqueline Kennedy to correct stories that appeared in *Newsweek*, the publication he edited at the time. Jackie wanted to clarify that domestic, not foreign, wines were served at certain meals and that dishes were no longer being referred to by their French names.[35] President Kennedy also took the extra, and somewhat unusual, step of taking American sparkling wine abroad with him on state visits in an effort to introduce Europeans to American wines.[36]

The Johnson administration decided to be bullish on American wines from the start. From 1964 on, the Johnsons exclusively served American wines whenever they entertained, and the same directive went to all U.S. embassy staffs.[37] The French seemed amused by the entire situation, with one French wine official blithely stating, "America produces some honest wines but only the great ones come from France."[38]

Public interest in the White House's wine policy continued during the 1970s, but it wasn't at the same fever pitch as in the 1960s. That doesn't mean critics missed opportunities to needle presidential wine selections. One such opportunity came when President Nixon hosted one of his iconic summit meetings with Soviet leader Leonid Brezhnev. At one of the summit meals, a cabernet wine was served with beef. French newspapers published scorching editorials claiming that the wine pairing "would make a gourmet faint in France." Nixon ordered an investigation into the matter, and unidentified sources blamed it on "backstairs personnel 'whose zeal exceeded their judgment.'"[39] Though President Nixon didn't call him out by name, the "backstairs personnel" was probably White House maître d' John Ficklin Sr. — an African American man who had become the de facto White House sommelier.

John Ficklin started working in the White House in 1940, following in the footsteps of his older brother Charles Ficklin, who also ended up working there for decades. Ficklin was born in Amissville, Virginia, in 1919. He moved to the Washington, D.C., area in the 1930s, and after a short stint in the army he started working in the White House as a part-time butler to help out when there was an extra workload. No doubt his brother helped him get that gig. By 1946, Ficklin had done so well at his job that he was brought on full-time. In 1965, he succeeded his brother Charles and became the White House maître d'. It is unclear how it started, but by the 1970s John Ficklin was in charge of selecting the wines.[40]

The "People Who Know Wine" were satisfied when California wines were served at White House functions, but the grapes of wrath fomented when Ficklin started choosing wines from other parts of the United States. Newspaper food sections ran headlines like "White House Serves Second Rate Wines" or "White House Wine Leaves Much to Be Desired." Given the torrent of criticism over his wine selections, the American Wine Society sent him an encouraging letter on 9 April 1975:

Dear Mr. Ficklin,

You are to be congratulated for your recommendations of American, particularly Eastern United States, wines to the President for service at official functions. Recent newspaper criticisms of your actions are uninformed and ill-advised. I am told several of the people quoted have not even tasted the wines they criticized. As chairman of the Society's 1975 Annual Conference, I would like to invite you to address our group on November 8. The conference will be held at the Carrousel Inn, Cincinnati. Our members will be very interested in learning of your experience and receiving your judgments of American wines. We sincerely hope you will be able to accept our invitation.

Cordially,

Gerald M. Bell

1975 Conference Chairman[41]

Ficklin didn't speak at this particular event, but he was grateful for the note. Apparently, Ficklin's White House bosses were fine with his wine selections, for he retained his sommelier duties for almost another decade.

In 1981, Ficklin agreed to a newspaper interview with the *Washington Post* that gave readers remarkable insight into how White House wine service worked:

Resting below the State dining room is the White House wine cellar. Behind a locked but otherwise unassuming blue door, just across a passageway from the downstairs kitchen, this one-time pantry is now the temperature-controlled repository (at 58°F) for all the president's wine. According to long-time White House maître d' and *de facto* sommelier John Ficklin, Sr., the cellar was begun in the Franklin Roosevelt administration and completed under President Eisenhower. Although only four feet wide and 16 feet long, the respectable if not imposing cellar contains individual wooden bins for almost 1,000 bottles of wine. The fact is, however, it is stocked largely with booze, including bourbon, gin and vodka.[42]

He also answered the question of what is done with leftover White House wine: "Also stored in the cellar and in a separate walk-in cooler (41°F) are re-corked bottles of previously opened wine which are used by the White House chef in cooking. Such are the economies of a deficit-ridden administration."[43]

Ficklin's long reign as sommelier ended with the Reagan administration, thanks to the assertiveness of one of Reagan's senior staffers.

In the past, Ficklin—who prefers rosé wines and sparkling cider—coordinated the selection of White House wines with advice and assistance from local wholesalers and retailers. [Deputy chief of staff and assistant to the president Michael K.] Deaver has preempted this process by making the wine recommendations himself. . . . Aware that the Carter administration "had left some wines," Deaver instructed Ficklin to use them "for large receptions." Although Ficklin says that the storekeeper has a complete list of the wines in the White House wine cellar and that Deaver "was supposed to have an inventory," it appears the list has been slow in arriving to the West Wing. Not to worry. The resourceful Deaver has his own cellar at the White House. Tucked away in a small closet below a television set in the corner of his office—not far from the Cabinet Room—Deaver keeps a stash of California wines.[44]

Though Deaver had usurped the sommelier duties, Ficklin had plenty to do as the White House maître d', a position he held until his retirement in 1983.

Ficklin was loved by many White House staffers, guests, and the First Families themselves, so much so that he was given a very rare honor. As *Jet* magazine reported, President and Mrs. Reagan made Ficklin and his wife, Nancy, their guests of honor at an August 1983 state dinner for His Highness Shaikh Isa Bin Salman Al-Khalifa, emir of Bahrain, an island kingdom near Saudi Arabia. In addition, "Mrs. Reagan put in front of his table a special gift—a pair of gold cuff links, generally reserved for heads of state."[45] The very next year, Ficklin died of cancer, and Eugene Allen, another African American, succeeded him as maître d'. Allen would also go on to a decades-long career at the White House, and a fictionalized account of Allen's life would form the basis of the 2013 movie *The Butler*.

Though wine has dominated over the years, what is served out of the White House punch bowl makes a decent showing in presidential drinking culture. Andrew Jackson served a whiskey-laced orange punch at his 1829 inauguration party, where thousands of well-wishers swamped the White House to consume said punch, ice cream, and a wedge of cheese. The Virginians who occupied the White House were also known for their punches, particularly Presidents Monroe and Tyler. For the most controversial punch episode before Prohibition, we must return to the Hayes administration.

The Hayeses eagerly took a hardcore stance because they were still suffering a bad publicity hangover from one of the earliest state dinners they had hosted for the Russian grand dukes, Alexis and Constantin, on 19 April 1877. From the Hayeses' perspective, the alcohol-free event went well, and, as Secretary Evarts would later reportedly describe, "the water flowed like champagne" that night.[46] Yet there seemed to be quite a buzz over the frozen Roman punch (a concoction of rum, tea, lemon, and orange juice) in orange skins created and served by steward William Crump. The punch tasted strongly of Saint Croix rum, and the grateful attendees deemed it "the life saving station" of the entertainment, thinking that the Hayeses were none the wiser.[47] One can hardly imagine the snickering that took place that such a fast one could be pulled off right under the noses of the First Couple.

Perhaps the Hayeses were the ones to have the last laugh. Writing in his diary on 10 January 1887, nearly a decade after the event, Hayes stated, "The joke of the Roman punch oranges was not on us, but on the drinking people. My orders were to flavor them *rather strongly* with the same flavor that is found in Jamaican rum. This took! There was not a drop of spirits in them!"[48] Crump was the only other person who knew the absolute truth. Over time, Crump would coyly suggest what happened that night, but he never confirmed or outright denied that he had spiked the drinks. One thing that we know for certain is that he basked in the attention.

As noted earlier, members of the general public frequently sent food to our presidents. The same went for drinks, especially alcoholic beverages. Obviously, such gifts were reduced to a trickle during the Prohibition years, but after repeal, the floodgates opened. Gifts were coming not only from the public but also from liquor manufacturers eager to tout the White House seal of approval. White House butler and maître d' Alonzo Fields became the point person for figuring out what to do with all of that liquor. Punch, it seems, was the only viable solution to the mounting potable problem:

> In no time at all gifts from wine manufacturers poured into the White House — even Japanese saki. Very little of it was palatable for the table, but we would serve a spiked punch and a fruit punch at receptions, so I experimented with combinations of wine to develop a punch to use up the gift wines. The spiked punch always went over big. Even with the most sedate groups, when we served 35 to 45 gallons of fruit punch we would need an average of 110 gallons of spiked punch for a crowd of 1,200, and most likely I would have to draw on a reserve supply. I first thought that, because of the newness of lifting the prohibition law, this consumption of spiked

Alonzo Fields (second from the left) *with other White House butlers, n.d.*
Courtesy Ronald Reagan Presidential Library and Museum.

. . .

punch would wear off, but in the years to follow the averages kept steady.[49]

Looking back on it now, it's quite astonishing how much liquor was actually being consumed in the White House without the public ever finding out.

Though spiking the punch seemed like a brilliant solution, Fields eventually acknowledged how stress-inducing it was to constantly stay one step ahead of potential disaster:

These are the punch combinations that always gave me sleepless nights after having served them at a White House party. In my days the White House budget was a very tight one and if a President indulged in heavy entertaining he would be forced to spend his own money. President Hoover always spent his own money, he did not even take home his pay. President Roosevelt wasn't about to do that so I was ordered to use up all gift wines for spike punch. There was sherry, sweet, dry and just sherry, sauterne, claret, muscatel, scuppernong, blackberry, concord, apple jack, white wines and Japanese saki. . . . One thing for sure—I did a lot of stirring and mixing and hoping some poor soul who might take in just a little too much wouldn't blow his top. I worked these recipes days before a party, for it required tasting and more tasting. Even just rolling the mixtures around in your mouth took courage, but my orders were: use up that gift wine. . . . Don't you wonder why these mixtures did not cause a tragic ending . . . [?] I could always see the headline "President's party has tragic end. Guests go besmirched after drinking spike punch at the White House. Chief Butler being held for investigation."[50]

Fortunately for Fields and several presidents, that day never came.

In addition to public entertaining, the White House punch bowl is always present for various winter holiday parties thrown for White House staffers. During my tenure there, we staffers eagerly anticipated these parties because it was our one and only chance to drink the famous White House eggnog. One sip of this elixir had me humming "It's the Most Wonderful Time of the Year." Eggnog is the most enduring party drink in White House history. It traces its roots to our first president and has several connections to African American servants.

Eggnog has British lineage as it is derived from a drink called "posset": "In England posset was a hot drink in which the white and yolk of eggs were whipped with ale, cider, or wine. Americans adapted English recipes to produce a variety of milk-based drinks that combined rum, brandy, or whiskey with cream."[51] As a good Virginian, George Washington kept up the custom of consuming eggnog between Christmas Eve and New Year's Day. Harnett T. Kane, in his history of Christmas traditions in the South, describes Washington's eggnog as a "virile drink; the first President not only used both rye and Jamaica or New England rum, but he also added a liberal dollop of mellow sherry for good measure and good fumes." Again as a testament to Washington's enduring influence, Kane states, "the men of Richmond, of Roanoke, of Charlottesville, and of other Virginia cities still emulate him."[52]

In the big houses of the antebellum South, the appearance of the eggnog bowl heralded gift time for the enslaved servants. The *Chicago Daily Inter Ocean* reported on a continuance of the tradition in the Executive Residence:

> From Jackson's time to Tyler's there were no festivities [in the White House] at Christmas time, for there were no children there. With

the advent of the Tyler family the Virginian idea of Christmas cele-bration came back, and the day's duties began with the preparation of a great bowl of eggnog. Then presents were distributed, the ser-vants one and all, being specifically remembered. A midday dinner and a family gathering, followed by a quiet evening, were the cus-tom. The latter was almost compulsory, for it was considered a duty to the colored servants that they should have a holiday after the din-ner hour.[53]

Thus, our slave-owning presidents were merely transplanting a family tra-dition in their home away from home.

Even northern-based presidents embraced the White House eggnog tradition; chief among them was President Franklin D. Roosevelt. Presi-dent Roosevelt's housekeeper Henrietta Nesbitt observed, "Speaking of liquids, I'm going to give once more the recipe of one other drink that came under my department. Cocktails and highballs were served upstairs and I had nothing to do with them, but the New Year's eggnog was tradi-tional, and the entire White House was concerned with its making. The creamy mixture was prepared in the same way, and the great punch bowl was carried before the President. And each time, lifting his cup, President Roosevelt gave the same toast: 'To the United States!'"[54] Lillian Rogers Parks, a White House maid, declared after tasting some of the eggnog that President Eisenhower made in the upstairs kitchen, "That was some kind of strong."[55] Looks like President Eisenhower's recipe would have kept good company with our first president's version.

By the Kennedy administration, eggnog had a starring role at the press parties. Unsurprisingly, the Kennedy White House was secretive about what exactly was in that eggnog. The rebuffed press inquiries eventu-ally led to a playful "scandal" with John Ficklin right in the middle of it. The *Washington Post*'s investigative team reported, "Every Christmas the rumor about the White House eggnog surfaces again. According to the story—from the usual, reliable, but anonymous, sources—John Ficklin, the White House maître d' for 36 years, saves eggnog from one year to the next and uses it as 'mother of nog,' adding the old to the new batch. As is customary in these rumors that shake the fate of a nation, Ficklin issued a denial: He said he never mixed the old with the new."[56] When faced with leaked eyewitness "testimony," Ficklin didn't confess to using an eggnog starter but merely to serving the press old eggnog in new glasses.[57] The White House eventually relented, and the eggnog recipe was ultimately revealed: "Ficklin uses a gallon and a half of bourbon, a gallon of brandy and a gallon of rum to 10 gallons of commercial eggnog mix. He serves it with a quart of eggnog ice cream for each punchbowl to make it richer and keep it cold, and tops it all with nutmeg."[58]

That White House eggnog recipe had a complex evolution. "The development of the White House eggnog has been a bipartisan effort," Ficklin said. "When we first worked it out, we had a lot of tasters until we got it just right. For a while, we used to put in whipped cream, but people complained that it was too rich. We found we had a lot more empty glasses when we didn't use egg white or cream. They don't seem to mind the ice cream."[59] Due to foot surgery, Ficklin later passed the baton to fellow butler Eugene Allen. Nancy Reagan approved of Allen's effort to replicate Ficklin's recipe and even emphasized to the press that "eggnog is a tradition in our house."[60] As anyone in the food industry would understand, Ficklin and Allen said that they served so much eggnog during the season that they were not enthusiastic about making it at home. Allen punctuated the point by saying, "I'm not a drinking man."[61]

While the White House put wine, punch, and eggnog on public display, its cocktail culture remained discreet. The earliest mention of the word "cocktail" in the English language happened in 1803, but cocktails didn't surface in campaign rhetoric until the late 1800s.[62] When steward Henry Pinckney served cocktails to President Theodore Roosevelt, it fit right in line with what his predecessors had done. Yet the public didn't see it that way. Perhaps no president has been haunted more by alcohol rumors than Theodore Roosevelt, who got guff as a candidate, as a sitting president, and even after his presidency.

Roosevelt had thought that his successor, William Howard Taft, was such a horrible chief executive that he decided to run against him as a third party candidate. After Roosevelt's political enemies floated rumors of his excessive drinking habits in order to torpedo his election chances, he filed a libel suit in order to clear his name. When it came his time to testify, Roosevelt dutifully recounted each drink he had imbibed in recent years: brandy and whiskey by a doctor's prescription, Madeira, champagne, sherry or white wine, and Poland water (in the summer). While on the witness stand, Roosevelt elaborated on one particular drink:

> At the White House we had a mint bed, and I should think that on the average I have drunk half a dozen mint juleps a year. Since I left the White House four years ago, to the best of my memory, I have

drunk mint juleps twice — on occasion at the Country Club at St. Louis, where I drank a part of a glass of mint julep, and on another occasion at a big luncheon given me at Little Rock, Ark., where they passed round the table a loving cup with the mint julep in it, and I drank when the cup was passed to me.[63]

The fact that Roosevelt could remember almost every alcoholic drink he'd taken impressed many, but not everyone.

President Roosevelt's court testimony created two pesky problems. First, the press had published conflicting accounts by White House employees as to the existence of the presidential mint bed. One staffer claimed that if a mint bed did exist, it was "never drawn upon except by the cook of the Executive Mansion when she was preparing mint sauce for a Presidential dinner."[64] The other troubling aspect of Roosevelt's claim was that he drank only "part" of the famous mint juleps at the St. Louis Country Club, concocted by its renowned African American bartender, Tom Bullock. For those times, this was the equivalent of candidate Bill Clinton's "I didn't inhale" denial. On 28 May 1913, the *St. Louis Times-Dispatch* skeptically editorialized the following in midtrial:

Colonel Roosevelt's fatal admission that he drank just a part of one julep at the St. Louis Country Club will come very near losing his case. Who was ever known to drink just part of one of Tom's? Tom, than whom there is no greater mixologist of any race, color or condition of servitude, was taught the art of the julep by no less than Marse Lilburn G. McNair, the father of the julep. In fact, the very cup that Col. Roosevelt drank it from belonged to Governor McNair, the first Governor of Missouri, the great-grandfather of Marse Lilburn and the great-great-grandfather of the julep. As is well know [*sic*], the Country Club mint originally sprang on the slopes of Parnassus and was transplanted thence to bosky banks of Culpepper Creek, Gaines County, Ky., and thence to our own environs; while the classic distillation with which Tom mingles it to produce his chief d'oeuvre is the oft-quoted liquefied soul of a Southern moonbeam falling aslant the dewy slopes of the Cumberland Mountains. To believe that a red-blooded man, and a true Colonel at that, ever stopped with just a part of one of those refreshments which have made St. Louis hospitality proverbial and become one of our most distinctive genre institutions, is to strain credulity too far. Are the Colonel's powers of self-restraint altogether transcendent? Have we found the living superman at last? When the Colonel says that he consumed just a part of one he doubtless meant that he did not swallow the mint itself, munch the ice and devour the very cup.[65]

Despite the newspaper's dire prediction, the former president won the lawsuit, procured an apology from the newspaper editor who slandered him, and pocketed six cents in court-awarded damages. As for the elite bartender Tom Bullock, he continued to mix drinks, and stay out of the headlines, until he died in 1964 at the age of ninety-one.

In sharp contrast to his presidential cousin, Franklin Roosevelt fully embraced cocktail culture when he became president and even flaunted that he drank cocktails in the White House. FDR imbibed different drinks with different companions, and according to longtime butler Alonzo Fields, "Scotch would evaporate" when Winston Churchill made a visit, but at heart, this Roosevelt was a martini man.[66] In fact, FDR may be the only president to claim the title "bartender in chief." White House maid Lillian Rogers Parks reminisced,

> FDR claimed he didn't know the exact formula of his martinis because they had been worked out by a family committee. Son Jimmy, he said, liked a mild martini, but not as mild as Anna's. Then son Franklin got old enough to speak up and argue for a still stronger martini. Then Johnny shot up so tall, he demanded to be heard and insisted on a martini so dry it could be mistaken for sand—a formula of seven-to-one. All this time the President would be mysteriously mixing vermouth and gin so that no one could see what his formula was. When he was finished he would say that as chairman of the committee, he had the power to decide the ultimate taste of a martini, and he would ostentatiously add Pernod to his concoction. At this point, some people—aghast at this addition—weren't sure they wanted a martini after all. . . . Missy would sip her favorite Haig & Haig while FDR mixed his own martini, or sometimes an old-fashioned. When they had guests, FDR would insist on mixing the martinis for everyone, and he would brag that he was the best martini mixer in the East.[67]

Consuming cocktails was not a complete family affair, and reminiscent of the Hayeses, First Lady Eleanor Roosevelt was more temperate than her husband. Again, Parks gives us valuable insight in her memoirs: "Eleanor said she hated to see all the trays of liquor around when she was there, and FDR was once quoted as saying after Churchill left that he hoped he wouldn't have to look at another drink for a week. For a day or so, he didn't."[68] Parks added that as much as Eleanor hated all of the drinking, she didn't interfere because what FDR did with guests "was his business."[69]

The Trumans were quite the opposite; they liked to drink together. Since the Trumans didn't mix their own drinks, that task fell upon White House maître d' Alonzo Fields. In his memoirs, White House chief usher J. B. West shares this anecdote about how Fields's first attempts to make an old-fashioned made him feel that his job was "on the rocks":

> At the end of the work day, the Trumans had cocktails in the West Hall, which is the family sitting room. One drink each, before dinner. But it took a while to learn their tastes. Shortly after they moved in, the First Lady rang for the butler. Fields came up, tray in hand. "We'd like two old-fashioneds, please," she requested. Fields, who often moonlighted at Washington's most elegant parties, prided himself on being an excellent bartender. "Yes, *Ma'am*," he answered. In no time flat, he was back with the order, in chilled glasses, with appetizing fruit slices and a dash of bitters. Mrs. Truman tasted the drink, thanked him, but made no other comment. The next evening she rang for Fields. "Can you make the old-fashioneds a little drier?" she said. "We don't like them so sweet." Fields tried a new recipe, and again she said nothing. But the next morning she told me, "They make the worst old-fashioneds here I've ever tasted! They're like fruit punch." The next evening, Fields, his pride hurt, dumped two big splashes of bourbon over the ice and served it to Mrs. Truman. She tasted the drink. Then she beamed. "Now that's the way we like our old-fashioneds!"[70]

Being away from the White House afforded the president a chance to drink in almost complete privacy, and that's when cocktails flowed freely. In the railroad days, according to the testimony of Chef Delefasse Green—an African American man who often cooked on presidential railcars—few took advantage of the opportunity. In contrast, temperance apparently has not been so highly valued among our jet age presidents. Recall that of the three-person crew detailed to serve *Air Force One* passengers, one person is a dedicated bartender. In addition to comforting the passengers, cocktails were served on the plane to calm unruly guests — some of them surprising: "Kennedy allowed the black Labrador of his brother, Robert, to romp unimpeded throughout the plane until the crew came up with a novel way to control the animal: They mixed a couple of martinis and served them to the dog on a plate, whereupon it promptly fell asleep. That was the tactic they used from then on whenever the canine started to bother passengers."[71]

At times, the president himself would be the most troublesome passenger on the plane; this was sometimes the case with President Lyndon Johnson. According to Kenneth Walsh in his history of presidents and their planes,

> Robert MacMillan, a steward, says Johnson made ridiculous demands. Once he ordered a root beer on the way back to Washington from Texas and his staff followed his lead, quickly exhausting the supply of a dozen cans. When Johnson asked for seconds, he flew into a rage when told there was none left and ordered the chief steward to keep several thousand cans on board. The staff ignored him and kept eight cases on hand, but Johnson never mentioned the incident again. Johnson would also throw his glass of Scotch and soda on the floor when stewards didn't mix it the way he liked — strong, with the glass three-quarters full of liquor.[72]

Fortunately, such temper tantrums were isolated incidents, and the serving of drinks on *Air Force One* usually went off without a ripple of controversy.

We end our exploration of presidential drinkways with a beverage that hasn't drawn as much scrutiny as the other drinks, even though presidential beer drinking dates back to President Washington, who "usually drank either beer or cider at every meal."[73] President William McKinley also liked the suds, but he was careful to frame its consumption as a stress reliever, as one newspaper reported: "Like most of his predecessors in office, whenever Mr. McKinley gave a state dinner at the White House wine was served to guests. The president himself usually, if not invariably, abstained from drinking it, for the only beverage he seemed to enjoy was a glass of beer, and this he drank but seldom and only after a strenuous day, usually in a campaign."[74]

Once again, President Theodore Roosevelt was right in the middle of another controversy, but unlike the mint julep matter, this controversy happened during his presidency:

The last time beer was served publicly at the White House was under another Roosevelt's administration — T.R.'s — when Prince Henry of Prussia, brother of Kaiser William, was entertained. The day before the Prince's arrival, somebody suggested that it would be a good idea to serve the beer in steins. T.R. approved the idea with several "Bullys" and "By George" exclamations, but it was discovered that the White House was shy on steins; so Jimmy Sloan, the Secret Service man, was commissioned to secure a supply. He dropped into Gunsenberg's, an old-fashioned German restaurant on Pennsylvania av [*sic*], [and] interviewed the proprietor, who loaned two barrels of steins which had never been unpacked. When T.R. [hosted] the Kaiser, a member of the White House staff noticed that the bottoms of the borrowed steins bore the words: "Stolen from Gunsenberg's, Pennsylvania av, Washington, D C," but he kept it to himself until after the Prince left and then told the President, who laughed heartily.[75]

Usually, it's the White House guests who "borrow" things, not vice versa. Fortunately, President Roosevelt did not suffer too much political fallout from this incident.

When Prohibition ended, beer started to get more attention than it had previously. President and Eleanor Roosevelt soon found this out after the First Lady held a press conference to announce that beer would be served in the White House:

When it is legal to serve beer in any government house, it will naturally be proper to do so for any one who desires it at the White House. I hope very much that any change in legislation may tend to improve the present conditions and lead to greater temperance. There has been a great deal of bootlegging in beer, and, once it was legal, this will be unprofitable, and I hope that a great many people who have used stronger things will be content with legal beer, so that the cause of temperance will be really served. No matter what the legislation, I myself do not drink anything with alcoholic content, but that is a purely individual thing. I should not dream of imposing my own convictions on other people as long as they live up to the law of our land.[76]

Seeing through a Glass Darkly

Though Eleanor Roosevelt acknowledged that she had a minority opinion, she still used her platform to express her convictions on drinking fewer or no alcoholic beverages.

Beer was still a presidential favorite. President Kennedy liked Heineken, and "during Gerald Ford's era, presidential aides arranged for much-coveted Coors beer to be transported on the presidential backup plane, since it was then a rare treat on the East Coast."[77] At that time, and it may seem ridiculous now, Coors wasn't available east of the Mississippi. In fact, a key plot line of the cult classic film *Smokey and the Bandit* was about smuggling some Coors beer to the East Coast. There is rumored to be a photograph of some Coors beer actually being loaded onto *Air Force One* during one of President Ford's visits to Colorado, but that potentially embarrassing photograph is difficult to find. Rivaling the embarrassment caused by President Ford's covetousness of Coors beer was the unabashed self-promotion of "Billy Beer" by Billy Carter during his older brother Jimmy Carter's presidency. Billy Beer lasted less than a year as a commercial venture, but Billy Carter milked as much publicity out of it as he could—much to the chagrin of President Carter.

Beer wasn't overtly linked to the presidency from the 1970s until the 2004 presidential election, when an unusual question started to be asked in polls to determine a candidate's "likeability." That question was, "With which candidate would you like to have a beer?" Beer, not unsurprisingly, has long been the official beverage of the common man. During that election, President George W. Bush easily beat John Kerry. In 2008, beer companies got in on the fun. The Half Moon Bay Brewing Company in Northern California created ale that was bottled and labeled separately as "McCain" and "Obama." In the mock "Alection," Obama steadily outperformed the McCain brew.[78] In 2012, it really wasn't a fair question since Obama's rival, Mitt Romney, didn't drink alcohol.[79]

With respect to presidential drinkways, beer comes with a twist, because our first African American president is also a home-brewed beer enthusiast, and beer has marked his presidency more than any other food or drink item. The first was a highly publicized "Beer Summit" that he convened to reconcile the tensions that erupted between Professor Henry Louis Gates Jr., African American scholar, and Sergeant James Crowley of the Cambridge, Massachusetts, police department. Crowley arrested and detained Gates after a neighbor reported a strange man breaking into the home next door. It turned out to be Gates's own home, and he was trying to get in because he had lost his keys. The false arrest made national news, and given the intersection of race, notoriety, and crime, President Obama was asked to comment on what seemed to be a local police matter. Obama made the remark that Sergeant Crowley had "acted stupidly," and all political hell broke loose. Obama proposed that Crowley and Gates come to the White House to have beer with him and Vice President Joe Biden to talk it out. That 30 July 2009 gathering has been christened the "Beer Summit." As for their drink selections? "The four drank out of beer mugs," the *New York Times* reported. "Mr. Obama had a Bud Lite, Sergeant Crowley had Blue Moon, Professor Gates drank Sam Adams Light and Mr. Biden, who does not drink, had a Buckler nonalcoholic beer." Mr. Biden put a lime slice in his beer. Sergeant Crowley, for his part, kept with Blue Moon tradition and had a slice of orange in his drink.[80]

Obama's next big beer splash came in September 2012, a few months before his second presidential election, when his White House announced that beer was being brewed in the kitchen. After an online campaign, public pressure nudged Obama and his private chef Sam Kass to release recipes for White House Honey Ale and White House Honey Porter. The honey used in the recipes was cultivated from a beehive kept on the grounds. Helpfully, the White House also released a short video of the brewers in action, and it is interesting to note that White House sous chef Tafari Campbell, an African American, is prominently featured. I immediately thought of the African Americans who brewed beer for Washington and Jefferson and was pleased to see the historical arc played out through the suds. As noted earlier, Washington loved ales and porters, and in my imagination I picture those early slaveholding presidents bonding over beer with the first African American president.

Our national obsession with alcoholic drinks gives presidential beverages a moral and political dimension that doesn't exist with food. Where food is arguably a window on the president's soul, intoxicating drinks represent a struggle for the presidential soul itself. The African American butlers and stewards who have helped satiate the presidential thirst play a singular role. Given all of the pressures that come with the job, they help create an escape, a retreat, a safe place for the president to unwind and relax. In essence, they provide the ultimate comfort and liquid courage.

Recipes

This recipe for a punch cocktail was inspired by President Obama and created by Brooklyn bartender extraordinaire Shannon Mustipher. It's modeled after the Roman Punch No. 2 recipe in *The White House Cookbook*, published in 1887, and it has sparked a number of variations. Tom Bullock, the first African American to publish a book on mixology, included one in *The Ideal Bartender*. The original recipe used a blend of rum and cognac and was topped with sparkling wine. This rendition uses applejack, an American spirit that is more affordable than cognac—and one of the most consumed spirits in colonial America. The citrus beer replaces the sparkling wine, which is a nod to President Obama's passion for brews and makes the punch easy to enjoy in any season.

Makes 12 servings

2 cups sugar

1 cup water

3 whole cloves

250 milliliters grapefruit juice

1.5 liters aged white rum (try Denizen Aged White, Angostura White, or Plantation 3Star)

500 milliliters Laird's applejack

500 milliliters lemon juice

100 milliliters Angostura bitters

100 milliliters Peychaud's bitters

1. Combine the sugar, water, and cloves in a small saucepan and bring to a low boil. Reduce the heat and simmer for 20 minutes.
2. Add the grapefruit juice and bring to a boil; reduce the heat and simmer for 20 minutes.
3. Combine the grapefruit mixture with the remaining ingredients and chill overnight to marry and integrate the flavors.
4. Fill a 16- to 20-ounce rectangular plastic container with water and freeze overnight.
5. To serve, place the block of ice in a punch bowl and pour the punch over it. Add 500 milliliters of cold water and stir.
6. Garnish the punch with grapefruit and lemon slices.
7. Serve in tumblers over ice and top with a saison or other light

beer with strong grapefruit or citrus notes. Another option is to add a bottle of your favorite hard cider.

WHITE HOUSE EGGNOG

The recipe for eggnog used for many years by White House butlers called for "a gallon of commercial eggnog mix." I thought that might be hard to find, so we have here the recipe for eggnog that I drank at the holiday parties that I attended while I served in the White House. This version comes from the recipe files of the late White House executive chef Walter Scheib.

Makes about 1/2 gallon

6–7 eggs (pasteurized if possible), separated
1 cup sugar
3/4 cup bourbon
3/4 cup Cognac
3/4 cup dark rum (Scheib recommended Meyers)
1 teaspoon salt
2 cups heavy cream
1 tablespoon vanilla extract
1 quart milk (or more if a thinner consistency is desired)
Freshly grated nutmeg, for serving

1. Combine the egg yolks and sugar in the bowl of a stand mixer fitted with a whisk attachment and whip to ribbon stage (lemon yellow in color), 5–7 minutes.
2. Add the alcohol, and mix well; scrape sides of the bowl and mix again.
3. Pour the mix into a 1 1/2-gallon bowl and set aside.
4. In a separate clean mixer bowl using a clean beater, whip the egg whites and salt into very stiff peaks and fold them into the mixture in the bowl.
5. Wipe out the mixer bowl, pour in the cream and vanilla, and whip until very stiff peaks form. Fold this into the eggnog mixture.
6. Add the milk and whisk until smooth. This may take 3–5 minutes, as the meringue and cream must be mixed completely.
7. Transfer the mixture to a sealable container and refrigerate for 3–5 days. If the foam rises from the eggnog mixture during refrigeration, reincorporate it by whisking right before serving.
8. Serve very cold topped with a sprinkle of nutmeg.

Seeing through a Glass Darkly

WHITE HOUSE HONEY ALE

This ale is a shout-out to President Thomas Jefferson, who loved ale. Martha Wayles Jefferson used to make small batches of ale early in their marriage. Though there isn't much evidence that Jefferson brewed beer while he was in the White House, he certainly brewed beer back at Monticello after his presidency. He often charged Peter Hemings to oversee all brewing activities, and evidently Hemings was quite good at it. Jefferson offered Hemings's tutoring services to other planters desiring to kickstart their brewing activities. I thank Tom Schurmann and his team at Tom's Brew Shop in Lakewood, Colorado, for brewing this beer, and taste-testing it with their customers. Tom also offered some very helpful tweaks to the recipe that appeared on the WhiteHouse.gov website should be of use to home brewers. Note that you'll need a 28-inch mesh bag for steeping malts.

Makes 53 twelve-ounce glasses of beer

12 ounces crushed amber crystal malt
8 ounces Biscuit Malt
2 (3.3-pound) cans light malt extract
1 pound light dried malt extract
1 1/2 ounces Kent Goldings hop pellets
2 teaspoons gypsum
1 1/2 ounces Fuggles hop pellets
1 pound honey
1 package Windsor dry ale yeast
3/4 cup corn sugar, for priming

1. In a 12-quart pot, steep all of the malts in the mesh bag in 1 1/2 gallons of sterile water at 155°F for half an hour. Remove the grains and set aside.
2. Add the liquid and dried malt extracts and bring to a boil.
3. For the first flavoring, add the Kent Goldings hop pellets and the gypsum. Boil for 45 minutes.
4. At the last minute of the boil, for the second flavoring, add the Fuggles hop pellets.
5. Add the honey and boil for 5 more minutes.
6. Add 2 gallons of chilled sterile water into the primary fermenter and add the hot wort. Top with more water to total 5 gallons. There is no need to strain.

7. Pitch the yeast when the wort temperature is between 70° and 80°F. Fill the airlock halfway with water or vodka or a sanitizer.
8. Ferment at 68°–72°F for about 7 days.
9. Rack to a secondary fermenter after 5 days and ferment for 14 more days.
10. To bottle, dissolve the corn sugar into 2 pints of boiling water for 15 minutes. Pour the mixture into an empty bottling bucket. Siphon the beer from the fermenter over it. Distribute the priming sugar evenly. Siphon into bottles and cap. Let sit for 2–3 weeks at 75°F.

7
Above Measure

THE FUTURE OF AFRICAN AMERICAN
PRESIDENTIAL CHEFS

You just don't exist for all intents and purposes. . . .
You are the most famous anonymous chef on Earth.
Everybody talks about it, but nobody really knows about it.
WALTER SCHEIB,
"Obamas Have a Habit of Inviting Celebrity Guest Chefs,"
HuffingtonPost.com, 4 April 2010

On 19 December 1789, presidential steward Samuel Fraunces placed an advertisement in the *New York Packet* newspaper to fill the first presidential cook position: "A *Cook* is wanted for the President of the United States. No one need apply who is not perfect in the business, and can bring indubitable testimonials of sobriety, honesty, and attention to the duties of the station."[1] As we look back on the personalities met and the stories shared in this book, a historical update of the job announcement would probably read, "In addition to the duties described above, you will be called upon from time to time to fill any one of the following roles: baby sitter, barbecue pit master, civil rights adviser, comfort food enabler, confidant, controversy sparker, culinary artist, diet enforcer, diplomat, disaster relief worker, entertainer, pet detective/sitter, property clerk, school transporter, security detail, sommelier, and spin doctor." With all of the additional duties, the at times high-stress environment, and relatively modest salary, one might wonder, "Who would want that job?" Mainly due to the prestige of the position, the short answer is "Plenty of people."

I suspect that you have never heard about many of the culinary professionals mentioned in this book. Much of the venerable presidential history we consume omits these people primarily due to a mix of condescension and contempt toward African Americans on the part of the white historians who wrote the stories. Black people simply were not considered important enough to be part of the narrative. If blacks were mentioned at all, they were portrayed more like curiosities than people. More contemporary presidential history is worse in a unique way: the writers tend to be lazy. Even though information is now readily available to researchers, lots of writers seem to think that ignorance is too blissful to avoid. Life in a bubble can be very good, but a good story could be richer if more voices were added to give perspective. When food service in the modern White House is examined, I hope that reporters and writers will acknowledge that there are more cooks in the kitchen than the executive chef and the pastry chef.

Given the rich, previously hidden legacy that we've now made plain, the question must be asked: could an African American once again helm the White House kitchen? The resounding answer is yes! Any future president can make that choice. Fortunately, the question of culinary competence is no longer an issue. Don't be fooled by the occasional "Where are the black chefs?" articles you may see in the mainstream media. Unlike in the days when Jacqueline Kennedy made European cooking de rigueur in the White House kitchen, thousands of African American chefs now working in private homes, hotels, resorts, and restaurants have the credentials and expertise to execute any cuisine they might be asked to prepare. Though few structural barriers exist to getting a job in the White House kitchen, several challenges do still persist. Much as it was in George Washington's day, becoming a White House chef depends on a combination of skill, knowing (or working for) the right people, timing, and some good old-fashioned luck. Of these elements, knowing the right people is the most challenging, because it's where the legacy of slavery and segregation has lingered the longest.

Despite decades of progress on civil rights and integration, many Americans still live, love, play, socialize, work, and worship with people who are like themselves. Unless people are intentional about diversifying their social circles, they tend to live in a homogeneous bubble. Thus, when a job opportunity arises, rather than cast a broad net to find the best person qualified for that opportunity (meritocracy), decision makers will often select someone in their own family (nepotism) or someone they know very well (cronyism). There are practical reasons for this. With some jobs, you want to be sure the person is up to the task and that he or she can be trusted, and there's a short time to make a decision.

Here's how this unintentionally affects the White House job prospects of a typical chef. Let's say that those who aspire to be a White House executive chef do all they can to burnish their résumé so that they can get that job: they go to a great culinary school; they get a nice job as a sous chef in a well-regarded hotel or restaurant; they join the right professional associations and network like crazy until they have a decent public profile. Those chefs has made all of the right moves but may never be considered for the White House executive chef position unless they happen to be friends with someone with access to the First Family or to the White House staff or they have an opportunity to cook in the kitchen of a political elite. Before the 1960s, most African American presidential cooks took the latter route to the White House kitchen. Since then, the African Americans who serve as assistant chefs have predominantly come with hotel and military experience. It's been two decades since the stars properly aligned and an African American was offered the White House executive chef position. That honor went to the late and acclaimed Chef Patrick Clark, and even he, as we'll see in a moment, wasn't a "perfect fit" for the job.

Patrick Clark grew up in Brooklyn, New York, the son of a professional chef (Melvin Clark) who took great care in his craft and even banned Velveeta from the family kitchen. Young Patrick, though discouraged from entering the arduous culinary profession by the very man whose cooking he admired, got his training the same place his father did—New York City Technical College. After obtaining further training in Europe, Clark went on to work and eventually helm some of the nation's finest restaurants—Bice in Beverly Hills; Café Luxembourg, Metro (his first solely owned restaurant), Odeon, and Tavern on the Green in New York City; and the restaurants at the Hay-Adams Hotel in Washington, D.C. While at Tavern on the Green, Clark was named best mid-Atlantic chef by the James Beard Foundation in 1995.

These achievements led Chef Marcus Samuelsson to write posthumously of Patrick Clark that he was considered to be the "first Black celebrity chef." Samuelsson added, "Clark helped make classical French cuisine—considered the bedrock of western cooking—more approachable when he created his own version of contemporary American cuisine with dishes like Horseradish Crusted Grouper and mashed potatoes, jerk chicken with sweet potato cakes, rack of lamb with fried white bean ravioli and salmon with Moroccan barbeque sauce."[2] Even celebrity chef Anthony Bourdain, who doesn't suffer fools, admired Clark's skills. "There was no one on the horizon we could see who could touch us," he wrote in *Kitchen Confidential*.

Okay—there was one guy. Patrick Clark. Patrick was the chef of the red-hot Odeon in nascent Tribeca, a [New York City] neighborhood that seemed not to have existed until Patrick started cooking there. We followed his exploits with no small amount of envy . . . he was an *American*, one of us, not some cheese-eating, surrender-specialist Froggie. Patrick Clark, whether he would have appreciated it or not, he was our hometown hero, our Joe DiMaggio—a shining example that *it could be done*.[3]

Reportedly, Chef Clark was offered the White House job after the First Family tasted a salmon dish that Clark had prepared.[4]

In 1993, Clark started getting some influential customers. *Black Enterprise* reported, "Luckily for Clark and the Clintons, they are neighbors. The Hay-Adams sits directly across the street from the nation's most famous residence. The Clintons frequently cart guests over to the hotel, making the Hay-Adams a venue of choice for Washington's power dining."[5] Unbeknownst to Clark, several meals that he cooked were edible auditions for another job. The magazine continued, "Hillary Clinton, then still settling into the White House, offered Clark the job of White House chef. Clark turned it down. 'I felt the White House would be too restrictive for me,' Clark explains simply, adding that he had a three-year commitment to fulfill with the Hay-Adams Hotel, where he had just started as executive chef."[6] Another factor was a Freedom of Information Act–type secret: chefs can make a lot more money in the private sector than they do at the White House. Chef Walter Scheib told me that when he was hired in the 1990s, the typical salary could be anywhere between $50,000 and $70,000.[7] When current White House executive chef Cristeta Comerford got the position in 2005, one newspaper reported her salary range as between $80,000 and $100,000.[8] Clark thus turned down the position because he had "five kids and five college tuitions to save for."[9] At the time he was offered the White House gig, Clark was making $170,000 a year at the Hay-Adams, and in his next job at the Tavern on the Green in New York City, he made a reported $500,000 annually, including perks such as traveling around the world to do cooking demonstrations.[10] Even though Clark met all of the criteria for being a White House executive chef, the "timing" was off. The job offer came at the wrong time in Clark's career (he was too prominent) and family life.

One may be surprised to learn this, but filling a vacant White House executive chef position has long had its challenges. Long hours, high pressure, the small work space, and less pay offset the prestige factor. As the Clark example shows, the White House has to call at the right time in the career of a chef who is ascending. This by no means implies that White House chefs are not at the top of their game; I'm just noting that a highly accomplished veteran chef or television personality would have to give up a lot of money to serve his or her country in this capacity. "Sacrifice" doesn't resonate as a rallying cry as it once did for those of the World War II era, the "Greatest Generation." A hungry, talented chef "on the rise" faces an easier choice. Though Clark turned down the job, he was willing to help out whenever the president called on him.

That gave Clark the chance to act as guest chef for the meal of a lifetime: the state dinner held for South African president Nelson Mandela in October 1994. This function was one of the most consequential state dinners of the Clinton administration, honoring Mandela's first visit to the White House since he was freed from prison in February 1990. According to Chef Scheib, rather than hosting the dinner in the usual State Dining Room, the Clintons held the dinner "in the East Room, because it was the room in which President Lyndon Johnson signed the Civil Rights Act of 1964."[11] Scheib continued,

> After our new protocol of featuring a dish that saluted the guest of honor's homeland, we served a starter of Layered Late-Summer Vegetables with Lemongrass and Red Curry—loosely based on the South African style of food called Cape Malay cuisine, which combines ingredients of South Africa, seasonings of South Asia and India, and cooking techniques of Europe. We also invited a guest chef-collaborator to this evening, African-American chef Patrick Clark . . . with whom we conceived the main course, Halibut with a Sesame Crust and Carrot Juice Broth.[12]

After the initial consultation on the Mandela state dinner menu, the White House unveiled another surprise to Chef Clark—an invitation to prepare the meal. As Clark's then sous chef Donnie Masterson recalled,

> Patrick was honored to accept the offer [to cook the state dinner]. The White House later informed Patrick that [instead] he was to attend the dinner with his wife, Lynette. Patrick was as passionate as he was protective of his food, so he told the White House that he would feel more confident if his own chef [Masterton] were to execute his entrée. I felt unbelievably honored and proud to be representing not only the White House but also Patrick Clark. . . . I was Patrick's chef, but he was always within arm's reach of his food. On

DINNER

Honoring
Mr. Nelson Mandela
President of the Republic of South Africa

Layered Late Summer Vegetables
with Lemongrass and Red Curry

Halibut with Sesame Crust
Carrot Juice Broth

Bibb Endive and Watercress
with New York Wild Ripened Cheese

Granadilla Sherbet
Lychees and Raspberries
Apple Sabayon
Cookies

JOSEPH PHELPS *Viognier 1993*
PETER MICHAEL *Chardonnay 1991*
PIPER SONOMA *Tête de Cuvée 1985*

The White House
Tuesday, October 4, 1994

Republic of South Africa State Dinner menu card, 1994.
Courtesy William J. Clinton Presidential Center/NARA.

. . .

that night, he had to let go. I prepared a sesame and wasabi–crusted halibut. The meal was flawless. The next day, Patrick told me I had done justice to his dish and had made him proud.[13]

Though Chef Clark didn't actually cook the state dinner's entrée, he savored that dish and the extraordinary moment.

Sadly, Chef Clark developed congestive heart failure a few years later and was desperately in need of a heart transplant. In 1997, the day after Thanksgiving, Clark checked into New York's Columbia-Presbyterian Medical Center to undergo a heart transplant. During his stay, he was so disappointed with hospital food that he had family members and loved ones sneak in cooking gear and food. At first, Clark kept a veil of secrecy over his clandestine culinary efforts that churned out dishes like grilled chicken with lemon and herbs and cauliflower steamed with garlic, but he later "sought attention because he hoped it would help force an improvement in the hospital food."[14] While in the hospital, Clark was diagnosed with another condition that prevented him from getting a new heart. He died two years later in Princeton, New Jersey.

In the nearly three decades that he cooked professionally, Patrick Clark, a dedicated husband and loving father, was acutely aware of the impact that he could make on American cuisine and of his place in American race relations. The *New York Times* reported, "'He didn't feel there was prejudice against him,' said Stephen Moise, the executive sous chef at the Tavern [on the Green]. 'But he could see how young African-American kids could feel that there was a lot against them, and he wanted to be an example of somebody who succeeded by working hard and believing in himself."[15] Bruce Wynn, an African American who worked as a pastry chef while Clark ran the Tavern on the Green, said, "He lived the flavor that he grew up on, and he spread that flavor."[16]

Chef Marcus Samuelsson has been the only other notable chef of African heritage to act as guest chef for a White House state dinner. Samuelsson was born in Ethiopia, was adopted and raised by a Swedish family in Sweden, and then immigrated to the United States to start what would become a highly decorated culinary career. The White House described Samuelsson's career in the press materials for the 24 November 2009 state dinner honoring the prime minister of India and his wife:

At the age of 39, Marcus Samuelsson has received more accolades than many chefs receive in a lifetime. A graduate of the Culinary Institute in Gothenburg, Samuelsson apprenticed in Switzerland,

Austria, France and the U.S. In 1995 he was hired as Aquavit's Executive Chef. Just 3 months later, Aquavit received a three-star review from *The New York Times*. Samuelsson was honored with the James Beard Foundation Award for "Rising Star Chef" in 1999 and "Best Chef, New York" in 2003. He was also celebrated as one of "The Great Chefs of America" by The Culinary Institute of America.[17]

Samuelsson obviously had the credentials to cook in the White House, but it took another special ingredient to get this dream cooking assignment that he didn't seek.

In between ending his association with New York's Aquavit restaurant and competing on *Top Chef Masters*, Chef Samuelsson got a call from a good friend. That good friend happened to be Chef Sam Kass, who was the personal White House chef for the Obamas at that time.

> Sam was calling to ask if I'd be interested in creating the menu for the Obamas' first state dinner. He told me he was speaking to a few other chefs, too, and that the state dinner was going to honor Prime Minister Manmohan Singh of India and his wife, Gursharan Kaur. Sam was asking if I'd make dishes that had a subtle Indian influence, and since the honored guests are both vegetarians, to make sure we could create a meal that would be very flavorful with no meat. The finalists would be chosen after evaluating each chef's menu. It was the kind of call chefs dream of receiving, and in many ways it was far more important to me than anything that was happening on TV.[18]

Given his established reputation as an excellent chef and his friendship with Kass, Samuelsson was able to get on the short list. After a Sunday audition in his New York home for Kass, Samuelsson won the assignment and went on to make the state dinner. Though the attendees would describe the meal as memorable, the event itself was notable due to a couple of party-crashers whose ability to get past White House security and attend the dinner ultimately cost White House social secretary Desirée Rogers her job. In the end, Samuelsson's experience is a useful roadmap for any chef who wants to be on the White House's short list for guest chef. It's all about being part of the conversation.

Aside from doing something illegal, actively and publicly campaigning is really the only "uncool" thing to do when seeking a White House chef job. This is a throwback to the early days of the presidency when the office was perceived as performing a duty for one's country. In fact, when the Democratic Party chose him as its presidential nominee in the election of 1844, James Polk said in his acceptance speech that the presidency "should neither be sought nor declined."[19] In this context, working in the White House kitchen is about serving your country. As Walter Scheib put it, "None of these people have any idea what the job is about. . . . And they're temperamentally not suited for it. You have to be a person who has a real heart of service, and it can't be someone who needs to see themselves on camera."[20]

Don't get the impression that being a White House guest chef is always a "lovefest." The politics of being a guest chef at the White House can get a little hectic, and the practice is not without its critics. Longtime White House pastry chef Roland Mesnier once said this on a panel of former White House staffers hosted by the White House Historical Association and broadcast on C-SPAN:

> "I am the chef of the White House, who does everything for the family and guests, day in and day out, but the day that I can shine I'm told that somebody else is coming in," he said. "I take it as a slap on the face as being White House chef." He compared it to him asking to be President for a day. "I don't believe in that, and I never will, because this is my job, and I would like to shine once in a while — and this is my chance."

Mesnier added that these chefs were doing it for self-promotion and probably would decline the chance if they had to keep their collaboration secret.[21]

Scheib underscored that point when speculation was rampant in 2008 about who would be the next White House chef, and many were clamoring for a celebrity chef or someone with an agenda. Chef Scheib said of agenda-driven chefs, "I get a kick out of all these people saying the No. 1 thing should be green, or sustainable or this, that or the other thing. They're missing the point. It's not about advancing your agenda. It's not about building your repertoire. It's not about getting your business promoted. It's about serving the first family, first, last and in every way. That's the only job." Mesnier underscored this point: "Celebrity chefs, in my book, are not chefs. They're entertainers. All these people on TV? Forget it."[22] One can tell that he's not a fan. Another path to the executive chef position is for a future president to choose someone currently on staff. That was the case for White House executive chef Cristeta Comerford, a

Filipina, who began working for the White House in 1995 and then got promoted when Scheib departed in 2005.

The general public tends to not hear much about assistant chefs, let alone the kitchen stewards, but Adam Collick was thrust into the spotlight thanks to First Lady Michelle Obama's "Let's Move!" initiative. Let's Move! was formally launched on 9 February 2010 with the following mission:

> *Let's Move!* is a comprehensive initiative, launched by the First Lady, dedicated to solving the challenge of childhood obesity within a generation, so that children born today will grow up healthier and able to pursue their dreams. Combining comprehensive strategies with common sense, *Let's Move!* is about putting children on the path to a healthy future during their earliest months and years. Giving parents helpful information and fostering environments that support healthy choices. Providing healthier foods in our schools. Ensuring that every family has access to healthy, affordable food. And, helping kids become more physically active.[23]

Let's Move! sparked celebrities, chefs, community leaders in all sectors, doctors, parents, and teachers to get involved with this effort. Though its main objective was to have an impact on children, the initiative has had a rippling effect that goes all the way to the White House kitchen, particularly with Collick.

Collick became a Let's Move! role model to the entire White House staff. Collick is a good-sized man, but he saw an opportunity to be healthier by eliminating extra calories. He eased up on drinking and traded "three 20-ounce cups [of coffee] topped with whipped cream drizzled with chocolate syrup" a day for calorie-free water and decided to eat dessert only a couple of times a week instead of with every meal. Those dietary changes coupled with exercise caused Collick to lose thirty pounds, which made him "a de facto coach to colleagues battling the bulge." He told the Associated Press in an interview that appeared in the *Washington Post*, "Once you see the changes in your body and the way you feel, it's going to make you want to keep doing it."[24] The amazing thing is that Collick did all of this while surrounded by serious temptations. The article continued:

> Overdoing it is easy as a chef in a place where there are few food-free functions — ranging from receptions and dinners for hundreds

Adam Collick, White House kitchen steward, 2003.
Courtesy George W. Bush Presidential Center.

. . .

of visitors to lunch for President Barack Obama and a guest in his private dining room off the Oval Office. One occupational hazard for the chefs is having to taste the food during all stages of preparation to check the flavorings, a seemingly simple task that when performed again and again every day can jeopardize anyone's well-intentioned efforts to eat right.

If not careful, Collick said, the chefs could easily eat an entire meal just by tasting their way through the work day.[25]

I'm sure any cook can relate to how remarkable Collick's accomplishment is.

In the 1960s, there was a popular saying that I believe needs reviving:

"Plant you now, dig you later."[26] In this context, I wonder what seeds are being planted in the dreams of young people that might flower into a desire to work in the White House kitchen. First Lady Michelle Obama has planted seeds that reimagine how the White House connects with our national foodways. The first is the vegetable garden and beehive that now exist on the South Lawn. There have been presidential gardens before, particularly during the nineteenth century (on the site where the current U.S. Treasury Building sits), but never with the scope and fanfare this iteration got when ground was broken on 20 March 2009. Aside from provisioning the White House kitchen and local food banks and schools, Michelle Obama had a larger, metaphorical vision for the garden: "I wanted it to be the starting point for something bigger. As both a mother and a first lady, I was alarmed by reports of skyrocketing childhood obesity rates and the dire consequences for our children's health. And I hoped this garden would help begin a conversation about the food we eat, the lives we lead, and how all of that affects our children."[27] Not surprisingly, given our polarized political environment, there has been mixed reaction to the White House garden—both lauded as a worthy endeavor and lambasted as a worthless expenditure of public resources. Regardless of political opinions, it's hard to argue with her desire to focus on childhood obesity given its rising incidence or with the fact that children don't recognize raw vegetables by sight or realize that potato chips come from potatoes.

Of course, another option is to cultivate and nurture in young people an interest in cooking. First Lady Michelle Obama created a tremendous platform when she created the Kids' State Dinners in 2012 as part of her Let's Move! initiative. In 2012 and every year since, fifty young people, representing their home states, enter a recipe contest to make a healthy food. The winners and their parents get to visit the White House and have a meal in the East Room. Of the now more than two hundred champions, I end this book by focusing on one of the past African American winners: Kiana Farkash of Colorado.[28]

Farkash wanted to cook ever since she was two or three years old, watching her mother, Maureen, who is a good cook in her own right. According to Kiana, her mom made "tasty" food, and Kiana wanted to be like her. In her early years, she was her mom's "sous chef," handing over ingredients and spices and asking questions as Maureen prepared things like tilapia with kale and rice. By the time she was five, she was able to cook on her own; she made scrambled eggs and grilled cheese sandwiches. It's no surprise that a few years later, while surfing the Epicurious website, Farkash's grandmother saw an advertisement to participate in something called the "Kids' State Dinner" and suggested Kiana enter the competition. Farkash asked for further explanation and blithely replied to her grandmother, "I'll think about it." Farkash decided to go for it and devised a recipe for grilled salmon with farro and a warm Swiss chard salad. All of the other ingredients pivoted off the Swiss chard, since her family garden was full of it. In addition, she paired her dish with a tropical fruit smoothie because she thought "kids would like something sweet."

Sometime later, Farkash's mom got an e-mail from the White House informing her that Farkash had won, and they both started jumping up and down with excitement. On 18 July 2014, Farkash, along with the other winners, enjoyed a private tour of the White House and its garden, special talks by Michelle Obama and White House chef Sam Kass, a surprise appearance by President Obama, a special performance of *The Lion King*, and participation in television interviews. On top of that, Farkash was one of two kids picked to help the White House kitchen chefs with plating the dishes that were served at the dinner. (She put microgreens on the spinach frittata.)

Michelle Obama hoped that the Kids' State Dinner, as an adjunct of the Let's Move! initiative, would be inspirational. At the very first dinner, she remarked,

> Let's Move! is all about . . . all of us coming together to make sure that all of you kids and kids like you across the country have everything you need to learn and grow and lead happy, healthy lives. It's about parents making choices for their kids—choices that work with their families, schedules, budgets and tastes, because there is no one-size-fits-all here; as parents we know what works for one kid in one household doesn't work for the other kid in the same household. So we've got to be flexible. And it's about kids like all of you doing your part to eat well and get active, which is an important part. We never want to underestimate the importance of getting up and moving. So stay active. Get involved in cooking delicious, good stuff—dishes like the ones we're going to try today.[29]

Farkash certainly took those rallying points home with her, especially the ones on healthy cooking. She emphatically told me that "healthy food doesn't have to sacrifice on taste." She also brought home the aspiration to become a professional chef when she grows up. A White House chef,

Kiana Farkash at the 2014 Kids' State Dinner. Courtesy Maureen Farkash.

. . .

perhaps? "I don't know if I could do that," she said. "Don't you have to audition?" I assured her that by the time she could be considered for that position, she'll have the skills.[30]

In the meantime, I wondered what Farkash will do with her burgeoning talent, now that she is at the point where she's creating her own dishes. She would love to cook a meal for the First Family, probably pan-seared cod with snow peas and curried rice—the latter inspired by a nice meal at Rasika, an Indian restaurant in Washington, D.C., recommended to her by her hotel concierge and which she found out the Obamas also love. I asked whom she would cook for if she could choose anyone in the world. Like other ten-year-olds, I expected her to list an actor, athlete, entertainer, politician—or someone with Kardashian in their name. No, Farkash said that she would like to "cook for a family who doesn't know how to cook or who doesn't have access to good ingredients."[31] Kiana is acutely aware of the growing problem of food deserts (areas where people lack access to healthy and affordable food, especially fresh produce) and malnourished, impoverished families. She knows kids whose main meal during the day consists entirely of junk food, and what the school offers is not much better. Don't be surprised if for a high school community service project she ends up creating a farmer's market in one of those food deserts. Farkash may wind up cooking for the president or advising the president on food policy—or may even be the president one day. As it should be, the sky's the limit.

Only time will tell if Kiana Farkash, or another young person like her, will become a White House chef, but she already sees herself as a "change agent." She can take inspiration in the legacy of the African American presidential chefs profiled in these pages. Even though they operated mostly out of public view, they asserted their humanity in ways that affected how presidents, First Families, White House staffers, the nation, and, in some cases, the world viewed African Americans. The term "kitchen cabinet" has traditionally been understood as an informal group of advisers and counselors whom a president consults when the need arises. Black chefs certainly participated in that role, and we now know how strong their agency often was and their importance to presidential history. They gave the most powerful chief executive of the United States of America a unique view of black life and black people. Through their work as culinary professionals, they confronted, contested, and ultimately creamed a racial caste system designed to keep them at society's margins. Instead, over a daily table, they nourished our presidents to truly taste the desire of an entire people to fully participate in American society.

Recipes

SESAME AND WASABI–CRUSTED HALIBUT

Chef Patrick Clark developed this recipe for the 4 October 1994 White House state dinner honoring Nelson Mandela, then president of the Republic of South Africa.

Makes 4 servings

For the halibut

> 1/2 cup black sesame seeds
> 1/2 cup white sesame seeds
> 4 (7-ounce) halibut fillets
> Salt and freshly ground black pepper
> Flour for dusting
> 2 tablespoons wasabi paste
> 1/4 cup plus 2 tablespoons olive oil

For the carrots

> 6 carrots, peeled
> 1 1/2 teaspoons cornstarch
> 2 tablespoons butter
> Salt and freshly ground black pepper, to taste
> Ground nutmeg, to taste
> Extra-virgin olive oil
> 12 sprigs chervil

To prepare the halibut:

1. Mix together the black and white sesame seeds on a plate.
2. Season the halibut with salt and pepper and dust the flat side of the halibut with flour.
3. With a spatula or small knife, spread the wasabi paste on the dusted side of the halibut, avoiding the sides of the fillet.
4. Lay the fillets, paste-side-down in the sesame seeds, pressing the fish into the seeds to ensure complete coverage.
5. Place on a plate, cover, and refrigerate until ready to cook.
6. Preheat the oven to 350°F. Heat the olive oil in a large, nonstick, ovenproof sauté pan over medium heat.
7. Place the fillets in the pan, crust-side-down and sear them until golden.
8. Turn the fillets over and place the pan in the oven for 4 or 5 minutes, or until cooked medium rare.

To prepare the carrots:
1. Scoop the carrots with a melon baller, reserving the scraps.
2. Blanch the carrot balls in salted water for 3 minutes, drain, and shock in ice water.
3. Remove from the water and set aide.

To prepare the carrot broth:
1. Purée the carrot scraps in a food processor and strain through a fine-mesh sieve.
2. In a small bowl, mix 4 tablespoons of the carrot juice with the cornstarch to create a slurry.
3. Put the remaining carrot juice in a saucepan and bring to a boil, then lower the heat to a simmer and whisk in the slurry and the butter.
4. Transfer the broth to a double boiler and add the carrot balls.
5. Season with salt, pepper, and nutmeg and keep warm.

To serve:
1. Place each fillet in the center of a large, shallow bowl.
2. Spoon the carrot balls and the sauce evenly around the fish.
3. Drizzle a few drops of the olive oil into the broth and garnish with the chervil sprigs.

LAYERED LATE-SUMMER VEGETABLES WITH LEMONGRASS AND RED CURRY DRESSING

Former White House executive chef Walter Scheib created this side dish with seasonal ingredients available in the United States to pay homage to South Africa's indigenous food culture. You'll need 4 ring molds (3 inches in diameter and 2 inches high) for this recipe.

Makes 4 servings

For the dressing
1/2 tablespoon olive oil
1 tablespoon minced shallot
2 teaspoons grated garlic
2 teaspoons grated lemongrass (white base portion only; peel off outer layer before grating)
1 teaspoon finely grated lime zest
1 teaspoon red curry paste
1 teaspoon grated fresh ginger
1 makrut lime leaf (optional)

1/2 cup homemade or store-bought low-sodium chicken stock

1/2 cup unsweetened coconut milk

1 tablespoon honey

1/4 teaspoon fish sauce

For the vegetables

1 medium cucumber (about 4 ounces)

1/2 tablespoon salt

1 tablespoon seasoned rice vinegar

1 tablespoon chopped fresh dill

4 ounces butternut squash, peeled, seeded, and sliced 1/4 inch thick (about 1/3 cup sliced)

2 tablespoons olive oil

Salt and freshly ground black pepper, to taste

2–4 small red-skinned potatoes (4 ounces), sliced 1/4 inch thick (about 1/2 cup slices)

1 medium zucchini (about 4 ounces), sliced 1/4 inch thick (about 1/2 cup sliced)

1/2 tablespoon minced garlic

1/4 cup uncooked corn kernels (fresh or frozen, thawed, and drained)

1/4 cup thinly sliced leek (white part only)

1 medium red bell pepper, roasted, skinned, seeds removed, and very thinly sliced

Crispy noodles, such as rice noodles, for garnish (optional)

4 sprigs Thai basil or regular basil, for garnish

To prepare the dressing:

1. Heat the oil in a small saucepan over medium heat.
2. Add the shallot, garlic, lemongrass, and lime zest and sauté until softened but not browned, 2–3 minutes.
3. Add the curry paste, ginger, and lime leaf, if using, and cook, stirring, for 2–3 minutes.
4. Add the stock, coconut milk, honey, and fish sauce.
5. Bring to a simmer and cook for 10 minutes.
6. Strain the mixture through a fine-mesh strainer set over a bowl, pressing down on the solids with a wooden spoon or spatula to extract as much flavorful liquid as possible.
7. Discard the solids and let the dressing cool to room temperature.
8. The dressing can be covered and refrigerated for up to 1 week. It will separate; whisk and warm it to reconstitute.

To prepare the vegetables:
1. Peel the cucumber, halve it lengthwise, scoop out the seeds, and cut it crosswise into 1/4-inch slices.
2. Put the cumber slices in a colander, toss with the salt, and set the colander in the sink to drain for 10–15 minutes to extract any excess moisture.
3. Pat dry with paper towels.
4. Stir together the rice vinegar and dill in a small bowl.
5. Add the cucumber, season with salt and pepper, and toss. Set aside.
6. Preheat a 12-inch, heavy-bottomed sauté pan over medium-high heat.
7. Brush the squash slices with 1/2 tablespoon of the olive oil, season with salt and pepper, add to the pan, and cook just until tender, 1–2 minutes per side.
8. Transfer to a baking sheet and set aside.
9. Carefully wipe out the sauté pan.
10. Brush the potato slices with a 1/2 tablespoon of olive oil, season with salt and pepper, add to the pan, and cook over medium-high heat until tender, 1–2 minutes per side.
11. Transfer to a baking sheet and set aside.
12. Wipe out the pan. Brush the zucchini slices with 1/2 tablespoon of the olive oil, season with salt and pepper, add to the pan, and cook over medium-high heat just until tender, about 30 seconds. (The zucchini is tender enough that you only need to cook the slices on 1 side.)
13. Transfer to the baking sheet with the squash.
14. Wipe out the pan. Add the remaining oil and heat it over medium heat. Add the garlic and sauté for 30 seconds.
15. Add the corn and leek and sauté just until al dente, about 3 minutes.
16. Layer the vegetables into the ring molds, in any order you like, so long as the zucchini is on top.

To serve:
1. Place a salad plate face down over a ring mold and invert the mold onto the plate. Repeat with the other molds.
2. Drizzle 2–3 tablespoons of the dressing around the ring mold on each plate, then carefully remove the mold.
3. Garnish with crisp noodles, if desired, and basil leaves. Serve.

Kiana Farkash won a trip to the White House with this recipe when she was just eight years old. "I made grilled salmon because it is one of my very favorite dishes," says Farkash. "I made the salad because it is very colorful and it reminds me of spring. I like warm, tropical places, so I decided to serve this with a tropical breeze smoothie because it reminds me of our family trip to Florida. I used farro because it's a healthy whole grain and I like the nuttier flavor it has!"

Makes 4 servings

For the salmon and farro
  1 cup farro
  2 tablespoons olive oil
  4 salmon fillets (about 1 pound)
  2 tablespoons herbes de Provence
  Salt and pepper, to taste
  Pinch of garlic powder
  Pinch of onion powder
  1 lemon, thinly sliced

For the salad
  1/2 tablespoon olive oil
  Bunch Swiss chard, roughly chopped
  1 large carrot, julienned
  1 large red bell pepper, julienned
  1 tablespoon balsamic vinegar
  Salt and pepper, to taste
  Crumbled feta cheese, to taste (optional)

For the smoothie
  1 cup orange juice
  1 cup "lite" coconut milk
  2 cups low-fat vanilla yogurt
  1 teaspoon vanilla extract
  2 frozen bananas
  1 cup frozen cut mango
  1/2 teaspoon freshly ground nutmeg

To prepare the farro and salmon:
  1. In a large pot, boil 2 cups of water over high heat.
  2. Add the farro and bring back to a boil.

3. Reduce the heat to low, cover, and simmer for 30 minutes, or until the grains are tender and all the water is absorbed.
4. Preheat the grill.
5. Drizzle the olive oil over both sides of the salmon fillets.
6. Mix the spices in a small bowl and sprinkle evenly to coat the salmon on both sides.
7. Grill the fillets for up to 5 minutes per side, depending on how thick the salmon is.
8. After flipping the salmon on the grill, place the lemon slices on the fish. Remove from the grill and keep warm in a 200° oven while you make the salad.
9. To serve, spoon a generous portion of farro on the plate and lay the salmon fillets on top of the farro.

To prepare the salad:
1. In a large pan, warm the olive oil over medium heat.
2. Add the Swiss chard and cook for 2 minutes.
3. Add the carrot and bell pepper and cook for 2 minutes more.
4. When Swiss chard wilts, add the balsamic vinegar and season with salt and pepper; sprinkle with feta cheese, if desired.

To prepare the smoothie:
1. Add the liquid ingredients to the blender first, and blend.
2. Add the rest of the ingredients.
3. Blend again and enjoy!

NOTES

PREFACE

1. Adler and Adler, *Kids' Letters to President Obama*, 57–58.

CHAPTER 1

1. "Forty Pound Turkey," 2.

2. "Yessah, Mistah Taft." The term "Lucullan" refers to the famous Roman general and politician named Lucullus (118–56 B.C.E.) who was known for his extravagant banquets.

3. Ibid.

4. Smith and Morris, *Dear Mr. President*, 67–68.

5. Ibid., 68.

6. "Chef," Oxford English Dictionary, http://bit.ly/2bqfaNX (accessed 30 December 2015).

7. Durst-Wertheim, "Chefs," 106.

8. Quoted in L. Walsh, "Lynda Bird," 3.

9. Fields, *My 21 Years*, 117.

10. Brooks, *Washington in Lincoln's Time*, 277.

11. Parks, *My Thirty Years*, 221. Maggie Parks, Parks's mother, was a longtime White House employee.

12. Ibid., 183.

13. Quoted in Bache, "New York," 12.

14. Parks, *My Thirty Years*, 123–24.

15. Bishop, *Day in the Life of President Johnson*, 7.

16. "Expenses at the White House."

17. Parks, *Roosevelts*, 70.

18. K. Walsh, *Air Force One*, 144.

19. J. B. West, *Upstairs at the White House*, 355–56.

20. Nesbitt, *White House Diary*, 196.

21. The actual spelling is McIntire.

22. Nesbitt, *White House Diary*, 189.

23. Odlin, "Center Market."

24. Gamarekian, "Keeping House."

25. Seale, *President's House*, 1:78.

26. Ibid., 203.

27. Ibid., 271.

28. "New Kitchens."

29. Colman, *Seventy-Five Years*, 232.

30. Evans, "New Stoves."

31. Moeller and Lovell, *Dining at the White House*, 48; Scheib and Friedman, *White House Chef*, 36.

32. Seale, *President's House*, 1:102.

33. Ibid.

34. Evans, "New Stoves."

35. Aikman, *Living White House*, 120.

36. Scrymser, *Personal Reminiscences*, 17–18.

37. Jaffray, *Secrets of the White House*, 123.

38. "Pepper and Salt."

39. *New York Times*, 28 July 1935, 1.

40. "Chafing Dishes."

41. "Women Scribes."

42. J. Fleming, "Tuskegee Culls Ideas for Chefs."

43. Moeller and Lovell, *Dining at the White House*, 31.

44. Bourdain, *Kitchen Confidential*, 55.

45. Jaffray, *Secrets of the White House*, 124.

46. "Keeping House at the White House"; Avery, "Costs of Living."

47. Nesbitt, *White House Diary*, 188.

48. Parks, *My Thirty Years*, 98.

49. Holland, *The Invisibles*, 10–11.

50. Jaffray, *Secrets of the White House*, 19.

51. Ibid., 125.

52. Parks, *Roosevelts*, 29–30; Nesbitt, *White House Diary*, 67.

53. J. B. West, *Upstairs at the White House*, 328.

54. "Dished in the Kitchen."

55. Nesbitt, *White House Diary*, 120–21.

56. Jaffray, *Secrets of the White House*, 126.

57. Nesbitt, *White House Diary*, 67, 182.

58. Parks, *Roosevelts*, 84.

59. Bryant, *Dog Days*, 137–38.

60. Ibid., 219–20.

61. "White House Dog Repentant." Actually, Winks had a fatal accident on the White House grounds soon after this event.

62. Bache, "Rats, Mice and Bugs."

63. J. B. West, *Upstairs at the White House*, 328–29.

64. Jaffray, *Secrets of the White House*, 62–63.

65. Parks, *My Thirty Years*, 90.

66. Claiborne, "Jefferson Paved the Way."

67. S. Johnson, *My Brother Lyndon*, 66.

68. Elliot and Ali, *Presidential-Congressional Dictionary*, 101.

69. Nelson, *Guide to the Presidency*, 1647.

CHAPTER 2

1. Paraphrasing John 2:1–10 in F. C. Thompson, *Thompson Chain Reference Study Bible*, 1375.

2. "Steward," *Oxford English Dictionary*.

3. Genovese, *Roll, Jordan, Roll*, 327–28.

4. Bodenhorn, *Color Factor*, 66.

5. *New York Gazette*, 4 April 1774, 3.

6. Graves, "He's Just a Man."

7. Quoted in Blockson, "Black Samuel Fraunces."

8. Hume, *Popular Media and the American Revolution*, 77.

9. Ibid.

10. Holte, "Unheralded Realities," E8.

11. Ibid.

12. Hume, *Popular Media in the American Revolution*, 77.

13. "54 Pearl Street History."

14. Riseley, "New York's Historic Landmarks."

15. Custis, *Recollections*, 421–22.

16. Piehler, "Fraunces, Samuel," 414.

17. Gourse, "Hoist a Glass of History."

18. Stevens, "Merchants of New York."

19. "No. 3 Cherry St."

20. Harrison, "Washington in New York."

21. Quoted in ibid.

22. Chernow, *Washington*, 582.

23. Rhodes, "Dining with George Washington."

24. Cannon and Brooks, *President's Cookbook*, 3.

25. Custis, *Recollections*, 421–22.

26. Quoted in ibid., 421.

27. Ibid.

28. Blockson, "Black Samuel Fraunces."

29. J. Smith, "Fraunces, Samuel," 368.

30. D. Smith, "Slave Site."

31. *Virginia Transcript*, 20 March 1868, 2.

32. Williams, *Life of Rutherford Birchard Hayes*, 301.

33. Whitcomb and Whitcomb, *Real Life at the White House*, 169.

34. Ibid.

35. "Better and Better."

36. *Critic*, 11 July 1881, 1.

37. "Crump," *Macon (Ga.) Weekly Telegraph.*

38. "Out of the Jaws of Death."

39. *Critic,* 11 July 1881, 1.

40. "Steward Crump Resigned."

41. "Presidents at Dinner."

42. Quoted in ibid.

43. "Crump," *Cincinnati Enquirer.*

44. "The District in Congress."

45. *New York World,* 6 September 1896, 8.

46. Ibid.

47. "Death of Henry Pinckney."

48. "President for all the People."

49. "Death of Henry Pinckney."

50. "Named After the President."

51. "In the White House."

52. "A Negro White House Steward."

53. Ibid.

54. "White House Steward."

55. Ibid.

56. "Real Leaders of Washington's Smart Set."

57. Howard, "White House Table."

58. "President Roosevelt Makes a Correction."

59. "At the White House," *Evening Star.*

60. *Boston Globe,* 30 November 1900, 12.

61. "At the White House," *New York Tribune.*

62. "City Full of Joy"; "President Gives Away Turkeys."

63. "Roosevelt's Guests Ate Aged Meat."

64. "Roosevelts Ate Best."

65. Fields, *My 21 Years,* 9–13.

66. Raymond Henle, "Alonzo Fields," oral history interview, 24 July 1970, 29–30, Harry S. Truman Presidential Library and Museum, Independence, Mo.

67. J. B. West, *Upstairs at the White House,* 99.

68. Henle, "Alonzo Fields," oral history interview, 3.

69. Ibid., 30.

70. Ibid.

71. Fields, *My 21 Years,* 7.

72. J. B. West, *Upstairs at the White House,* 82.

73. Fields, *My 21 Years,* 99.

74. J. B. West, *Upstairs at the White House,* 73.

75. Fields, *My 21 Years,* 109.

76. Ibid., 69–70.

77. Ibid., 77–78.

78. Ibid., 35–36.

79. "Personnel Announcement."

80. Shields, "Man of the House."

81. Cahalan, "Invisible Hands."

82. "All Black 1800s Lifesaving Unit Gets Medal."

83. Carter, "Welcome Aboard."

84. "White House Announces New Chief Usher"; Benac, "New White House Usher."

85. "White House Announces New Chief Usher."

86. "Angella Reid, the First Woman Named Chief Usher."

87. Kantor, "Electing to Sleep Elsewhere."

CHAPTER 3

1. Holland, *Black Men Built the Capitol*, 124.

2. "Ending Slavery in the District of Columbia."

3. Washington, *They Knew Lincoln*, 120.

4. Custis, *Recollections*, 422.

5. Wood, *Black Majority*, 183.

6. LaBan, "Hercules."

7. Scheib, Foreword, 7–9.

8. LaBan, "Hercules."

9. Lee, "1786 Laboring Hands George Washington."

10. "Kitchen."

11. Ritter, *Philadelphia and Her Merchants*, 19.

12. Harris, *Beyond Gumbo*, 93.

13. Twohig, *The Papers of George Washington*, 8:189–90.

14. For a detailed exploration of the history of fireplace cooking in the American South, see Crump, *Early American Southern Cuisine Hearthside Cooking*.

15. Custis, *Recollections*, 422–23.

16. Ford, *George Washington*, 172–73.

17. LaBan, "Hercules."

18. DaveManuel.com, http://www.davemanuel.com/inflation-calculator.php (accessed 15 December 2015).

19. Custis, *Recollections*, 422.

20. Ibid.

21. Ibid., 423.

22. Holland, *The Invisibles*, 53–54.

23. LaBan, "Hercules."

24. LaBan, "Birthday Shock."

25. Ibid.

26. Quoted in Wiencek, *Imperfect God*, 323–24.

27. Quoted in Hirschfeld, *George Washington and Slavery*, 15.

28. T. Fleming, *Great Divide*, 310.

29. Quoted in Hirschfeld, *George Washington and Slavery*, 70.

30. Quoted in ibid., 64.

31. Quoted in LaBan, "Birthday Shock."

32. Quoted in ibid.

33. Lee, *Experiencing Mount Vernon*, 68.

34. LaBan, "Birthday Shock."

35. Ibid.

36. Conkling, *Memoirs*, 151.

37. Frémont, *Souvenirs of My Time*, 97–98.

38. Bear, *The Hemings Family of Monticello*, 9–11.

39. Ibid.

40. Gordon-Reed, *Hemingses of Monticello*, 171–72.

41. "About Thomas Jefferson and Monticello."

42. Bear, *The Hemings Family of Monticello*, 11.

43. McElveen, "James Hemings."

44. Bear, *The Hemings Family of Monticello*, 11.

45. Quoted in ibid., 12.

46. Quoted in ibid.

47. Stanton, "Well-Ordered Household," 8.

48. Ibid., 10.

49. Vlach, *Back of the Big House*, 43.

50. Pegge, *Forme of Cury*, 46.

51. Cutler and Cutler, *Life Journals*, 71–72.

52. Nathan, "Gourmet President."

53. Stanton, "Well-Ordered Household," 13–14.

54. Washington, *They Knew Lincoln*, 33.

55. Leni Sorensen interview with the author.

56. Stanton, "Well-Ordered Household," 10.

57. Ibid., 10–11.

58. Ibid., 17–18.

59. Ibid., 19.

60. Hess, "Mr. Jefferson's Table," 44; "Thomas Jefferson's Negro Grandchildren."

61. Morley, *Snow-Storm in August*, 106.

62. Ibid.

63. Unless otherwise indicated, the next three paragraphs summarize material found in Rohrs, "Antislavery Politics," and Edwards and Winston, "Commentary."

64. Taylor, *Slave in the White House*, 171.

65. Rohrs, "Antislavery Politics," 25; Edwards and Winston, "Commentary."

66. "Modern Pharaoh," 1.

67. Junior League of the City of Washington, *City of Washington*, 119.

68. Washington, *They Knew Lincoln*, 100.

69. Quoted in ibid., 77–78.

70. Ibid., 82–84.

71. Ibid.

72. Pinkser, *Lincoln's Sanctuary*, 2.

73. Quoted in ibid., 88.

74. Ibid., 94.

75. Ibid., 179.

76. Quoted in Washington, *They Knew Lincoln*, 116.

77. "White House Appoints First Black Cabinet Member."

78. McLeod, *Dining with the Washingtons*, 200.

79. Fowler, *Dining at Monticello*, 178.

CHAPTER 4

1. Berlin, *Slaves without Masters*, 136.

2. Junior League of the City of Washington, *City of Washington*, 95.

3. Ibid., 230.

4. Jaffe and Sherwood, *Dream City*, 4.

5. Ibid., 28–29.

6. Eighmey, *Abraham Lincoln in the Kitchen*, 213.

7. Washington, *They Knew Lincoln*, 119–20.

8. Ibid.

9. "Washington Gossip."

10. Leland, "Ana of the War."

11. "New York Ice-Cream"; G. Johnson, *Profiles in Hue*, 62.

12. Pate, "Ice Cream Stores to Close."

13. "Ice Cream as a Novelty."

14. Quote from an unnamed newspaper in Junior League of the City of Washington, *City of Washington*, 246.

15. "Reminiscences of Wormley."

16. "James Wormley's Death," 1.

17. "Beef Tea and Terrapin."

18. "Reminiscences of Wormley." This fortune was reportedly $200,000 (about $4,546,000 in 2015 dollars); "Colored People"; Emerson, "In and about Washington."

19. "James Wormley."

20. "Local Affairs."

21. Goodbody, "Meal in the Nation's Capital."

22. "Stories of John Chamberlin."

23. "Dishes of a Famous Cook"; "How to Cook Terrapin."

24. "The White House Cook."

25. Ibid.; Hardwick, "From Cleveland," 693.

26. In many sources her name is alternatively spelled "Dolly," and her last name is given as "Dandridge." I use "Dollie" because that seems to be her preferred spelling.

27. Eblen, "Lexington Caterer."

28. Quoted in ibid.

29. Ibid.

30. Ibid.

31. "A White House Cook."

32. "With Mr. Roosevelt's Consent."

33. "The State's Survey."

34. "With Mr. Roosevelt's Consent."

35. Other sources spell the name "Pelonard" or "Petronard."

36. "Zieman on the President's Diet."

37. *St. Louis Post-Dispatch*, 20 August 1889, 4.

38. Grundy, "In the White House."

39. Ibid.

40. " Zieman on the President's Diet"; "Red Ants."

41. "Eating for Christmas."

42. "Knows Good Cooking."

43. "New White House Cook."

44. "Flush Congressman."

45. Eblen, "Lexington Caterer"; "Boarding School Miss Lost Watch."

46. "Boarding School Miss Lost Watch."

47. "Singing Evangelist"; *Morning Herald*, 2 October 1905, 1; "Pecan Cake for Miss Roosevelt"; "White House Cook Dead"; Eblen, "Lexington Caterer"; "Boarding School Miss Lost Watch."

48. "Little Yellow Woman."

49. Ibid.

50. Ibid.

51. "Hostilities at the White House."

52. "Little Yellow Woman."

53. "Intimidation."

54. Some sources list the assailed as "J. D. A. Whitlaw." "Police Court."

55. "Little Yellow Woman."

56. *Summit County Beacon*, 21 December 1881, 4.

57. "Little Yellow Woman."

58. "Wedding Bells."

59. "Wilson Will Enjoy Southern Cooking"; Parks, *My Thirty Years*, 125–26.

60. "Wedding Bells"; "White House Cook Elopes with Stonemason."

61. "Getting Booker T."

62. "What It Means to Be Colored."

63. Welch, "South as It Might Be"; *Baltimore Afro-American*, 30 May 1931, 12; "White House Is Being Changed."

64. Nesbitt, *White House Diary*, 78, 118.

65. Ibid.

66. Ibid., 141, 189.

67. Ibid., 141.

68. J. B. West, *Upstairs at the White House*, 28.

69. Parks, *Roosevelts*, 69.

70. Ibid., 136, 141.

71. Dr. Maclyn Burg, "John Moaney," oral history interview, 21 July 1972, 13, Dwight D. Eisenhower Presidential Library, Museum and Boyhood Home, Abilene, Kans.

72. Ibid., 14.

73. Ibid., 1–3.

74. Ibid., 45.

75. Eisenhower Medical Center Auxiliary Cookbook Committee, *Five-Star Favorites*, 99; "John Moaney, Orderly."

76. Butcher, *My Three Years*, 81.

77. Burg, "John Moaney," oral history interview, 29–31.

78. Ibid., 39.

79. Drew, "Washington Merry-Go-Round."

80. Parks, *My Thirty Years*, 41.

81. Ibid., 53.

82. J. B. West, *Upstairs at the White House*, 159–60.

83. Burg, "John Moaney," oral history interview, 15.

84. Booker, "Broke Barriers for D.C.'s Blacks."

85. S. Eisenhower, *Mrs. Ike*, 286.

86. Bryant, *Dog Days*, 17.

87. Booker, "Broke Barriers for D.C.'s Blacks," 16–17.

88. "Legion of Merit."

89. D. Eisenhower, *At Ease*, 308n.

90. J. B. West, *Upstairs at the White House*, 212–13.

91. Ibid.

92. Michael L. Gillette, "Zephyr Wright," oral history interview, 5 December 1974, 1–2, Correspondence File, Lyndon Baines Johnson Presidential Library, Austin, Tex.; "Johnson Cook," 21.

93. Gillette, "Zephyr Wright," oral history interview, 4.

94. "Johnson Cook Has Seat of Honor."

95. L. Walsh, "Lynda Bird."

96. "Johnson Cook Has Seat of Honor."

97. J. B. West, *Upstairs at the White House*, 324–25.

98. Ibid., 327–28.

99. Gillette, "Zephyr Wright," oral history interview, 27–28; M. Smith, "White House Cook."

100. M. Smith, "Zephyr's Wants Out Of the Kitchen"; "Heat in the Kitchen"; Gillette, "Zephyr Wright," oral history interview, 27–28; M. Smith, "White House Cook."

101. "Johnson Cook Has Seat of Honor."

102. Brown, "Johnson and His 'Boss.'"

103. "Power's in LBJ Kitchen."

104. Gillette, "Zephyr Wright," oral history interview, 8.

105. Ibid., 11–14.

106. Caro, *Master of the Senate*, 888; Gillette, "Zephyr Wright," oral history interview, 6–7; Thomas, *Thanks for the Memories*, 50.

107. Carpenter, *Ruffles and Flourishes*, 305.

108. Quoted in Tolbert, *Bowl of Red*, 11.

109. "Roberts Asks Wright for Information on LBJ's Preference for Various Kinds of Beans," Citation No. 2250, Tape: WH6403.11, Program No. 26, 18 March 1964, Audiovisual Collection, Lyndon Baines Johnson Presidential Library, Austin, Tex.

110. Tolbert, *Bowl of Red*, 12.

111. "Johnson Cook to Retire."

112. Gillette, "Zephyr Wright," oral history interview, 37.

CHAPTER 5

1. Ellis, *Presidential Travel*, 8.

2. Ibid., 169–70.

3. Ibid., 4.

4. Hardesty, *Air Force One*, 29.

5. Ellis, *Presidential Travel*, 74.

6. "The Pullman Company."

7. Quinzio, *Food on the Rails*, 27.

8. Ibid., 29.

9. M'Bee, "He Has Prepared Food."

10. Ibid.

11. Ibid.

12. "Grover Has Arrived."

13. "Month's Home on Wheels."

14. Quoted in Landau, *President's Table*, 42.

15. "Yessah, Mistah Taft."

16. Quoted in ibid.

17. Standish, "Safety First."

18. Haskin, "King of Cooks," 24.

19. Ibid.

20. Ibid.

21. Parks, *Roosevelts*, 20.

22. *Philadelphia Tribune*, 6 January 1938, 20.

23. "Servant Campaigns."

24. "Wife of F. D. R.'s Valet Campaigns."

25. Parks, *Roosevelts*, 33–34; "F. D. R. Hails First Lady's Maid."

26. Parks, *Roosevelts*, 171.

27. Warm Springs, Georgia, promotional handout, n.d., n.p.

28. Lippman, *Squire of Warm Springs*, 235; R. Stevens, *Hi-Ya Neighbor*, 33.

29. Bishop, *FDR's Last Year*, 764–65.

30. "Warm Springs Cook of Roosevelt Dies."

31. Burns, "Thousands Visit Georgia Site."

32. Berger, "At the White House Switchboard."

33. Burns, "Thousands Visit Georgia Site."

34. "Woman Who Cooked for Roosevelt Died."

35. Ibid.

36. Vaccaro, "Truman Campaign Trip."

37. Kerr, "U.S. Car No. 1."

38. Bishop, *A Day in the Life of President Kennedy*, 21.

39. Jaffee, *Presidential Yacht*, 15; Kelly, Sequoia: *Presidential Yacht*, 32–33.

40. Jaffee, *Presidential Yacht*, 15.

41. Kelly, Sequoia: *Presidential Yacht*, x.

42. Ibid., 68.

43. "Negroes Wanted."

44. "Filipino Mess Boys."

45. Guzman, *Bush Family Cook Book*, 18.

46. Carr, "Negroes in the Armed Forces."

47. Doyle, *Inside the Oval Office*, 3.

48. Quoted in Jaffee, *Presidential Yacht*, 31–32.

49. Ibid., 32.

50. Ibid.

51. Ibid., 40.

52. Ibid., 40–41.

53. J. B. West, *Upstairs at the White House*, 123.

54. Ibid., 124.

55. Guzman, *Bush Family Cook Book*, 18.

56. "Cheap White House Lunch."

57. Patterson, *White House Staff*, 368–69.

58. Ibid., 369.

59. Gamarekian, "It's Cheap."

60. *San Mateo Times*, 31 October 1969, 27.

61. "Nixons to Eat Turkey Dinner."

62. Ron Jackson, memorandum for Madeline MacBean: "Proposed Menu Thanksgiving Day Dinner, Aspen Lodge, Camp David, 24 November 1977," 17 November 1977, Jimmy Carter Presidential Library and Museum, Atlanta, Ga.

63. Lukas, "And Then a New Wrinkle."

64. "Nixon Gives Flooded City a Free Cookout."

65. Ellis, *Presidential Travel*, 12.

66. "Carter Sold Yacht."

67. O'Leary, "Reagan Won't Sail."

68. Except where noted, the following information is from Charlie Redden's telephone interview with the author, 23 May 2016.

69. Greeley, "From the White House."

70. Huetteman, "On Air Force One."

71. K. Walsh, *Air Force One*, 28.

72. Ibid., 27; Hardesty, *Air Force One*, 17.

73. K. Walsh, *Air Force One*, 27.

74. Wanda Joell, telephone interview with the author, 14 November 2015.

75. K. Walsh, *Air Force One*, 29.

76. Hardesty, *Air Force One*, 13.

77. Ibid.

78. K. Walsh, *Air Force One*, 30.

79. Ibid., 28 (quoting Bob Schieffer).

80. Ibid., 30.

81. Huetteman, "On Air Force One."

82. Ibid.

83. Richard Norton Smith, "Lee Simmons," oral history interview, 1 December 2008, 9, 16, Gerald R. Ford Presidential Library and Museum, Ann Arbor, Mich; Huetteman, "On Air Force One."

84. Smith, "Lee Simmons," oral history interview, 9.

85. Ibid., 12.

86. Ibid., 13.

87. "Serving on Number 1."

88. Ibid.

89. Smith, "Lee Simmons," oral history interview, 15.

90. Ibid., 18–19.

91. "Serving on Number 1."

92. Smith, "Lee Simmons," oral history interview, 18–19.

93. "Serving on Number 1."

94. Smith, "Lee Simmons," oral history interview, passim.

95. Except where otherwise noted, the following information is from Joell's telephone interview with the author.

96. Estep, "Suwanee Woman Recalls 9/11 aboard Air Force One."

97. Ibid.

98. Ibid.

1. Wharton, *Social Life*, 25.

2. Stanton, "Well-Ordered Household," 9–10.

3. A. Smith, *Drinking History*, 212.

4. Charlton, "Wet or Dry."

5. Prial, "Wine at the White House."

6. Hailman, *Thomas Jefferson on Wine*, 128.

7. Prial, "Wine at the White House."

8. "Studebaker's White House Brandy."

9. Hennessy, "Coolidge Used the White House Cellar."

10. "Hayes's Compromise."

11. *Anderson Intelligencer*, 17 February 1881, 2.

12. *American Citizen*, 6 April 1878, 1.

13. "Minor Notes."

14. *New York Tribune*, 29 April 1878, 4.

15. "White House."

16. "Famous Chef Dead."

17. "President's Table."

18. "Famous Chef Dead."

19. "Congressional Gastronome."

20. "Echoes."

21. "President's Table."

22. "Our Washington Letter."

23. "Act of 'Drys.'"

24. "Death of Major Brooks."

25. "Custodian of White House Dies."

26. "Death of Major Brooks."

27. *New York Times*, 8 September 1926, 1.

28. "Death of Major Brooks."

29. Jaffray, *Secrets of the White House*, 22–23.

30. Ibid., 62–63.

31. "Major Brooks Passes Away at Capital."

32. *New York Times*, 8 September 1926, 1.

33. Appiah and Gates, "Brooks, Arthur."

34. Mohr, "U.S. Prods Diplomats."

35. Bradlee, *Conversations*, 187–88.

36. Gamarekian, "All the President's Wines."

37. Mohr, "U.S. Prods Diplomats."

38. "Embassies Ready."

39. D. West, "French Alarmed by Summit Wine."

40. Pearson, "John Ficklin."

41. Gerald M. Bell, letter to John Ficklin, 9 April 1975, Correspondence, Gerald R. Ford Presidential Library and Museum, Ann Arbor, Mich.

42. R. Thompson, "Choosing the President's Wines."

43. Ibid.

44. Ibid.

45. "Maître d' to Presidents John Ficklin Retires."

46. Gilder, "Some Recent Autobiography."

47. Raconteur, "Washington Society."

48. Williams, *The Life of Rutherford Birchard Hayes*, 312–13n.

49. Fields, *My 21 Years*, 36.

50. Ibid., 129–31.

51. Jenkins, "Eggnog."

52. Kane, *Southern Christmas Book*, 11.

53. Langford, "In the White House."

54. Nesbitt, *Presidential Cookbook*, 156.

55. "White House Workers Recall Their Service."

56. Conroy, "White House Elixir."

57. Ibid.

58. Ibid.

59. Ibid.

60. Ibid.

61. Ibid.

62. "Cocktail," *Oxford English Dictionary*, http://bit.ly/2bBp7Fu (accessed 8 December 2015).

63. "What Roosevelt Told the Jury."

64. "That White House Mint Bed."

65. Quoted in Bullock, *173 Pre-Prohibition Cocktails*, 13–14.

66. Fields, *My 21 Years*, 57.

67. Parks, *Roosevelts*, 87, 182.

68. Ibid., 99.

69. Ibid., 116.

70. J. B. West, *Upstairs at the White House*, 75.

71. K. Walsh, *Air Force One*, 65.

72. Ibid., 80.

73. Van Gelder, "Books of the *Times*."

74. "Cocktail Issue Old."

75. Hennessy, "T. R. Was Last."

76. "Beer to Be Served."

77. K. Walsh, *Air Force One*, 55.

78. "Obama, McCain Beer Generates Election Buzz."

79. Grise, "Obama Reaches for the 'Beer Vote.'"

80. Cooper and Goodnough, "In a Reunion over Beers, No Apologies."

CHAPTER 7

1. Quoted in De Voe, *Market Book*, 304.

2. Samuelsson, "Celebrating Black Culinarians," 150.

3. Bourdain, *Kitchen Confidential*, 121.

4. Blum, "Man Who Loved to Cook."

5. Clarke, "What a Great Job," 105.

6. Ibid.

7. Walter Scheib, telephone interview with author, 12 October 2010.

8. Baldwin, "White House Gets First Lady Chef."

9. Blum, "Man Who Loved to Cook."

10. Scheib and Friedman, *White House Chef*, 131–32.

11. Ibid., 134.

12. Ibid.

13. Trotter, *Cooking with Patrick Clark*, 180.

14. Quoted in Kennedy, "Chef Spices Up Hospital Life."

15. Asimov, "Patrick Clark."

16. Ibid.

17. "State Dinner Press Preview."

18. Samuelsson, *Yes, Chef*, 286–87.

19. Ellis, *Presidential Travel*, 7.

20. "White House Chefs Look for Sensitivity."

21. Joynt, "Roland Mesnier."

22. Ibid.

23. Let's Move! website, http://www.letsmove.gov/learn-facts/epidemic-child hood-obesity (accessed 12 December 2015).

24. Superville, "White House Staff Lose Weight."

25. Ibid.

26. Major, *Juba to Jive*, 354.

27. Obama, *American Grown*, 9.

28. Information in the following section is from Kiana Farkash, interview with the author, 28 December 2015, Denver, Colo.

29. Obama, "Remarks by the First Lady."

30. Farkash interview with the author.

31. Ibid.

BIBLIOGRAPHY

Abilene, Kans.

    Dwight D. Eisenhower Presidential Library, Museum and Boyhood Home

        Burg, Dr. Maclyn, "John Moaney," oral history interview, 21 July 1972

Ann Arbor, Mich.

    Gerald R. Ford Presidential Library and Museum

        Correspondence

            Bell, Gerald M., letter to John Ficklin, 9 April 1975

            Smith, Richard Norton, "Lee Simmons," oral history interview,

                1 December 2008

Atlanta, Ga.

    Jimmy Carter Presidential Library and Museum

        Audiovisual Collection

Austin, Tex.

    Lyndon Baines Johnson Presidential Library and Museum

        Audiovisual Collection

            "Roberts Asks Wright for Information on LBJ's Preference for Various

                Kinds of Beans," Citation No. 2550, Tape: WH6403.11, Program No.

                26, 18 March 1964

        Correspondence File

            Jones, C. F., letter to Honorable Lyndon B. Johnson, June 24, 1964

            Gillette, Michael L., "Zephyr Wright," oral history interview, 5 December

                1974

        Claudia T. Johnson Recipe File

Boston, Mass.

    John F. Kennedy Presidential Library and Museum

        Audiovisual Collection

College Park, Md.

    National Archives

    Audiovisual Collection

Dallas, Tex.

    George W. Bush Presidential Center

        Audiovisual Collection

        Cookery and Foodways Collection

Denver, Colo.

    University of Denver, Cookery and Foodways Collection

        Margaret Husted Collection

Hyde Park, N.Y.
    Franklin D. Roosevelt Presidential Library and Museum
        Audiovisual Archives
Independence, Mo.
    Harry S. Truman Presidential Library and Museum
        Henle, Raymond, "Alonzo Fields," oral history interview, 24 July 1970
Indianapolis, Ind.
    Benjamin Harrison Presidential Site
Little Rock, Ark.
    William J. Clinton Presidential Center
        Cookery and Foodways Collection
Simi Valley, Calif.
    Ronald Reagan Presidential Library and Museum
        Audiovisual Collection
        John Woodson Ficklin Papers, 1946–1994
Washington, D.C.
    Library of Congress
Yorba Linda, Calif.
    Richard Nixon Presidential Library and Museum
        Cookery and Foodways Collection

AUTHOR INTERVIEWS

Farkash, Kiana. 28 December 2015, Denver, Colo.
Joell, Wanda. Telephone interview, 14 November 2015.
Redden, Charlie. Telephone interview, 23 May 2016.
Robb, Lynda Bird Johnson. Telephone interview, 17 October 2011.
Scheib, Walter. Telephone interview, 12 October 2010.
Sorensen, Leni. Telephone interview, 8 August 2015.

SECONDARY SOURCES

"About Thomas Jefferson and Monticello." Embassy of the United States, Paris,
    France, website, http://france.usembassy.gov/jefferson.html. Accessed 18
    December 2015.
"Act of 'Drys' May Embarrass Roosevelt." *Willmar (Minn.) Tribune*,
    6 November 1907, 3.
Adler, Bill, and Bill Adler Jr. *Kids' Letters to President Obama*. New York:
    Ballantine Press, 2009.
"Admits to Police He Shot Watchman." *Evening Star* (Washington, D.C.),
    5 April 1918, 15.
"AF Trains Stewards for Presidential Jet." *Washington Post*, 31 July 1968, A6.
Aikman, Lonnelle. *The Living White House*. Washington, D.C.: White House
    Historical Association, 2007.

A. J. S. "An Old Virginia Cook." *Detroit Free Press*, 5 June 1886, 4.

"All Black 1800s Livesaving Unit Gets Medal." *Los Angeles Sentinel*, 14 March 1996, A12.

"Angella Reid, the First Woman Named Chief Usher at the White House." *Washington Post*, 4 October 2011, http://wapo.st/2bjYftT. Accessed 28 November 2015.

Anthony, Carl Sferrazza. *The Kennedy White House: Family Life and Pictures, 1961–1963.* New York: Touchstone, 2001.

Appiah, Anthony, and Henry Louis Gates Jr. "Brooks, Arthur." *Africana: The Encyclopedia of African and African American Experience.* 2nd ed., 1:629-30. London: Oxford University Press, 2005.

"Arthur Simmons Transferred." *Evening Star* (Washington, D.C.), 1 February 1905, 6.

Asbell, Bernard. *When F. D. R. Died.* New York: Holt, Rinehart and Winston, 1961.

Asimov, Eric. "Patrick Clark, 42, Is Dead; Innovator in American Cuisine." *New York Times*, 13 February 1998, A25.

"At the White House." *New York Tribune*, 24 December 1904, 8.

"At the White House." *Evening Star* (Washington, D.C.), 27 November 1901, 1.

Avery, Patricia. "Costs of Living Rises at White House, Too." *U.S. News and World Report*, 23 July 1979, 51.

Bache, Rene. "New York as George Washington Saw It in 1789." *New York Times Sunday Magazine*, 20 February 1916, 12.

———. "Rats, Mice and Bugs." *Evening Star* (Washington, D.C.), 5 August 1893, 11.

Baldrige, Letitia. *A Lady, First: My Life in the Kennedy White House and the American Embassies of Paris and Rome.* New York: Penguin Books, 2001.

Baldwin, Tom. "White House Gets First Lady Chef for Tex-Mex Delicacies." *London Times*, 15 August 2005, 29.

Bear, James A., Jr. *The Hemings Family of Monticello.* Ivy, Va., 1980.

"Beef Tea and Terrapin." *Detroit Free Press*, 17 September 1885, 7.

"Beer to Be Served at White House." *New York Times*, 4 April 1933, 5.

Beil, Gail K. "Four Marshallites' Roles in the Passage of the Civil Rights Act of 1964." *Southwestern Historical Quarterly*, 106, no. 1 (July 2002): 1–29.

Benac, Nancy. "New White House Usher Angella Reid Comes from Hotel Industry." *Deseret (Utah) News*, 24 October 2011, http://bit.ly/2bqgAbh. Accessed 3 August 2015.

Berger, Meyer. "At the White House Switchboard." *New York Times*, 23 March 1947, SM20.

Berlin, Ira. *Slaves without Masters: The Free Negro in the Antebellum South.* New York: New Press, 1974.

"Better and Better." *Critic*, 14 July 1881, 1.

Bishop, Jim. *A Day in the Life of President Johnson*. New York: Random House, 1967.

———. *A Day in the Life of President Kennedy*. New York: Bantam Books, 1964.

———. *FDR's Last Year: April 1944–April 1945*. New York: Pocket Books, 1975.

Blockson, Charles L. "Black Samuel Fraunces: Patriot, White House Steward and Restaurateur Par Excellence." Temple University Libraries, http://library .temple.edu/collections/blockson/fraunces. Accessed 16 November 2015.

Blum, David. "The Man Who Loved to Cook." *New York Times*, 3 January 1999, SM44.

"Boarding School Miss Lost Watch." *Kentucky Morning Herald* (Lexington), 13 February 1906, 1.

Bodenhorn, Howard. *The Color Factor: The Economics of African-American Well-Being in the Nineteenth Century South*. New York: Oxford University Press, 2015.

Booker, Simeon. "Broke Barriers for D.C.'s Blacks." *Jet*, 17 April 1969, 14–21.

Bourdain, Anthony. *Kitchen Confidential*. Updated ed. New York: Harper Perennial, 2007.

Bradlee, Benjamin C. *Conversations with Kennedy*. New York: Pocket Books, 1976.

Brooks, Noah. *Washington in Lincoln's Time*. New York: Century Co., 1895.

Brown, Nona. "Johnson and His 'Boss.'" *New York Times*, 8 May 1966, E5.

Bruce, Preston, with the assistance of Katherine Johnson, Patricia Haas, and Susan Hainey. *From the Door of the White House*. New York: Lothrop, Lee and Shepard, 1984.

Bryant, Traphes, with Frances Spatz Leighton. *Dog Days at the White House: The Outrageous Memoirs of the Presidential Kennel Keeper*. New York: Macmillan, 1975.

Bullock, Tom. *173 Pre-Prohibition Cocktails*. Jenks, Okla.: Howling Moon Press, 2001.

Burns, Francis. "Thousands Visit Georgia Site of President Roosevelt's Death." *Canton (Ohio) Repository*, 12 April 1946, 23.

Butcher, Harry C. *My Three Years with Eisenhower: A Personal Diary of Captain Harry C. Butcher, USNR*. New York: Simon and Schuster, 1946.

Cahalan, Susannah. "Invisible Hands to Keep Obamas' White House in Order." *New York Post*, 16 November 2008, 25.

Cannon, Poppy, and Patricia Brooks. *The President's Cookbook: Practical Recipes from George Washington to the Present*. New York: Funk and Wagnalls, 1968.

Caro, Robert A. *Master of the Senate*. New York: Alfred A. Knopf, 2002.

Carpenter, Frank G. *Carp's Washington*. New York: McGraw Hill, 1960.

———. "The Presidents as Gastronomers." *Lippincott's Monthly Magazine*, December 1886, 38.

Carpenter, Liz. *Ruffles and Flourishes: The Warm and Tender Story of a Simple*

Girl Who Found Adventure in the White House. Garden City, N.Y.: Doubleday, 1970.

Carr, Robert K. "Negroes in the Armed Forces." Prepared by Milton D. Stewart and Joseph Murtha, Memorandum to the President's Committee on Civil Rights, 10 June 1947, http://bit.ly/2brq6Ke. Accessed 28 November 2015.

Carter, Angela. "Welcome Aboard." *McClatchy-Tribune Business News* (Washington, D.C.), 19 May 2011, n.p.

"Carter Sold Yacht—Hill May Buy It Back." *Evening Star* (Washington, D.C.), 2 May 1978, A-2.

"Chafing Dishes Alone Survive in New White House Kitchen." *Washington Post*, 17 December 1935, 4.

Charlton, Linda. "Wet or Dry, the Carter White House Inherits Some Instructive Customs." *New York Times*, 20 January 1977, 52.

"Cheap White House Lunch." *Kingston (N.Y.) Daily Freeman*, 2 December 1974, 6.

Chernow, Ron. *Washington: A Life*. New York: Penguin Press, 2010.

Church, Ruth Ellen. "Happy Days Arrive for Wine Devotees." *Chicago Tribune*, 6 March 1975, W-A5.

"The City Full of Joy." *New York Tribune*, 24 December 1905, 7.

Claiborne, Craig. "Jefferson Paved the Way for a French Chef in the White House." *New York Times*, 10 April 1961, 34.

Clarke, Caroline. "What a Great Job." *Black Enterprise*, February 1995, 94–106.

"Cocktail Issue Old." *Detroit Free Press*, 2 October 1907, 7.

Colman, Edna M. *Seventy-Five Years of White House Gossip: From Washington to Lincoln*. New York: Doubleday, Page, 1926.

"The Colored People: How They Prosper in Washington and Elsewhere." *Brooklyn Eagle*, 15 December 1886, 4.

"A Congressional Gastronome." *Rocky Mountain News*, 10 March 1885, 8.

Conkling, Margaret C. *Memoirs of the Mother and Wife of Washington*. Auburn, N.Y.: Derby, Miller, 1850.

Conroy, Sarah Booth. "White House Elixir." *Washington Post*, 19 December 1982, K1.

Cooper, Helene, and Abby Goodnough. "In a Reunion over Beers, No Apologies, but Cordial Plans to Have Lunch Sometime." *New York Times*, 30 July 2009, A10.

Crackel, Theodore J., ed. *The Papers of George Washington, Digital Edition*. Charlottesville: University of Virginia Press, Rotunda, 2008, http://rotunda.upress.virginia.edu/founders/GEWN-05-08-02-0148. Accessed 17 November 2010.

"Crump." *Cincinnati Enquirer*, 11 September 1886, 9.

"Crump." *Macon (Ga.) Weekly Telegraph*, 16 December 1881, 4.

Crump, Nancy Carter. *Early American Southern Cuisine Hearthside Cooking:*

Updated for Today's Hearth and Cookstove. 2nd ed. Chapel Hill: University of North Carolina Press, 2008.

"Crump Funeral on Tuesday." *Evening Star* (Washington, D.C.), 28 March 1909, pt. 2, 8.

Custis, George Washington Parke. *Recollections and Private Memoirs of Washington by His Adopted Son.* New York: Derby and Jackson, 1860. Google Books, http://bit.ly/2bqgFf6. Accessed 26 November 2015.

"Custodian of White House Dies." *New York Amsterdam News*, 15 September 1926, 1.

Cutler, William Parker, and Julia Perkins Cutler. *Life Journals and Correspondence of Rev. Manasseh Cutler, LL.D., Vol. II.* Cincinnati: Robert Clarke, 1888. Google Books, http://bit.ly/2bBpUpW. Accessed 21 December 2015.

"Daniel W. Baker Pneumonia Victim." *Evening Star* (Washington, D.C.), 2 January 1919, 4.

"Death of Henry Pinckney." *Washington Post*, 7 April 1911, 2.

"Death of Major Brooks Felt at the White House." *New Journal and Guide* (Newport, Va.), 18 September 1926, 1.

Depold, Hans. *Bolton Historic Tales.* Charleston: History Press, 2008. Google Books, http://bit.ly/2boCGAH. Accessed 9 December 2015.

De Voe, Thomas F. *The Market Book Containing a Historical Account of the Public Markets in the Cities of New York, Boston, Philadelphia and Brooklyn.* New York, 1862.

"Dished in the Kitchen." *Evening Star* (Washington, D.C.), 13 June 1979, A2.

"Dishes of a Famous Cook." *Bay City (Mich.) Sunday Times*, 4 January 1903, 18.

"The District in Congress." *Evening Star* (Washington, D.C.), 24 May 1888, 1.

Doyle, William. *Inside the Oval Office: The Story of the White House Tapes from FDR to Nixon.* New York: Kodansha America, 1999.

Drew, "Washington Merry-Go-Round." *Springfield (Mass.) Republican*, 28 March 1954, 13C.

"Drought in 'Nog' Due to the Expense of 'Hen Fruit.'" *Washington Herald*, 24 December 1911, 1.

Durst-Wertheim, Carol. "Chefs." In *Savoring Gotham: A Food Lover's Companion to New York City*, edited by Andrew Smith, 106–7. New York: Oxford University Press, 2015.

"Eating for Christmas." *Chicago Tribune*, 22 December 1889, 26.

Eblen, Tom. "Lexington Caterer Became One of White House's Most Notable Black Chefs." *Lexington Herald-Leader*, 2 February 2016, http://www.kentucky.com/news/local/news-columns-blogs/tom-eblen/article57966958.html. Accessed 2 February 2016.

"Echoes." *Indianapolis Leader*, 27 May 1882, 1.

Edwards, G. Franklin, and Michael R. Winston. "Commentary: The Washington

of Paul Jennings — White House Slave, Free Man, and Conspirator for
Freedom." *White House History* 1, no. 1 (1983): 42–63.

Eighmey, Rae Katherine. *Abraham Lincoln in the Kitchen: A Culinary View of
Lincoln's Life and Times.* Washington, D.C.: Smithsonian Books, 2013.

Eisenhower, Dwight D. *At Ease: Stories I Tell to Friends.* New York: Avon Books,
1967.

Eisenhower Medical Center Auxiliary Cookbook Committee. *Five-Star Favorites:
Recipes from Friends of Mamie and Ike.* New York: Golden Press, 1974.

Eisenhower, Susan. *Mrs. Ike: Memories and Reflections on the Life of Mamie
Eisenhower.* New York: Farrar, Straus and Giroux, 1996.

Elliot, Jeffrey M., and Sheikh R. Ali. *The Presidential-Congressional Political
Dictionary.* Santa Barbara: ABC-Clio, 1984.

Ellis, Richard J. *Presidential Travel: The Journey from George Washington to
George W. Bush.* Lawrence: University of Kansas Press, 2008.

"Embassies Ready to Serve U.S. Wine." *New York Times*, 25 May 1965, 4.

Emerson, "In and about Washington." *Christian Union*, 20 November 1884, 30.

"Ending Slavery in the District of Columbia." DC.gov website, http://
emancipation.dc.gov/page/ending-slavery-district-columbia. Accessed 27
January 2016.

Estep, Tyler. "Suwanee Woman Recalls 9/11 aboard Air Force One." *Gwinnett
(Ga.) Daily Post*, 9 September 2011, http://www.gwinnettdailypost.com
/archive/suwanee-woman-recalls-aboard-air-force-one/article_bce7d771-f4f9
-5e80-bfbe-28aa6f2aa7ad.html. Accessed 29 November 2015.

Eustis, Celestine. *Cooking in Old Creole Days.* New York: R. H. Russell, 1908.

Evans, Jessie Fant. "New Stoves at White House Recall Fillmore Troubles."
Evening Star (Washington, D.C.), 28 June 1936, B4.

"Expenses at the White House." *Circular*, 30 December 1858, 149.

"Experienced Railway Man Handles Train of Queen." *Oregonian* (Portland,
Ore.), 4 November 1926, 8.

"Famous Chef Dead." *Evening Star* (Washington, D.C.), 25 March 1914, 20.

"F. D. R. Hails First Lady's Maid as Chief Campaigner." *Baltimore Afro-
American*, 14 November 1936, 18.

Fields, Alonzo. *My 21 Years in the White House.* New York: Crest Books, 1961.

"54 Pearl Street History." Fraunces Tavern Museum, http://frauncestavern
museum.org/history-and-education/history-of-fraunces-tavern. Accessed 26
November 2015.

"Filipino Mess Boys Replace Aliens in U.S. Navy." *Fort Wayne (Ind.) Journal
Gazette*, 11 October 1918, 2.

Fleming, James G. "Tuskegee Culls Ideas for Chefs, Cooks from White House."
New York Amsterdam News, 8 August 1936, 13.

Fleming, Thomas. *The Great Divide: The Conflict between Washington and
Jefferson That Defined a Nation.* Boston: Da Capo Press, 2015.

"Flush Congressman." *Louisville Courier-Journal*, 14 December 1889, 1.

Ford, Paul Leicester. *George Washington*. Philadelphia: J. B. Lippincott, 1896.

"Forty Pound Turkey in White House Oven." *Evening Star* (Washington, D.C.), 30 November 1911, 2.

Fowler, Damon Lee. *Dining at Monticello: In Good Taste and Abundance*. Charlottesville, Va.: Thomas Jefferson Foundation, 2005.

Frémont, Jessie Benton. *Souvenirs of My Time*. Boston: D. Lothrop, 1887.

Gallagher, Mary Barelli. *My Life with Jacqueline Kennedy*. New York: David McKay, 1969.

Gamarekian, Barbara. "All the President's Wines." *New York Times*, 15 January 1986, B10.

———. "It's Cheap, It's Exclusive, It's Handy—It's the White House Mess," *New York Times*, 2 February 1980, C1.

———. "Keeping House to the Tune of $4 Million a Year." *New York Times*, 29 October 1982, A18.

Gates, Henry Louis, Jr., and Evelyn Brooks Higginbotham, eds. *African American National Biography*. Vol. 3. London: Oxford University Press, 2008.

Genovese, Eugene D. *Roll, Jordan, Roll: The World the Slaves Made*. New York: Pantheon Books, 1974.

"George DeBaptiste." Clarke Historical Library, Central Michigan University website, https://www.cmich.edu/library/clarke/AccessMaterials /Bibliographies/UndergroundRailroad/Pages/George-DeBaptiste.aspx. Accessed 22 May 2015.

"Getting Booker T. Out of the Dining Room." *Baltimore Afro-American*, 6 June 1931, 6.

Gilder, Jeannette L. "Some Recent Autobiography." *Critic*, January 1904, 49.

Goodbody, Col. "A Meal in the Nation's Capital." *Pittsburgh Courier*, 7 May 1932, 7.

Gordon-Reed, Annette. *The Hemingses of Monticello: An American Family*. New York: W. W. Norton, 2008.

Gourse, Leslie. "Hoist a Glass of History." *New York Times*, 13 June 1999, M5.

Graves, Lee. "He's Just a Man—Not a Match with the Birthday or the Month." *Richmond Times-Dispatch*, 20 February 1997, D8.

Greeley, Alexandra. "From the White House to Yours." *Washington Examiner*, 5 August 2010, 23.

Grise, Chrisanne. "Obama Reaches for the 'Beer Vote.'" The Fix website, https://www.thefix.com/content/obama-romney-beer-vote90476. Accessed 10 December 2015.

"Grover Has Arrived." *Kansas City Times*, 3 March 1893, 1.

Grundy, Sal, Jr. "In the White House." *Oregonian* (Portland, Ore.), 1 June 1890, n.p.

Guzman, Ariel de. *The Bush Family Cook Book: Favorite Recipes and Stories from One of America's Great Families*. New York: Scribner, 2005.

Hailman, John R. *Thomas Jefferson on Wine*. Jackson: University Press of Mississippi, 2006.

Haller, Henry, with Virginia Aronson. *The White House Family Cookbook: Two Decades of Recipes, a Dash of Reminiscence, and a Pinch of History from America's Most Famous Kitchen*. New York: Random House, 1987.

Hardesty, Von. *Air Force One: The Aircraft That Shaped the Modern Presidency*. Chanhassen, Minn.: NorthWord Press, 2003.

Hardwick, John W. "From Cleveland to McKinley in the White House." *Chautauquan*, March 1897, 690–96.

Harris, Jessica B. *Beyond Gumbo: Creole Fusion Food from the Atlantic Rim*. New York: Simon and Schuster, 2003.

Harrison, Constance Cary. "Washington in New York in 1789." *Century Magazine*, April 1889, 853.

Haskin, Frederic J. "The King of Cooks." *Washington Times*, 12 October 1919, 24.

"Hayes's Compromise Temperance Party." *Stark County Democrat* (Canton, Ohio), 10 May 1877, 8.

"Heat in the Kitchen." *Washington Post*, 2 December 1968, A20.

Hennessy, M. E. "Coolidge Used the White House Cellar to Keep Cigars In." *Boston Globe*, 4 February 1934, C1.

———. "T. R. Was Last to Serve Beer in White House." *Boston Globe*, 9 April 1933, A40.

Hess, Karen. "Mr. Jefferson's Table: The Culinary Legacy of Monticello." *Petits Propos Culinaires*, May 2001, 39–48.

Heymann, C. David. *The Georgetown Ladies' Social Club: Power, Passion, and Politics in the Nation's Capital*. New York: Atria Books, 2003.

Hirschfeld, Fritz. *George Washington and Slavery: A Documentary Portrayal*. Columbia: University of Missouri Press, 1997.

"Hobo Conceals Himself on Presidential Train." *Montgomery Advertiser*, 14 November 1909, 14.

Holland, Jesse J. *Black Men Built the Capitol: Discovering African-American History in and around Washington, D.C.* Guilford, Conn.: Globe Pequot Press, 2007.

———. *The Invisibles: The Untold Story of the African American Slaves in the White House*. Guilford, Conn.: Lyons Press, 2016.

Holte, Clarence L. "Unheralded Realties North America—1619-1776." *New York Amsterdam News*, 28 February 1976, E3–E10.

"Hostilities at the White House." *Boston Journal*, 22 November 1876, n.p.

Howard, William K. "White House Table Supplied with Best Market Affords, but Wholesomeness First Considered." *Washington Post*, 24 June 1906, SM6.

"How to Cook Terrapin." *Boston Daily Globe*, 27 February 1898, 21.

Huetteman, Emmarie. "On Air Force One, No Lightening Up on Burgers and Cake." *New York Times*, 27 June 2014, http://www.nytimes.com/2014/06/28/us/politics/on-air-force-one-no-lightening-up-on-burgers-and-cake.html?_r=0. Accessed 5 September 2015.

Hume, Janice. *Popular Media and the American Revolution: Shaping Collective Memory*. New York: Routledge, 2014.

"Ice Cream as a Novelty." *New York Tribune*, 15 July 1990, A8.

"In the White House." *Evening Star* (Washington, D.C.), 5 August 1889, 24.

"Intimidation—Open War—in the White House." *Observer*, 8 December 1876, 3.

Jaffe, Harry S., and Tom Sherwood. *Dream City: Race, Power, and the Decline of Washington, D.C.* New York: Simon and Schuster, 1994.

Jaffee, Capt. Walter W. *The Presidential Yacht* Potomac. Palo Alto, Calif.: Glencannon Press, 1998.

Jaffray, Elizabeth. *Secrets of the White House*. New York: Cosmopolitan Book Corp., 1927.

"James Wormley." *San Francisco Daily Evening Bulletin*, 1 November 1884, column E, n.p.

"James Wormley's Death." *Critic-Record* (Washington, D.C.), 20 October 1884.

Jenkins, Virginia Scott. "Eggnog." In *The Oxford Companion to American Food and Drink*, edited by Andrew F. Smith, 205. New York: Oxford University Press, 2007.

"John Moaney, Orderly, Valet to Ike in War, White House." *Washington Post*, 22 February 1978, C6.

"Johnson Cook Has Seat of Honor for Speech." *New York Times*, 28 November 1963, 21.

"Johnson Cook to Retire When He Quits Capital." *New York Times*, 27 November 1968, 28.

Johnson, George D. *Profiles in Hue*. Bloomington, Ind.: Xlibris Corporation, 2011. Google Books, http://bit.ly/2bNiovq. Accessed 14 August 2015.

Johnson, Lady Bird [Claudia T.]. *A White House Diary*. New York: Holt, Rinehart and Winston, 1970.

Johnson, Sam Houston. *My Brother Lyndon*. Edited by Enrique Hank Lopez. New York: Cowles, 1970.

Joynt, Carol Ross. "Roland Mesnier Calls Guest Chefs 'A Slap on the Face' to the White House Chef." Washingtonian.com, 21 February 2013, http://bit.ly/2boDghD. Accessed 16 September 2015.

Junior League of the City of Washington, D.C. *The City of Washington: An Illustrated History*. Edited by Thomas Froncek. New York: Alfred A. Knopf, 1977.

Kane, Harnett T. *The Southern Christmas Book*. New York: David McKay, 1958.

Kantor, Jodi. "Electing to Sleep Elsewhere." *New York Times*, 12 April 2012, D1.

"Keeping House at the White House." *U.S. News and World Report*, 2 June 1975, 40.

Kelly, Capt. Giles M., USNR (Ret.), with photographs by Ann Stevens. Sequoia: *Presidential Yacht*. Centreville, Md.: Tidewater, 2004.

Kennedy, Randy. "A Chef Spices Up Hospital Life." *New York Times*, 10 December 1997, B1.

Kerr, Frances. "U.S. Car No. 1." *Evening Star* (Washington, D.C.), 13 August 1950, Pictoral Magazine 6-7.

"Kitchen." George Washington's Mount Vernon website, http://www .mountvernon.org/research-collections/digital-encyclopedia/article/kitchen/. Accessed 15 December 2015.

"Knows Good Cooking." *Maysville (Ky.) Daily Public Ledger*, 28 February 1893, 1.

LaBan, Craig. "A Birthday Shock from Washington's Chef." *Philadelphia Inquirer*, 22 February 2010, http://articles.philly.com/2010-02-22/news /24957476_1_oney-judge-hercules-slave. Accessed 11 November 2015.

———. "Hercules: Master of Cuisine, Slave of Washington." *Philadelphia Inquirer*, 21 February 2010, http://articles.philly.com/2010-02-21/news /24956757_1_hercules-slave-compelling-historical-drama. Accessed 11 November 2015.

Landau, Barry H. *The President's Table: Two Hundred Years of Dining and Diplomacy*. New York: Collins, 2007.

Langford, Laura Holloway. "In the White House." *Chicago Daily Inter Ocean*, 24 December 1893, 25.

Lee, Jean B., ed. *Experiencing Mount Vernon: Eyewitness Accounts, 1784–1865*. Charlottesville: University of Virginia Press, 2006.

"Legion of Merit for Former Ike Aide." *Baltimore Afro-American*, 8 November 1969, 6.

Leland, Charles Godfrey. "Ana of the War." *United States Service Magazine*, January 1866, 17.

Lincoln, Evelyn. *My Twelve Years with John F. Kennedy*. New York: Bantam Books, 1965.

Lippman, Theo, Jr. *The Squire of Warm Springs: F. D. R. in Georgia, 1924–1945*. Chicago: Playboy Press, 1977.

"A Little Yellow Woman Who Served as Cook for Four Presidents." *Washington Times*, 11 May 1902, 4.

"Local Affairs." *National Republican*, 9 October 1865, 3.

Louis-Philippe, "They Hoped They Would No Longer Be Slaves in Ten Years." In *Experiencing Mount Vernon: Eyewitness Accounts, 1784–1865*, edited by Jean B. Lee, 67–69. Charlottesville: University of Virginia Press, 2006.

"Lucullan." *Oxford English Dictionary*, http://www.oed.com.ezproxy .denverlibrary.org/view/Entry/110916#eid38676601. Accessed 7 May 2016.

Lukas, J. Anthony. "And Then a New Wrinkle: High Priced 'Security' Goodies." *Bennington (Vt.) Banner*, 18 January 1974, 8.

"Maître d' to Presidents John Ficklin Retires; Guest at White House." *Jet*, 15 August 1983, 24. Google Books, http://bit.ly/2bxtwbz. Accessed 9 December 2015.

"Major Brooks Passes Away at Capital." *Chicago Defender*, 11 September 1926, 1.

Major, Clarence, ed. *Juba to Jive: A Dictionary of African-American Slang*. New York: Penguin Books, 1994.

Manchester, William. *Portrait of a President*. New York: MacFadden, 1964.

M'Bee, Avery. "He Has Prepared Food for Stomachs of Great." *Baltimore Sun*, 20 March 1938, M3.

McCardle, Dorothy. "In White House Cellar, Only American Wines." *Boston Globe*, 29 May 1965, 5.

McElveen, Ashbell. "James Hemings, Slave and Chef for Thomas Jefferson" (letter to the editor). *New York Times*, 4 February 2016, http://www.nytimes.com/2016/02/05/opinion/james-hemings-slave-and-chef-for-thomas-jefferson.html?_r=0. Accessed 4 February 2016.

McLeod, Stephen A., ed. *Dining with the Washingtons: Historic Recipes, Entertaining, and Hospitality from Mount Vernon*. Chapel Hill: Mount Vernon Ladies' Association, distributed by the University of North Carolina Press, 2011.

Miller, James Nevin. "New Deal Hits the White House Kitchen." *Daily Boston Globe*, 30 June 1935, B3.

"Minor Notes." *Vermont Phoenix*, 8 November 1878, 2.

"A Modern Pharaoh." *Liberator*, 1 July 1842, 1.

Moeller, John, and Mike Lovell. *Dining at the White House: From the President's Table to Yours*. Lancaster, Pa.: American Lifestyle, 2013.

Mohr, Charles. "U.S. Prods Diplomats to Serve Domestic Wine at Posts Abroad." *New York Times*, 24 May 1965, 1.

"A Month's Home on Wheels." *Omaha World Herald*, 14 May 1892, 2.

Morley, Jefferson. *Snow-Storm in August: Washington City, Francis Scott Key, and the Forgotten Race Riot of 1835*. New York: Nan A. Talese/Doubleday, 2012.

"Named after the President." *New York Times*, 29 October 1901, 2.

Nathan, Joan. "The Gourmet President." *Washington Post Magazine*, 18 April 1982, 33.

"Negroes Wanted in United States Navy." *Asheville (N.C.) Citizen*, 12 September 1917, 5.

"A Negro White House Steward." *Kansas City Star*, 6 December 1903, 18.

Nelson, Michael, ed. *Guide to the Presidency and Executive Branch*. 5th ed. Vol. 1. Los Angeles: CQ Press, 2013.

Nesbitt, Henrietta. *The Presidential Cookbook: Feeding the Roosevelts and Their Guests*. Garden City, N.Y.: Doubleday, 1951.

————. *White House Diary*. Garden City, N.Y.: Doubleday, 1948.

"The New Belief." *Cincinnati Daily Enquirer*, 28 October 1862, 1.

"New Kitchens at the White House." *Daily Boston Globe*, 6 November 1904, 49.

"The New White House Cook." *Evening Star* (Washington, D.C.), 2 March 1893, 1.

"New York Ice-Cream." *Boston Cooking-School Magazine*, March 1904, 426.

"Nixon Gives Flooded City a Free Cookout." *Kingsport (Tenn.) Times-News*, 10 September 1972, 1.

"Nixons to Eat Turkey Dinner." *Bennington (Vt.) Banner*, 22 November 1972, 5.

"No. 3 Cherry St., New York, First White House." *Kalamazoo (Mich.) Gazette*, 21 November 1922, 7.

"Obama, McCain Beer Generates Election Buzz." *USA Today*, 17 October 2008, http://usatoday30.usatoday.com/news/offbeat/2008-10-16-alection_N.htm. Accessed 10 December 2015.

Obama, Michelle. *American Grown: The Story of the White House Kitchen Garden and Gardens across America*. New York: Crown, 2012.

————. "Remarks by the First Lady at Kids' State Dinner." Office of the First Lady, White House, 20 August 2012, https://www.whitehouse.gov/the-press-office/2012/08/20/remarks-first-lady-kids-state-dinner. Accessed 29 December 2015.

Odlin, William S. "Center Market Passes into History." *Washington Post*, 4 January 1931, MF5.

O'Leary, Jeremiah. "Reagan Won't Sail on Sequoia." *Washington Star*, 18 June 1981, A-3.

"On the Presidential Train." *Coalville (Utah) Times*, 17 May 1901, 5.

"Our Washington Letter." *Donaldson (La.) Chief*, 30 May 1885, 4.

"Out of the Jaws of Death." *Evening Star* (Washington, D.C.), 16 July 1881, 1.

Parks, Lillian Rogers, in collaboration with Frances Spatz Leighton. *My Thirty Years Backstairs at the White House*. New York: Fleet, 1961.

————. *The Roosevelts: A Family in Turmoil*. Englewood Cliffs, N.J.: Prentice-Hall, 1981.

Pate, Kelly. "Ice Cream Stores to Close." *Denver Post*, 22 February 2001, http://extras.denverpost.com/business/biz0222a.htm. Accessed 9 May 2016.

Patterson, Bradley H., Jr. *The White House Staff: Inside the West Wing and Beyond*. Washington, D.C.: Brookings Institution Press, 2000.

Pearson, Richard. "John Ficklin, Was Maître d' at White House." *Washington Post*, 18 December 1984, C4.

"Pecan Cake for Miss Roosevelt." *Louisville Courier-Journal*, 15 February 1906, 3.

Pegge, Samuel. *The Forme of Cury: A Roll of Ancient English Cookery*. London: J. Nichols, 1780. Google Books, http://bit.ly/2bmqdno. Accessed 21 December 2015.

"Pepper and Salt." *Wall Street Journal*, 14 September 1936, 2.

"Personnel Announcement." Office of the Press Secretary, White House, 27 February 2007, http://georgewbush-whitehouse.archives.gov/news /releases/2007/02/20070227-3.html. Accessed 3 August 2015.

Piehler, Kurt G. "Fraunces, Samuel." *American National Biography*, edited by John A. Garrity and Mark C. Carnes, 3:414–15. New York: Oxford University Press, 1999.

Pinkser, Matthew. *Lincoln's Sanctuary: Abraham Lincoln and the Soldier's Home.* Oxford: Oxford University Press, 2003.

"Police Court—Judge Snell." *Evening Star* (Washington, D.C.), 21 November 1876, 4.

"The Power's in LBJ Kitchen." *New York Times*, 6 May 1966, B1.

"The President and the Wine Cup." *New York Times*, 26 November 1899, 22.

"President for all the People." *Philadelphia Times*, 22 September 1901, 1.

"President Gives Away Turkeys." *New York Tribune*, 24 December 1907, 6.

"The Presidential Train." *Railway Age*, 18 April 1891, 365.

"President Roosevelt Makes a Correction." *Washington Post*, 25 June 1906, 2.

"Presidents at Dinner." *Washington Bee*, 24 May 1884, 1.

"The President's Table." *Evening Star* (Washington, D.C.), 19 July 1884, 2.

Prial, Frank. "Wine at the White House: Jefferson Set the Standard." *New York Times*, 20 January 1993, C12.

"The Pullman Company." The Pullman State Historic Site website, http://www .pullman-museum.org/theCompany/. Accessed 6 February 2016.

Quinzio, Jeri. *Food on the Rails: The Golden Era of Railroad Dining.* Lanham, Md.: Rowman and Littlefield, 2014.

Raconteur. "Washington Society." *Chicago Daily Tribune*, 19 February 1879, 12.

"The Real Leaders of Washington's Smart Set." *Washington Times*, 27 April 1902, 29.

"Red Ants in the White House." *Washington Post*, 29 April 1905, A6.

"Reminiscences of Wormley." *St. Albans (Vt.) Daily Messenger*, 3 December 1884, 2.

Rhodes, Jesse. "Dining with George Washington," 17 February 2011, Smithsonian.com, http://www.smithsonianmag.com/arts-culture/dining -with-george-washington-29372121/?no-ist. Accessed 4 August 2016.

Riseley, H. M. "New York's Historic Landmarks of the Revolutionary Period." *Overland Monthly and Out West Magazine*, February 1904, 122.

Ritter, Abraham. *Philadelphia and Her Merchants, as Constituted Fifty @ Seventy Years Ago.* Philadelphia: Privately published, 1860.

Rohrs, Richard C. "Antislavery Politics and the Pearl Incident of 1848." *Historian* 56, no. 4 (Summer 1994): 711–24.

Roosevelt, James, and Sidney Shalett. *Affectionately F. D. R.: A Son's Story of a Lonely Man.* New York: Harcourt, Brace, 1959.

"Roosevelts Ate Best, Says Steward Pinckney." *Evening Star* (Washington, D.C.),
    8 February 1910, 2.

"Roosevelt's Guests Ate Aged Meat." *New York Times*, 8 February 1910, 2.

Rousseau, Caryn. "Obamas Have a Habit of Inviting Celebrity Guest Chefs."
    Huffington Post, 4 April 2010, http://www.huffingtonpost.com/2010/02/02
    /obamas-have-habit-of-invi_n_445564.html. Accessed 14 December 2015.

Samuelsson, Marcus. "Celebrating Black Culinarians." *Ebony*, November 2006,
    148–52.

———. *Yes, Chef: A Memoir*. New York: Random House, 2012.

Scheib, Walter. Foreword to *Dining with the Washingtons: Historic Recipes,
    Entertaining, and Hospitality from Mount Vernon*, edited by Stephen A.
    McLeod, 7–9. Chapel Hill: Mount Vernon Ladies' Association, distributed by
    the University of North Carolina Press, 2011.

Scheib, Walter, and Andrew Friedman. *White House Chef: Eleven Years, Two
    Presidents, One Kitchen*. Hoboken, N.J.: John Wiley and Sons, 2007.

Scrymser, James A. *Personal Reminiscences of James A. Scrymser in Times of
    Peace and War*. New York: Eschenbach, 1915.

Seale, William. *The President's House: A History*. 2 vols. Washington, D.C.:
    White House Historical Association with the cooperation of the National
    Geographic Society and Harry N. Abrams, New York, 1986.

"The Servant Campaigns." *Baltimore Afro-American*, 31 October 1936, 4.

"Serving on Number 1." *Roswell (N.M.) Daily Record*, 10 June 1979, 32.

Shields, Gerard. "Man of the House—N.O. Native Stephen Rochon Keeps
    White House Running as Facility's Chief Usher." *Baton Rouge Advocate*,
    6 July 2008, 1D.

Shuster, Alvin. "Kennedy Trip Planned in Detail: Meals, Protocol and Security."
    New York Times, 29 May 1961, 3.

———. "A Trip Aboard 'Air Force One.'" *New York Times*, 19 November 1961,
    SM 59–60.

"A Singing Evangelist." *Cleveland Gazette*, 1 February 1896, 2.

Smith, Andrew F. *Drinking History: Fifteen Turning Points in the Making of
    American Beverages*. New York: Columbia University Press, 2012.

Smith, Dinitia. "Slave Site for a Symbol of Freedom." *New York Times*, 20 April
    2002, B7.

Smith, Ira T., and Joe Alex Morris. *Dear Mr. President: The Story of 50 Years in
    the White House Mail Room*. New York: Julian Messer, 1949.

Smith, John Howard. "Fraunces, Samuel." In *African American National
    Biography*, edited by Henry Louis Gates Jr. and Evelyn Brooks
    Higginbotham, 3:366–68. New York: Oxford University Press, 2008.

Smith, Marie. "White House Cook Eagerly Awaits Retirement from Duty
    Hardships." *Oregonian* (Portland, Ore.), 2 December 1968, 5.

————. "Zephyr's Wants Out of the Kitchen." *Washington Post*, 28 November 1968, DI.

Standish, Burton K. "Safety First for President." *Ann Arbor News*, 25 November 1914, 2.

Stanton, Lucia. "A Well-Ordered Household: Domestic Servants in Jefferson's White House." *White House History* 17 (Winter 2006): 4–23.

"State Dinner Press Preview." The White House website, https://www .whitehouse.gov/files/documents/2009/november/state-dinner-press-preview .pdf. Accessed 14 December 2015.

"The State's Survey." *State* (Columbia, S.C.), 16 March 1893, 4.

Stevens, John Austin. "The Merchants of New York, 1765 to 1775." *Galaxy*, June 1875, 787.

Stevens, Ruth. *Hi-Ya Neighbor: Intimate Glimpses of Franklin D. Roosevelt at Warm Springs, Georgia, 1924–45*. New York: Tupper and Love, 1947.

"Steward." *Oxford English Dictionary*, http://www.oed.com.ezproxy .denverlibrary.org/view/Entry/190087?rskey=cMjvur&result=1&isAdvanced =false#eid. Accessed 19 May 2015.

"Steward Crump Resigned." *Evening Star* (Washington, D.C.), 28 April 1882, 3.

"Stories of John Chamberlin." *Broad Ax* (Salt Lake City, Utah), 14 August 1897, 3.

"Studebaker's White House Brandy." *Trenton Evening News*, 13 September 1884, n.p.

Superville, Darlene. "White House Staff Lose Weight, Credit First Lady." *Washington Post*, 1 November 2011, http://www.washingtonpost.com/politics /white-house-staff-lose-weight-credit-first-lady/2011/11/01/gIQAkuibcM_story .html. Accessed 14 August 2015.

Taylor, Elizabeth Dowling. *A Slave in the White House: Paul Jennings and the Madisons*. New York: Palgrave Macmillan, 2012.

"That White House Mint Bed." *New York Times*, 29 May 1913, 2.

Thomas, Helen. *Thanks for the Memories, Mr. President: Wit and Wisdom from the Front Row at the White House*. New York: Scribner, 2002.

"Thomas Jefferson's Negro Grandchildren." *Ebony*, November 1954, 78–80.

Thompson, Flora McDonald. "Housekeeping in the White House." *Junior Munsey*, May 1901.

Thompson, Frank Charles, comp. and ed. *The Thompson Chain Reference Study Bible, New King James Version*. Updated and expanded by John Stephen Jauchen. Indianapolis, Ind.: Kirkbride Bible Company, 1997.

Thompson, Robert Lewis. "Choosing the President's Wines." *Washington Post*, 10 December 1981, 155.

————. "Reds, Whites, but No Blues: The 'New' White House Wine Cellar." *American Bar Association Journal*, July 1982, 858–59. Google Books, http:// bit.ly/2b2QXOi. Accessed 3 March 2015.

Tolbert, Frank X. *A Bowl of Red: The Classic Natural History of Chili con Carne with Other Delectable Dishes of the Southwest*. Dallas, Tex.: Taylor, 1988.

Trotter, Charlie. *Cooking with Patrick Clark: A Tribute to the Man and His Cuisine*. Berkeley: Ten Speed Press, 1999.

Twohig, Dorothy, ed. *The Papers of George Washington*. 11 vols. Charlottesville: University of Virginia Press, 1987–.

Vaccaro, Ernest B. "Truman Campaign Trip Will Cover 24 States." *Aberdeen (S.D.) Daily News*, 27 September 1952, 8.

Van Gelder, Robert. "Books of the *Times*." *New York Times*, 30 December 1933, 11.

Verdon, René. *The White House Chef Cookbook*. Garden City, N.J.: Doubleday, 1968.

Vlach, John Michael. *Back of the Big House: The Architecture of Plantation Slavery*. Chapel Hill: University of North Carolina Press, 1993, 43.

Walsh, Kenneth T. *Air Force One: A History of the Presidents and Their Planes*. New York: Hyperion, 2003.

Walsh, Lee. "Lynda Bird Prepares for Queen's Role." *Washington Star*, 5 March 1961, C1.

"Warm Springs Cook of Roosevelt Dies." *Washington Post and Times Herald*, 23 April 1958, B2.

Washington, George, "1786, Laboring Hands." In *Experiencing Mount Vernon: Eyewitness Accounts, 1784–1865*, edited by Jean B. Lee, 36–47. Charlottesville: University of Virginia Press, 2006.

"Washington Gossip—The President's Salary—How Cheap Living Is Obtained." *Detroit Free Press*, 19 January 1865, 3.

Washington, John E. *They Knew Lincoln*. New York: E. F. Dutton, 1942.

"Watchman King's Slayer Is on Trial." *Evening Star* (Washington, D.C.), 20 December 1918, 2.

"Wedding Bells Ringing for the White House Bride." *Evening Star* (Washington, D.C.), 12 January 1914, 3.

Welch, Robert W. "The South as It Might Be." *New York Times*, 3 November 1901, SM10.

West, Dick. "French Alarmed by Summit Wine." *Long Beach (Calif.) Independent*, 28 June 1973, 29.

West, J. B., with Mary Lynn Kotz. *Upstairs at the White House: My Life with the First Ladies*. New York: Coward, McCann & Geoghegan, 1973.

Wharton, Anne Hollingsworth. *Social Life in the Early Republic*. New York: Benjamin Blom, 1902.

"What It Means to Be Colored in the Capital of the United States." *Independent*, 24 January 1907, 181.

"What Roosevelt Told the Jury." *New York Times*, 28 May 1913, 2.

Whitcomb, John, and Claire Whitcomb. *Real Life at the White House: 200 Years of Daily Life at America's Most Famous Residence*. New York: Routledge, 2002.

"The White House." *Wheeling (Ohio) Register*, 22 December 1882, 1.

"White House Announces New Chief Usher, Angella Reid." Office of the First
Lady, White House, 4 October 2011, https://www.whitehouse.gov/the-press
-office/2011/10/04/white-house-announces-new-chief-usher-angella-reid.
Accessed 3 August 2015.

"White House Appoints First Black Cabinet Member." African American
Registry website, http://aaregistry.org/historic_events/view/white-house
-appoints-first-black-cabinet-member. Accessed 31 January 2016.

"White House Chefs Look for Sensitivity, Not a Star." *Telegram* (St. John's
Newfoundland, Canada), 29 November 2008, http://www.thetelegram.com
/Living/2008-11-29/article-1446967/White-House-chefs-look-for-sensitivity
%2C-not-a-star/1. Accessed 14 December 2015.

"The White House Cook." *Boston Herald*, 22 July 1886, 2.

"A White House Cook." *Lexington (Ky.) Drummer*, 14 December 1889, 3.

"White House Cook Dead." *Washington Post*, 12 February 1918, 9.

"White House Cook Elopes with Stonemason." *Washington Times*, 12 January
1914, 12.

"White House Dog Repentant." *Los Angeles Times*, 3 March 1934, 2.

"White House Is Being Changed." *Grand Forks (N.D.) Daily Herald*, 14 October
1909, 7.

"The White House Steward." *Hartford Courant*, 1 November 1904, 8.

"White House Workers Recall Their Service with Pride." *Deseret (Utah) News*,
19 February 1995.

Wiencek, Henry. *An Imperfect God: George Washington, His Slaves, and the
Creation of America*. New York: Farrar, Straus and Giroux, 2013.

"Wife of F. D. R.'s Valet Campaigns." *Baltimore Afro-American*, 31 October
1936, 17.

Williams, Charles Richard. *The Life of Rutherford Birchard Hayes, Nineteenth
President of the United States*. Vol. 2. Boston: Houghton Mifflin, 1914.

"Wilson Will Enjoy Southern Cooking." *New York Times*, 26 June 1913, 14.

"With Mr. Roosevelt's Consent." *Washington Post*, 12 December 1889, 1.

Wolff, Perry. *A Tour of the White House with Mrs. John F. Kennedy*. New York:
Dell, 1963.

"Woman Who Cooked for Roosevelt Died." *Hartford Courant*, 23 April 1958, 5.

"Women Scribes Inspect White House Kitchen." *Baltimore Afro-American*, 21
December 1935, 5.

Wood, Peter H. *Black Majority: Negroes in South Carolina from 1670 through the
Stono Rebellion*. New York: W. W. Norton, 1974.

"Yessah, Mistah Taft Likes a Big Thick Steak." *St. Louis Post-Dispatch*, 26
November 1911, B2.

Y. M. C. A. "Hayes and the Poor Colored Man." *Washington Post*, 9 December
1878, 2.

"Zieman on the President's Diet." *Philadelphia Inquirer*, 21 October 1889, n.p.

Page numbers in italics refer to illustrations.

131, 140, 169, 190; and Jacqueline
Kennedy, 26, 114, 169, 190; enslaved
cooks trained in, 70–71, 72, 76, 89;
criticism of, 99, 101, 103; and alco-
holic beverages, 169–70; and Patrick
Clark, 191
French Revolution, 72
Fugitive Slave Act of 1793, 66, 68, 69
Fulbright, William, 117–18

Gallatin, Albert, 77
Ganeshram, Ramin, 58
Garfield, James, 42–43, 44, 97, 98, 130
Garfield, Lucretia, 42, 43, 44
Garrison, William Lloyd, 82
Gates, Henry Louis, Jr., 183–84
Gender attitudes, 18
General Service Administration, 147
Genovese, Eugene D., 34
George III (king of England), 36
George W. Bush Presidential Library,
57
Gerald R. Ford Presidential Library,
153
Gone with the Wind (film), 134–35
Gradual Abolition Act of 1780, 65
Grant, Julia, 105, 106
Grant, Ulysses S.: presidential steward
of, 41; and White House Thanks-
giving turkey, 47; Lucy Fowler as
presidential cook of, 105–6; Lucy
Fowler as private cook of, 106; travel
of, 131
Grayson, Cary T., 107
Great Awakening, 163
Green, Delefasse, 127, 132–33, 180–81
Green peas, Minted Green Pea Soup,
57
Grilled Salmon with Farro, Swiss
Chard Salad, and a Tropical
Smoothie, 208–9
Guiteau, Charles J., 42, 43, 130

Haiti, 63
Haldeman, Bob, 154
Halibut, Sesame and Wasabi-Crusted
Halibut, 204–5
Haller, Henri, 11, 117
Hamilton, Alexander, 35, 72, 162
Hamilton, Elizabeth Schuyler, 95
"Happy slave" stereotype, 82–83
Hardesty, Von, 127–28
Harding, Warren, 13, 139
Harless, Paul, 143
Harris, Jessica B., *Beyond Gumbo*, 63
Harrison, Benjamin: and kitchen
equipment, 16; diet of, 99, 101; Dol-
lie Johnson as presidential chef
of, 99–103; Sinclair as presidential
steward of, 100; Christmas dinner
menu, 103; travel of, 127, 128, 131,
139
Harrison, Caroline, 99, 101, 124–25
Harrison, William Henry, 12, 13, 41,
163
Hartford Courant, 46
Hatch Act, 135
Hawaiian French Toast, 159
Hay-Adams Hotel, Washington, D.C.,
191, 192
Hayes, Lucy, 130, 165
Hayes, Rutherford B.: Crump as presi-
dential steward of, 41–42; domestic
staff for, 96; as president, 97; Lucy
Fowler as presidential cook of, 106;
travel of, 128, 130, 139; and alcoholic
beverages, 164, 165, 172–73
Hearth cooking, 14, 63–64, 77
Heke (Mende noun), 61
Hemings, Elizabeth "Betty," 71
Hemings, James (enslaved cook): as
Jefferson's cook, 60, 70–71, 72, 89;
training in French cuisine, 70–71,
72, 76, 89; and French language,
71; wages of, 71; Freedom Principle

Soldiers' Home, 84–85, 94–95; Mitchell as presidential cook for, 94–95; travel of, 139

Lincoln, Mary Todd, 6, 15–16, 85–86, 94

Lincoln, Tad, 96

Little Rock High School, desegregation of, 113

Little White House, Warm Springs, Georgia, 54, 136–38

Loeb, William, Jr., 48

Longworth, Nicholas, 105

Louis-Philippe (king of France), 69

Louis V Joseph de Bourbon, Prince de Condé, 71

Lucullus, 1, 211n2

Lukash, William, 155

Lynch, Jack, 143–44

Macaroni and cheese: Jefferson's serving of, 75–76, 90; Baked Macaroni with Cheese, 90–91

Mackall family, 105

Maclay, William, 39

MacMillan, Robert, 181

Madison, Dolley, 95–96

Madison, James, 77, 82

Mammy stereotype, 98, 102

Mandela, Nelson, Clinton state dinner for, 193, *194*, 195, 204

Marshall, Ann Parks, *Martha Washington's Rules for Cooking*, 58

Marshall, George, 111

Martha, Princess of Norway, 54

Martha Washington's Rules for Cooking (Marshall), 58

Masterson, Donnie, 193, 195

Mayflower (yacht), 139, *140*

McCain, John, 183

McClellan, George, 85

McCrary, George W., 167–68

McCurry, Mike, 152

McDaniel, Hattie, 135

McDuffie, Lizzie: and Franklin Roosevelt, 118, 133–37; and presidential travel, 127, 133, 136

McDuffie, O. J., 133

McElveen, Ashbell, 72

McIntire, Ross, 11

McKinley, William: Seabrook as cook of, 29; Sinclair as presidential steward of, 45; travel of, 127, 128; and alcoholic beverages, 181

McLeod, Stephen, 88

McNair, Lilburn G., 178

Mesnier, Roland, 197

Miami (cutter), 139

Miles, Ellen, 69

Military personnel, 28. *See also* U.S. Air Force; U.S. Navy cooks

Minted Green Pea Soup, 57

Mise en place approach, 5

Mitchell, Cornelia, 94–95

Mitchell, Samuel Clayton, 127, 139

Moaney, Delores, 111, 113, 114, 118

Moaney, John, Jr.: as professional cook, 94; as Eisenhower's valet, 110–14; grilling with Eisenhower, *112*; Legion of Merit awarded to, 114; and civil rights leaders, 118

Moeller, John, 17–18

Moise, Stephen, 195

Monroe, James, 6, 172

Montgomery bus boycott of 1955, 113

Monticello, Virginia: Jefferson's enslaved labor at, 71, 75, 78; Jefferson's return visits to, 72, 78, 79; James Hemings's inventory of kitchen utensils, 73, 74; Jefferson's growing of West African food at, 76

Moore, Elizabeth, 16–17, 53, 109, 110

Morgan, John Tyler, 93

Morley, Jefferson, 80

Morris, Joe Alex, 2

Udo, Pedro, color insert
Uncle Tom's Cabin (Stowe), 82
Underground Railroad, 80, 84, 97
U.S. Air Force, 149, 157
U.S. Civil Service Commission, 100
U.S. Commission of Fine Arts, 56
U.S. Congress: budget for presidential residential staff and entertaining, 8, 21, 25; as influence on presidential foodways, 25; compensation for Fraunces for patriotic services to country, 37, 44; Crump's appeal for money from, 44; and treaty negotiations with European nations, 71; and voting rights for African Americans, 93; creation of free school for African Americans, 97; and Civil Rights Act of 1964, 118–19; Truman's relationship with, 144; and plane travel, 157
U.S. Department of Labor, *Dictionary of Occupational Titles*, 4
U.S. Navy cooks: in White House Mess, 4, 141–42, 145, 146, 149; African Americans as mess boys, 141, 142; Filipinos recruited by, 141, 142, 143, 144–45
U.S. Patent Office, 15
U.S. Secret Service, 12, 18, 26–27, 147–48
U.S. Supreme Court, 108, 113
Ursula (enslaved cook), 75
USS *Constitution*, 146

Van Buren, Martin, 23, 163
Varick, Richard, 69
Vegetables, Layered Late-Summer Vegetables with Lemongrass and Red Curry Dressing, 205–7
Verdon, René, 114, 116–17, 122–23
Vietnam War, 117, 118
Virginia, 59, 60

The Virginia Housewife (Randolph), 80
Vlach, John, 75
Vose, Horace, 47
Voting Rights Act of 1965, 118

Wallace, Madge G., 52
Wall Street Journal, 16
Walsh, Kenneth T., 151–52, 181
Walters, Barbara, 152
Washington, Booker T., 108
Washington, George: food philosophy of, 6; schedule of, 7, 8; and public perception, 25, 65, 126, 127; and White House Way, 27; Fraunces as presidential steward of, 33, 34–35, 38–40, 44, 46, 56, 63, 64, 72; and Fraunces Tavern, 36–37, 58; as president, 37–38; and alcoholic beverages, 39, 175, 181, 184; presidential entertaining of, 40, 64, 70; enslaved labor of, 60–62, 65–69, 71; Hercules as enslaved cook for, 60–67, 70, 72, 74; personality of, 65, 68; and Hercules's escape, 67–70; appointment of Jefferson as secretary of state, 72; hoecakes as among favorite foods, 88; and John Adams, 95; travel of, 126, 127
Washington, John E., 83
Washington, Martha Dandridge, 39, 61, 66, 67, 68, 69
Washington, D.C.: enslaved labor in, 59–60, 78, 80–83, 92; Black Codes of, 59–60, 96; French cuisine in, 70; establishment as U.S. capital, 72; race relations in, 80–81, 92, 96, 97; slave trade abolished in, 83; Lincoln's dismantling of slavery in, 86; opportunities for free African Americans in, 92–93; black middle class in, 93, 107–8